CHOICE AND DIVERSITY IN SCHOOLING

EDUCATIONAL MANAGEMENT SERIES
Series editor: Cyril Poster

CHOICE AND DIVERSITY IN SCHOOLING

Perspectives and Prospects

Edited by Ron Glatter, Philip A. Woods
and Carl Bagley

London and New York

First published 1997
by Routledge
11 New Fetter Lane, London EC4P 4EE

Simultaneously published in the USA and Canada
by Routledge
29 West 35th Street, New York, NY 10001

Typeset in Palatino by
BC Typesetting, Bristol BS15 5YD

Printed and bound in Great Britain by
Biddles Ltd, Guildford and King's Lynn

British Library Cataloguing in Publication Data
A catalogue record for this book is available from the British Library

Library of Congress Cataloguing in Publication Data
Choice and diversity in schooling: perspectives and prospects/
edited by Ron Glatter, Philip Woods, and Carl Bagley.
    p.   cm. – (Educational management series)
Based on material presented at an invitation seminar hosted by
Open University's Centre for Educational Policy and Management in
June 1995, and sponsored by the UK Economic and Social Research
Council.
    Includes bibliographical references and index.
    1. School choice–Great Britain–Congresses.   2. School management
and organization–Great Britain–Congresses.   3. Education and
state–Great Britain–Congresses.   4. Education–Great Britain-
-Marketing–Congresses.   I. Glatter, Ron, 1939–.   II. Woods, Philip, 1950–.
III. Bagley, Carl, 1958–.   IV. Series.
LB1027.9.C486   1996
379.1'1–dc20   96-11590
                    CIP

ISBN 0-415-13978-3 (pbk)

CONTENTS

ILLUSTRATIONS

FIGURES

TABLES

CONTRIBUTORS

Carl Bagley is a Senior Lecturer in Sociology at Staffordshire University where his responsibilities include the teaching of social policy and the welfare state. Professionally qualified as a social worker, he worked in the continuing education department of Leeds Local Education Authority before concentrating on research and teaching. He has written in the field of education and racism and is co-author with Philip A. Woods and Ron Glatter of a forthcoming book from Routledge on educational markets and choice.

Tony Edwards is Professor of Education at the University of Newcastle-upon-Tyne, and Dean of the Education Faculty 1989–96. He is a co-opted member of Newcastle Education Committee, and chair of governors at a Northumberland high school. Government initiatives to promote consumer choice in education are a main research interest.

Jennifer Evans is currently Lecturer and MA Course Leader in the Policy Studies Group at the Institute of Education, University of London. She has worked in the field of policy research in relation to special education since 1983. She is an adviser to the House of Commons Education Committee and a consultant to the Organisation for Economic Co-operation and Development (OECD).

John Fitz is a Senior Lecturer in Education at the University of Wales Cardiff. He has undertaken extensive research in educational policy-making, school choice and school autonomy. He is presently co-directing funded research on national school inspection.

Sharon Gewirtz is Research Fellow at the School of Education, King's College London. She has published extensively on education policy and is co-author of *Specialisation and Choice in Urban Education* (Routledge 1993) and *Markets, Choice and Equity in Education* (Open University Press 1995).

Ron Glatter is Professor of Education and Director of the Centre for Educational Policy and Management, School of Education, the Open University. He directed the ESRC-sponsored Parental and School Choice Interaction (PASCI) Study at the Open University. His interests and publications are in educational management development, school management and government, and relationships between educational institutions and their environments.

Ellen B. Goldring is Professor of Educational Leadership and Associate Dean for Academic Affairs at Peabody College, Vanderbilt University. Her research focuses on the organisation and control of schools, and their impact on educational leadership and the principalship. Much of her work examines the changing roles of principals and parents in an international perspective. She has published in such journals as *Educational Administration Quarterly*, *Educational Policy* and *Urban Education*. She is co-author with Sharon F. Rallis of *Principals of Dynamic Schools: Taking Charge of Change* (Corwin Press 1994).

David Halpin is Professor of Educational Research at Goldsmiths' College, University of London. His most recent publications include, with John Fitz and Sally Power, *Grant Maintained Schools: Education in the Market Place* (Kogan Page 1993) and, with Barry Troyna as co-editor, *Researching Education Policy: Ethical and Methodological Issues* (Falmer Press 1994).

Jason Hardman is a Research Assistant in the Centre for Educational Policy and Management, School of Education, the Open University. He is currently responsible for Phase I of the ICOSS project, a quantitative study of the impact of competition on secondary schools' rolls and budgets.

Donald Hirsch is author of *School: A Matter of Choice*, an international study by the Organisation for Economic Co-operation and Development's Centre for Educational Research and Innovation. A former official of the Centre, Mr Hirsch is now an independent policy consultant and a Visiting Fellow of the Institute of Education, University of London.

Martin Hughes is Professor of Education at the University of Exeter. He has recently directed two major funded projects on parents' response to the National Curriculum and assessment at Key Stage One (see Hughes, Wikeley and Nash, *Parents and their Children's Schools*, Blackwell 1994).

Rosalind Levačić is Senior Lecturer in the Centre for Educational Policy and Management, School of Education, the Open University. She has written extensively on financial management in education. The Open University Press has recently published her book, *Local Management of*

Schools: Analysis and Practice (1995). The research on the impact of competition on schools reported here is being extended with a grant from the Economic and Social Research Council.

Benjamin Levin is in the Department of Educational Administration and Foundations of the University of Manitoba. Previously he was a civil servant with the Manitoba Department of Education. His main research interests are in education policy, politics and economics.

Gulam-Husien Mayet is head of the North West Provincial Education, Sport and Recreation Department in South Africa. Before that he was Chief Welfare Adviser for the Greater London Council/Inner London Education Authority (ILEA), Divisional Education Officer in ILEA's Lambeth Division, and Assistant Director of Education for Birmingham City Education Department. He has worked to achieve racial equality in the UK, Europe and South Africa. In April 1995 he returned to South Africa after twenty-nine years in exile to assist in the transformation of the education service and in addition to work for a caring, transparent, open and democratic society.

Hazel Pennell is a Research Fellow at the Centre for Educational Research, London School of Economics and Political Science. Previously she held senior positions in the Research and Statistics Branch of the Inner London Education Authority and the London Residuary Body. Her research interests are extensive, although she retains a particular interest in education in inner London.

Sally Power is a Research Officer in Policy Studies, Institute of Education, University of London, where she is currently engaged in research into student experiences of state and private schooling. Other research interests include education policy analysis, the curriculum and homelessness and education.

J. Anthony Riffel is a member of the Department of Educational Administration and Foundations of the University of Manitoba. He has been a teacher, civil servant and university administrator. His main interests are in education and social policy, behaviour in organisations and administrative ethics.

Carol Vincent is a Research Fellow in Education Policy at Warwick University. Her research interests include special education and the role of parents in relation to the education system. She has recently published a book on parent–teacher relationships (*Parents and Teachers: Power and Participation*, Falmer Press 1996) and is currently directing a research project studying parents' organisations.

Anne West is Director of Research at the Centre for Educational Research, London School of Economics and Political Science. She was previously a Senior Research Fellow in the Research and Statistics Branch of the Inner London Education Authority. Her research interests are diverse and include choice of schools and schools' admissions policies. She has published widely in academic journals and is co-author of *Mother's Intuition? Choosing Secondary Schools* (with Miriam David and Jane Ribbens, Falmer Press 1994).

Geoff Whitty is the Karl Mannheim Professor of Sociology of Education and Co-Director of the Health and Education Research Unit at the Institute of Education, University of London. He was previously Professor and Dean of Education at Bristol Polytechnic and the Goldsmiths' Professor of Policy and Management in Education at Goldsmiths' College, University of London. He is co-author of *The State and Private Education: An Evaluation of the Assisted Places Scheme* (Falmer Press 1989), and *Specialisation and Choice in Urban Education: The City Technology Experiment* (Routledge 1993), as well as numerous papers on devolution and choice in education.

Philip A. Woods is Research Fellow at the Centre for Educational Policy and Management, School of Education, the Open University, and Principal Investigator on the PASCI (Parental and School Choice Interaction) Study. He has published extensively on the impact of choice and competition on schools, school responsiveness and home–school relationships, and consumerism, as well as on educational policy and spiritual development.

ACKNOWLEDGEMENTS

This book arose from an invitation seminar (described in Chapter 1) sponsored by the Economic and Social Research Council (ESRC) and hosted by the Open University's Centre for Educational Policy and Management (CEPAM). We would like to thank the ESRC for providing the funds to make the seminar possible, and also CEPAM for giving some additional resource to support the international aspect of the seminar.

We are grateful to all the contributors for their co-operation with the editorial process. In addition to the authors whose work appears in these pages, there were other participants all of whom made important contributions, for example as discussants or panel members, which have had an influence on this book and particularly Chapter 14. They were: Sandy Adamson, Funding Agency for Schools; Michael Adler, University of Edinburgh; Stephen Ball, King's College London; Nigel Bennett, The Open University; Miriam David, South Bank University; Bill Dennison, University of Newcastle-upon-Tyne; Andy Dorn, Advisory Centre for Education; Robert Godber, Secondary Heads Association; Ian Langtry, Association of County Councils; Alastair Macbeth, University of Glasgow; Alan Parker, Association of Metropolitan Authorities; Andrew Sargent, Department for Education and Employment; Tim Simkins, Sheffield Hallam University; Meryl Thompson, Association of Teachers and Lecturers; Margaret Tulloch, Campaign for State Education; and Felicity Wikeley, University of Bath.

In addition, we would like to thank Bob Morris, who at the time was Visiting Senior Research Fellow in CEPAM and is now at the University of Reading, for his invaluable help with the planning of the seminar and for providing background documentation. Daphne Johnson, another CEPAM Visiting Senior Research Fellow, made numerous significant contributions including a report of the final session which was sent to all participants. Sue Parker's expert management of the seminar was greatly appreciated by ourselves as co-organisers and by the other participants. Our secretaries, Caroline Dickens and Sindy York, have provided sustained support of the highest order in connection with both the seminar and the preparation of this book.

None of these people carry responsibility for any errors or omissions in what follows.

Ron Glatter
Philip A. Woods
Carl Bagley

1

INTRODUCTION

Ron Glatter, Philip A. Woods and Carl Bagley

In England and Wales we have witnessed since 1988 an extensive and determined national project in structural reform aimed at introducing market pressures into school education. Major policy components in this project include increasing the diversity of types of school through the creation of grant-maintained (GM) schools and technology colleges, introducing more open enrolment and per capita school funding, devolving management responsibilities (including responsibility for budgets) to schools, and increasing the range of information made available to parents about schools. A number of these developments have parallels in other countries. There has been, and continues to be, intense interest internationally in the capacity for parental choice and a more market-like environment to act as a motor for school improvement and for creating a more responsive school system (OECD 1994).

The reforms in England and Wales have prompted substantial research activity intended to investigate their impact and to examine the values and political aims underpinning them. There has also been much debate and argument concerning these fundamental values and aims, and the detail and consequences of specific educational policies. To examine both research and policy on these issues, the Open University's Centre for Educational Policy and Management hosted in June 1995 a unique invitation seminar sponsored by the UK Economic and Social Research Council. A variety of perspectives was represented. It brought together *leading UK scholars* engaged in research and analysis of parental choice and school responsiveness to market pressures in education; *members of the policy community* concerned with formulating, implementing or influencing educational policy (drawn from central and local government, teachers' unions and consumer bodies); and *international researchers and policy analysts* able to provide insights into similar policy initiatives and relevant research findings overseas. Reported research drew from a range of methodologies and approaches, and from work with secondary and primary schools.

This volume is designed to make available to a wide audience research findings, key themes and issues of concern that were considered. A range of issues central to understanding and evaluating market-like systems in schooling is tackled. First amongst these are diversity, hierarchy and school responsiveness, which are intimately related notions at the heart of questions concerning the impact and operation of a more market-like education system. A typology of school diversity is set out by Glatter, Woods and Bagley (Chapter 2). On the basis of their longitudinal investigation (deploying both qualitative and quantitative methods) of parental choice and school response – the PASCI study – they ask whether the new market-like environment has enhanced diversity and whether parents want increased diversity. They conclude that an increase in diversity is not evident in their three case study areas: in general, neither 'popular' nor 'unpopular' schools are regarding differentiation as a route to success except where a school responds to specific funding incentives offered by the Government. The evidence on whether parents want more diversity is equivocal. Issues relating to the promotion of diversity as a policy goal are reviewed, and changes that would be required to secure greater diversity are identified.

Edwards and Whitty (Chapter 3) present an analytical review of research and policy relating to diversity and choice in England, taking an historical perspective. They examine the impact of private schools and their shift towards a more academic orientation under the influence of competition from grammar schools. They also discuss the tension between promoting traditional or modern versions of educational excellence as experienced, for example, by city technology colleges (CTCs), and conclude that the entrenched prestige of the traditional academic form, and the opportunities to which it is perceived to lead, have persistently devalued progressive alternatives and restricted diversity. Only a more concerted policy drive than anything offered so far could successfully establish alternative conceptions of excellence.

School responsiveness is further addressed from differing angles in the three chapters which follow. Levin and Riffel (Chapter 4) set their analysis of the unresponsiveness of school systems to external change against a background of theory concerned with organisation–environment interactions. This emphasises the unclear and problematic nature of the link between environmental change and organisational response. On the basis of their empirical work with school districts in Canada, they hypothesise that schools' responses to parental choice policies will be limited, short-term and conservative. They argue that economic incentives alone are insufficient to induce schools to make changes of the scale the context demands: this would require attention to deep-seated institutional and cultural factors, as well as a much fuller understanding of contemporary social changes on the part of professional educators.

Halpin, Power and Fitz (Chapter 5) report findings from their studies of GM schools and the impact of self-governing status on institutional continuity and change and the extent to which this contributes to conservatism and innovation in their working patterns, curriculum and educational identities. They conclude that there is no evidence that institutional autonomy is transforming the work of classroom teachers. Indeed, far from 'breaking the mould' and attempting innovative practices, GM schools appear to be celebrating and reinforcing past visions of educational practice. Drawing on Giddens' analysis of modern-day society, these apparent conservative tendencies are seen as a form of educational 'fundamentalism' which seeks to 'reinvent the past'.

The capacity of schools to identify and respond to the preferences of their 'consumers' is an important characteristic of any market-like educational system if it is to have any chance of producing the benefits that the advocates of choice and competition claim. Hughes (Chapter 6) reports some of the findings from a project on Parents and Assessment at Key Stage One. Based on interviews with primary school teachers and parents, the findings cast doubt on the extent to which schools are aware of their parents' views and will change their practice to accommodate these views. Hughes argues that factors such as teachers' sense of their own professionalism and their deeply-held views about the role of parents present a substantial barrier to the development of a school system that resembles an effective market.

The danger of market-like systems in education intensifying social inequalities has been a major concern of the critics of such systems. On the other hand, advocates have claimed that under market pressures schools will become more effective and involve parents more (which much research has shown is itself a significant factor in school effectiveness). Goldring (Chapter 7) draws on research in Israel and the US concerned with 'schools of choice' – i.e. schools that enrol students from outside their zone or catchment area. Goldring examines the extent to which schools of choice are segregated by social class, why parents choose outside their local school, and whether this choice leads to closer relations between home and school. She highlights, amongst other things, evidence of 'creaming' – the tendency for schools of choice to attract pupils from higher social classes – and the complexity of designing educational policies that enhance choice *and* promote parental involvement and socially-mixed schools. In particular, Goldring suggests that policies which create a market-like system will not automatically lead to improved home–school relations and more active involvement by parents in their child's education. Attention needs to be paid to how schools can achieve this within a policy framework that encourages school choice and diversity.

Evans and Vincent (Chapter 8) focus on a particular group of parents and the disempowering potential of market pressures. They explore a neglected area of study, namely the impact of a market-like system on the ability of parents to exercise choice if their children have learning difficulties. Evans and Vincent use special education as a lens through which to explore the changes in education as a whole. They deconstruct the discourses of individualism and consumerism which underpin current policy, stressing how an increase in emphasis upon the social, cultural and financial resources of parents is determining the type of educational provision pupils receive. In this individualistic consumer-orientated environment parents whose children are experiencing difficulties in learning – already discursively constructed as abnormal – are, they contend, increasingly likely to find themselves positioned as ineffective and disempowered consumers with schools unresponsive to their needs.

If market pressures appear to exacerbate certain social divisions, as is suggested by Goldring and by Evans and Vincent, are there nevertheless benefits in terms of the general level of school effectiveness resulting from competition? Were this to be so, it may be considered worthwhile to preserve the positive aspects of market pressures whilst seeking ways of eliminating their negative results. Hardman and Levačić (Chapter 9) begin to explore the extent to which the English and Welsh reforms are in fact promoting competition and encouraging schools to improve. They report findings from a longitudinal, quantitatively-based investigation. Drawing from six English local education authorities (LEAs) and a data base of over 300 schools, Hardman and Levačić conclude that, as a result of parental choice, competition between schools is rising but that the connection between recruitment success and financial success is far from straightforward. The single factor marking out successful from less successful schools is that the most 'popular' schools appear to be those with a high proportion of GCSE passes. While careful not to imply that competition alone will lead to a rise in standards, Hardman and Levačić believe there is some indication that competition has provided some schools with the impetus to improve.

Gewirtz (Chapter 10) focuses on an area on which little has been written. She discusses the impact of market pressures on labour relations in schools and on the potential for organised industrial action by teachers. She draws on findings from a three-year investigation into the operation of market forces in education. Gewirtz highlights a rather complicated picture. The market-like environment creates difficulties for unionism but also enhances the need for it. It accentuates tensions in the teaching workforce but also produces solidarities. It is somewhat early, Gewirtz argues, to provide a definitive evaluation of the impact of market pressures on labour relations and union activity in schools. School managers, teachers and union activists are continuing to interpret their roles in relation to these matters, and, she points out, there is a need for more in-depth research into this process.

A market-like system of schooling is not a given, but is a political creation. Its impact will depend on the particular educational policies implemented in order to generate market pressures. Chapters 11, 12 and 13 are concerned to examine variations, both nationally and locally, in these policies. Particular attention is given in the latter two of these chapters to the rules and practices concerning admissions to schools and their impact on family choice: these are key factors in understanding the operation and effects of a market-like system in schooling (and, indeed, are referred to in several other chapters).

Hirsch (Chapter 11) presents an international review of policies for school choice based on his work on this theme for the Organisation for Economic Co-operation and Development (OECD). He points to striking paradoxes relating to school governance: for example, independent schools in the Netherlands are subject to much greater regulation than state schools in New Zealand. In drawing lessons for Britain, he argues that we should concentrate on finding ways in which equality of access and the mixing of abilities, classes and races can be combined with choice and genuine educational differences among schools. In this context, both selection and allocation based on residence are to be avoided it is argued, because they tend to promote the clustering of élites around particular schools.

Mayet (Chapter 12) reports on a study centred on eight LEAs which was conducted for the Society of Education Officers (SEO). He describes some of the wide range of admissions systems in operation, including one based on random selection and another on annually-redrawn catchment areas. Mayet highlights the potential for confusion and the differing accountabilities where there is a variety of admissions authorities – individual GM and voluntary aided schools as well as LEAs – in an area, and calls for full information to be assembled and published about all admission and appeals systems, not just those conducted by LEAs. A beginning is made to filling this information gap, at least in respect of inner London, by West and Pennell (Chapter 13). Their documentary study charts the development of varying admissions policies and practices since the abolition of the Inner London Education Authority (ILEA), which operated a unique system of banding which sought, with mixed results, to ensure that its secondary schools received intakes that were balanced in terms of ability. A patchwork of systems has emerged, including apparent covert selection through the interviewing of pupils and parents and the use of probing and demanding application forms. The authors put forward a range of policy proposals to promote equity and transparency, and argue that research should be conducted, among other things, to see whether the ability intake to secondary schools is changing.

In the final chapter common inter-related themes which emerge from the contributions are brought together. After several years of market-orientated reforms in the English and Welsh education system, there are pressing policy and research issues which the chapter identifies. The schooling system can be given a different character and direction depending on how these challenges are addressed and how policies governing school choice, budgets and decision-making are developed or revised. For example, incentive systems, such as school funding formulae, can be changed to support particular social goals. It is argued that the development and revision of policy can benefit greatly from an active and continuing dialogue between the research and policy communities. The chapter concludes by summarising areas of shared concern that need to be addressed through that dialogue.

REFERENCES

OECD (1994) *School: A Matter of Choice*, Paris: Centre for Educational Research and Innovation (CERI), Organisation for Economic Co-operation and Development.

2

DIVERSITY, DIFFERENTIATION AND HIERARCHY

School choice and parental preferences

Ron Glatter, Philip A. Woods and Carl Bagley

INTRODUCTION: TYPES OF DIVERSITY

Much has been written in recent years about choice, both conceptually and empirically – for instance concerning the question whether parents' scope for choosing schools has increased or decreased following the school reforms. Surprisingly little attention has been paid to diversity of provision.

The purpose of this paper is not to argue that diversity of school provision is or is not a good thing, but to ask what it means, whether parents want it and whether it is increasing. We shall be drawing on our work in the ESRC-funded Parental and School Choice Interaction (PASCI) study[1], in which one of our research questions is 'How "good" a market is being created?' and one of the sub-questions to this is 'What significant market imperfections are there?' Clearly the answers to such questions will depend on one's view of the market, but a key element in any functioning market must be that there are differences between the 'products' on offer, and that these differences to some extent reflect and accord with the variety of needs and preferences amongst consumers.

A wide range of *types of diversity* is possible in principle. Table 2.1 shows seven types and is by no means exhaustive.

Some of these forms of diversity could in principle be offered within rather than across schools, as in the 'programme diversity' of the 'mini-schools' in the East Harlem district of New York City (Carnegie Foundation 1992). Such a system puts the emphasis more on creating a wide range of choices than on fostering competition between providers.

There are, of course, numerous constraints upon offering highly diverse provision in any given local competitive arena (Woods *et al.* 1996). Two of the most potent are:

1 the complex interaction of funding, geography and demographics, well illustrated in the debate about surplus places in schools (Baxter 1995; DfE 1994a); and

Table 2.1 Types of school diversity

Type	Description/comments
Structural	concerning arrangements for governance, funding and ownership (e.g. private, grant-maintained, LEA-maintained schools)
Curricular	where schools specialise in or emphasise particular aspects of the curriculum (e.g. technology, music)
Style	where schools emphasise a particular learning or teaching style or educational approach (such as child-centred or formal teaching), including related aspects such as approach to discipline, pupil grouping practices
Religious/philosophical	where schools promote or emphasise a particular religious belief system or philosophy (pressures for a greater range of faith-based schools have received much publicity, but in principle schools could also be based on political philosophies for example, as some are in Denmark)
Gender	concerning variations in schools according to the gender of pupils (schools may be girls', boys' or mixed, or hybrids such as Shenfield School in Essex, which, though a mixed school, has begun to teach girls and boys separately for the most part)
Market specialisation	where schools cater to a particular market segment or segments (e.g. selective schools for the more able and schools for particular categories of special need): this might be related to hierarchy (see below), though the link is not a necessary one
Age range	where schools vary according to the age range of pupils, e.g. 11–16, 11–18, 12–18

Note: The above categories can, and usually do, overlap.

2 the requirements of the National Curriculum, though these have been reduced.

In addition, there is a fundamental and continuous tension between pressures towards, on the one hand, increasing the diversity of provision and on the other 'the desire to use schools to promote social cohesion . . . and . . . to avoid educational fragmentation, inconsistency and inequality' (Riffel *et al.* 1994: 1).

The school system in England and Wales was very diverse by inter-national standards prior to 1988. Curricular decisions were largely in the hands of heads and teachers taking into account the syllabuses of the examination boards. Even comprehensives varied greatly, as the author of a research report for the Schools Council observed in the mid-1970s: 'The present secondary school system is more remarkable for its variations than for any clear-cut division between those schools that can and those that cannot be called "comprehensive"' (Richardson 1975: 36). This point has been taken up recently as part of the developing political debate: 'Diversity is not a Conservative word, it is a reality that has existed in the education system since the 1944 Education Act' (Blunkett 1994).

However, such diversity in the postwar period was not an explicit policy objective: it appeared to be more a product of the relative power and influence of the 'partners' in the educational system (central government, the local education authorities (LEAs) and the teachers). Widespread dissatisfaction with the position led through a series of well-documented stages (for example Maclure 1992) to the establishment of the National Curriculum in 1988. The recent policy approach to diversity has been more deliberate and controlled, starting with the introduction of the Assisted Places Scheme in 1980 (Edwards *et al.* 1989) and proceeding through the provisions of the 1988 Education Reform Act relating to city technology colleges (CTCs) and grant-maintained (GM) schools to the later initiative on technology schools.

Further developments in the 1993 Education Act include the possibility of establishing new GM schools (DfE 1994b) and the 'Specialist Schools Programme', originally dubbed the Technology Colleges Initiative with eligibility limited to GM and voluntary aided (VA) schools, but later extended to all maintained secondary schools and including schools wishing to develop a special strength in modern foreign languages (DfE 1994c; DfE 1995). The 1992 White Paper *Choice and Diversity* (DfE/ Welsh Office 1992), which paved the way for the Act, praised diversity in contrast to uniformity and proposed the now celebrated distinction between specialisation and selection.

As well as the Government, LEAs as distinct as Wandsworth (Whitty *et al.* 1993) and Manchester (Jobson 1995) have become interested in promoting school diversity and specialisation, somewhat on the lines of magnet schools in the USA.

Diversity is essentially a policy concept. Policy makers assume that some form of diversity is desired by parents (and perhaps pupils). It is not generally clear what is meant by diversity, as in the recent definition: 'the range of types of education provision, geared to local circumstances and individual need' (DfE 1994a: para. 5), nor whether it is thought desirable that all the forms of diversity identified in our typology above should be available to every parent. It is important, however, to be

9

aware of the distinction between diversity as a policy goal and diversity as actually experienced by the chooser (Woods 1994).

Two other concepts merit brief discussion. *Differentiation* is a marketing concept relevant to schools' responses to a competitive climate. It involves understanding, and being able and willing to provide, what 'consumers' want or can be persuaded to 'buy'. 'The key to a successful differentiation strategy is to be unique in ways that are valued by buyers' (Bowman 1990: 53). This raises issues such as how schools try to find out what parents want (Bagley *et al.* 1996a), what are the significant differences among parents in what they are looking for (West *et al.* 1995), and how schools decide on their differentiation strategy.

There is some evidence that, in the eyes of parents and pupils, schools gain in terms of their image if they have some kind of appealing defining feature that sets them apart from others, almost regardless of the precise nature or quality of the 'difference' (Fitz *et al.* 1993; Whitty *et al.* 1993). 'It is the special*ness* as much as the special*ism* that seems to influence parents' (OECD 1994: 29). Differentiation by schools does not necessarily lead to diversity within the system, particularly if schools in trying to be different end up making similar kinds of changes.

Hierarchy in this context refers to a specific criticism, that the new system is designed not so much to promote choice and diversity as to reinforce and consolidate the grouping of schools into tiers, starting with prestige public schools and going through grammar, GM, specialists/ CTCs and finishing with LEA or 'council schools' in deprived areas at the bottom (Simon 1988; Walford and Miller 1991; Ball 1994). Middle-class parents with their greater material and cultural resources will, it is claimed, find their way to the schools in the higher tiers. This is clearly a crucial issue, not least because, in the 1992 White Paper, the Government committed itself firmly to diversity *without* hierarchy: 'The Government wants to ensure that there are no tiers of schools within the maintained system but rather parity of esteem between different schools, in order to offer parents a wealth of choice' (DfE/Welsh Office 1992: para. 1.49).

In the remainder of this paper we will report on our fieldwork in three contrasting 'local competitive arenas' (Glatter and Woods 1994: Woods *et al.* 1996) in different parts of the country, asking:

- whether the introduction of a market-like environment has resulted in increased diversity among schools;
- whether hierarchy has been reduced or increased;
- what differentiation strategies (if any) schools have adopted; and
- what our data on parental preferences suggest about parents' wishes for school diversity.

In the next section, we look at our three case study areas in which we are undertaking a series of interviews with school personnel and monitoring competitive responses by the secondary schools. Following that, we discuss the data on parental preferences obtained from the first of our annual surveys in the three areas. The final section presents some conclusions and reflections for future policy and research.

THE SCHOOLS RESPOND

Marshampton

Marshampton is a town of approximately 100,000 people with an above average representation of professional and middle-class households. It has a long history of competition between schools (both state and private, though the latter educate less than 10 per cent of pupils in Marshampton). All six state secondary schools have become GM. Five are comprehensive schools (Bridgerton, Thurcleigh Hill, St Asters Catholic High, Daythorpe and Endswich). One is a grammar school (Salix Grammar).

Marshampton state secondaries have moved full circle in recent years in terms of structural diversity: from being all LEA-maintained to being all GM. As a result, there is no structural diversity, apart from the alternative of private schooling. Religious or philosophical diversity is represented by the Catholic High School. Diversity based on market specialisation is present in the form of the grammar school. The age range covered by the schools also differs: Salix Grammar and Bridgerton are 11–18 schools with sixth forms; the remainder are 11–16 schools.

Salix Grammar and Bridgerton are the most academically-orientated, most successful in terms of examination passes, and are over-subscribed each year. Thurcleigh Hill has in recent years increased its intake and appears to have come closer to Bridgerton in terms of reputation. St Asters, Daythorpe and Endswich are under-subscribed. Endswich is in the most difficult position, with the poorest reputation and falling admission numbers.

There is a fair amount of diversity amongst Marshampton schools. For those schools that have distinctive and attractive attributes and are doing well – Salix Grammar and Bridgerton – the incentive to differentiate along new lines is not strong. The grammar school has sought to sharpen the distinction that already exists between it and other schools. It has sought to extend its appeal beyond the town, without increasing its intake, thus making it more élitist and exclusive. It is therefore narrowing its market specialisation.

At St Asters Catholic High, school managers consider that it is not doing well enough in attracting Marshampton's Catholic community. It appears that the school's religious/philosophical diversity is not a

11

sufficiently attractive feature in itself. Hence, St Asters is taking steps to improve its examination results and to pay attention to other aspects of school life such as discipline policy.

One of the competitive moves by Thurcleigh Hill, St Asters, Daythorpe and Endswich is to seek sixth forms (which they can do as they are GM). It is unlikely that they will all be successful. But it is evident that competitive pressures in this regard are encouraging schools away from diversity. These schools have long felt that their attractiveness has been markedly diminished by removing the sixth forms they once had. If successful, however, it may be that Daythorpe and Endswich sixth forms would focus more on vocational qualifications than those of other schools. This would constitute a form of curricular diversity, but it could also reinforce the hierarchy of schools, confirming the lesser reputations of Daythorpe and Endswich. Nevertheless, the main competitive focus for Thurcleigh Hill, St Asters, Daythorpe and Endswich is not on differentiating themselves, but on improving their reputation, working at links with feeder schools and making changes where school managers feel necessary, often along 'traditional' lines intended to improve academic performance and discipline.

Altering the hierarchy of schools is extremely difficult. Only Thurcleigh Hill to date appears to have made headway, becoming more of a competitor to Bridgerton (the comprehensive school with the highest reputation). Endswich is trying, through a change of name and with the help of some extra money acquired as a result of going GM, to lift its reputation and increase its intake. This is not a differentiation strategy, but an attempt to make itself less 'cut off' in reputational terms from other comprehensives.

Northern Heights

Northern Heights is an area within Northborough LEA. It has an above average number of working-class households, and a sizeable Bangladeshi community. The concept and practice of parental choice is well established, the LEA having operated a system of open enrolment since 1977.

Northborough LEA offers a wide range of types of school: three single-sex grant-maintained schools (two boys' and one girls'); two LEA-maintained single-sex schools (one boys' and one girls'); three Roman Catholic schools; three special schools; and one independent school. The most recent example of diversification is the decision three years ago of the single-sex schools to structurally diversify and go GM.

Around one-third of Northern Heights parents prefer a Northborough school outside the Northern Heights area. A small percentage of parents elect to send their children to schools in neighbouring LEAs. There is evidence of a similar number of parents in neighbouring LEAs electing to send their children to schools in Northborough, including Northern Heights.

Northern Heights itself has three LEA-maintained 11–16 co-educational comprehensive schools: Braelands, Newcrest and Leaside. Significant differences of character exist between the schools. Braelands is academically-orientated, and the most successful in terms of examination passes, being over-subscribed each year. It also receives a small but growing percentage of parents from an adjacent LEA, who live closer to the school than many parents in Northern Heights. In contrast, Newcrest and Leaside are more pastorally-orientated and located in the bottom half of the academic league table. While Newcrest struggles to maintain its standard number, Leaside is 50 per cent under-subscribed.

For Braelands, as a characteristically distinctive and successful school with a good reputation, there is no perceived need or incentive to differentiate. In 1993 the previous headteacher unsuccessfully proposed that the school should opt out of LEA control. The major reason given was financial, although it was also seen that GM status could enhance the school's existing image as an academic institution. A major reason for the proposal's rejection was the fear that having gone grant-maintained the school might then introduce some form of academic selection and become a *de facto* grammar. In essence, the headteacher's desire for structural diversification was rejected due to parents' and governors' fears of it leading to a sharpening and formalising of diversity based on market specialisation.

At Newcrest, school managers, having secured money under the Technology Schools Initiative, used the additional funds to facilitate a differentiation strategy around technology. The school's name was changed, a school uniform introduced and technology brought into all curricular areas, with in-service training for staff. In introducing a type of curricular diversity into Northern Heights, Newcrest aims to attract more middle-class parents and thereby increase its intake of above average ability pupils. Moreover, as the only school in the Northborough LEA to present itself as a technology school, Newcrest hopes to attract pupils from outside Northern Heights.

In response to competitive pressures Braelands, Newcrest and Leaside all express a desire to offer vocational qualifications. Consequently, the moves in this direction are unlikely in themselves to increase diversity. Each of the three schools if successful is nevertheless likely to put its own 'educational spin' on the initiative: Newcrest as complementing the school's commitment to technology; Leaside as providing opportunities for the less academically-orientated pupils who make up the majority of its student body; and Braelands as enhancing its reputation as a centre for educational achievement, in both vocational and non-vocational subjects.

In terms of hierarchy, Braelands remains the most popular and Leaside the least popular of the three schools. There has been some movement in that Newcrest has recorded a consistent rise in its number of parental first preferences, closing the gap with Braelands.

East Greenvale

East Greenvale is an administrative district of Greenvale LEA. It is a semi-rural area consisting of three small towns and a large number of villages. Each of the towns is served by an LEA-maintained 13–18 co-educational comprehensive upper school (Molehill, Dellway and Elderfield).

A 'pyramid' system of schooling operates with an upper school at the pyramid head taking pupils at age 13 from its feeder middle schools and the latter receiving pupils at age 9 from their first schools. Parents are allocated a particular pyramid school by the LEA according to where they live. While parents retain the right to select an alternative school, the vast majority of pupils transfer in accordance with LEA allocations.

As a result of this allocations policy, and also the schools' rural location and the limited availability of public transport, the three schools tend to serve their own communities. Moreover, the schools are virtually assured of a constant and sufficiently high intake of pupils to feel financially secure. To maintain and reinforce the mutual benefits of this situation the three schools have a 'gentleman's agreement' not to undertake any measures which would result in their 'poaching' another school's intake. This non-competitive agreement effectively rules out any form of differentiation or diversity as it could threaten the status quo.

In line with this, no move towards differentiation or diversity has been observed. All three schools (located in the lower middle of the academic league table for Greenvale LEA) continue to be broadly similar in character, reputation, status and popularity, offering a comprehensive education to a wide ability range of pupils.

DO PARENTS WANT DIVERSITY?

One of the PASCI study's methods of investigation consists of annual surveys of parents in each of the case study areas. Three surveys were conducted in each year from 1993 to 1995. The survey population was made up of all parents with a child transferring to secondary schooling in the survey year. Parents were asked about their first-preference school and their reasons for this preference: they were asked to indicate factors[2] influential in making the school their first preference, and to select the three most important factors, ranking these as first, second and third most important. Qualitative data was also obtained via personal interviews with a sample of parents.

Below, we present some of the quantitative data from the first round of surveys, undertaken in 1993.[3] The surveys were not designed to enable construction of a 'wish-list' of parental preferences showing the diversity of schooling that parents might ideally want.[4] Thus, rather than being concerned with the range of types of school parents might like, the focus is on their preferred school out of those perceived as being available. Parental responses to the survey are bounded by the particular diversity (or lack of diversity) that is available in their area. The general point is that the *formation* of parental preferences does not occur in a vacuum (this also means that even a parental 'wish-list' cannot be seen as representing completely freely-chosen preferences). The increased sociological attention now being given to consumer behaviour has drawn attention, amongst other things, to ways in which consumer choices may reproduce social hierarchies and how producers can influence consumers by attempting to define the meaning and value attached to products and services (Abercrombie 1994; Warde 1994). Recognition of this has to temper interpretation of the data presented below as we consider what these might suggest concerning the question of whether parents want diversity.

Certain factors appear to be influential for the majority of parents across all three case study areas (Woods 1994). These are:

- child's preference for the school;
- standard of academic education;
- nearness to home/convenience for travel;
- child's happiness at the school.

In each area, these were indicated as having some degree of influence by more than half of parents *and* were ranked in the top three most important factors by around a fifth or more of parents. They are the 'core' around which we may develop our thinking further about parental approaches to school preferences. In addition to these, 'school reputation', 'examination results' and 'child's friends will be there' were notably influential in particular areas (Woods 1994).

Here, we focus on the factors that parents indicated were *most* important to them (i.e. ranked first) in deciding which school was their first preference and on comparing the data according to parents' first-preference school – see Table 2.2[5] (analysis of the data according to other factors, such as social class and gender of the child, is underway and will be reported in due course). A wide range of factors is represented in the table. They include characteristics of the school itself (perceived academic success, facilities, its leadership as represented

15

Table 2.2 1993 PASCI data: most important reason for first-preference school being preferred option, by first-preference school

Salix	Bridgerton	Braelands	St Asters	Thurcleigh Hill	Daythorpe
• standard of academic education: 42%	• school's reputation: 18.5%	• exam results: 21%	• child will be happy there: 10%	• school's reputation: 13%	• child will be happy there: 15%
• school's reputation: 13%	• standard of academic education: 17%	• standard of academic education: 19%	• nearness/convenience: 10%	• child will be happy there: 13%	• school's head: 11%
• exam results: 11%	• nearness/convenience: 10%	• child will be happy there: 10%	• is a church school: 8%	• nearness/convenience: 13%	• child preferred school: 9%
• child will be happy there: 7%	• child will be happy there: 8%	• child preferred school: 8%	• child preferred school: 8%	• child preferred school: 8%	• nearness/convenience: 8%
• child preferred school: 6%	• older brother/sister will be there: 6%	• school's reputation: 7%	• policy on discipline: 6.5%	• school atmosphere: 8%	• facilities: 5.5%
	• child preferred school: 5%	• nearness/convenience: 4.5%	• school's reputation: 5%	• caring approach to pupils: 8%	• policy on discipline: 5.5%
	• what school teaches/subject choices: 5%	• older brother/sister will be there: 4%	• standard of academic education: 5%	• standard of academic education: 7%	• older brother/sister will be there: 5.75%
	• exam results: 4%	• policy on discipline: 3%	• older brother/sister will be there: 4%	• older brother/sister will be there: 6%	• school atmosphere: 4%
	• has sixth form: 4%	• caring approach to pupils: 3%	• school's head: 4%	• way school managed: 3%	• standard of academic education: 3%
	• facilities: 3%	• school atmosphere: 3%	• exam results: 3%	• exam results: 2%	• school's reputation: 2%
	• child's friends will be there: 2%		• school atmosphere: 3%		
			• caring approach to pupils: 3%		
			• pupil's behaviour in school: 3%		
			• what school teaches/subject choices: 3%		
			• size of classes: 3%		
			• other schools not acceptable: 3%		
base: 108	195	156	77	139	91

Table 2.2 (cont.)

Endswich	Newcrest	Leaside	Elderfield	Molehill	Deltway
• child will be happy there: 15% • child preferred school: 12.5% • older brother/sister will be there: 11% • nearness/convenience: 10% • exam results: 10% • facilities: 10% • standard of academic education: 7% • policy on discipline: 4% • caring approach to pupils: 3% • school's staff: 3%	• caring approach to pupils: 13% • school's head: 11% • child will be happy there: 10% • child preferred school: 9% • school's reputation: 7% • exam results: 6% • nearness/convenience: 4% • facilities: 4% • what school teaches/subject choices: 3% • older brother/sister will be there: 3% • child's friends will be there: 2% • school atmosphere: 2%	• child will be happy there: 13% • standard of academic education: 11.5% • nearness/convenience: 11.5% • exam results: 10% • child preferred school: 7% • school's head: 5% • school's staff: 5% • older brother/sister will be there: 5%	• nearness/convenience: 16% • child will be happy there: 10% • standard of academic education: 9% • exam results: 9% • child preferred school: 8.5% • school's reputation: 8% • what school teaches/subject choices: 5% • caring approach to pupils: 4% • school's head: 3% • school's staff: 2%	• nearness/convenience: 18% • standard of academic education: 11% • child will be happy there: 10% • school's reputation: 6% • child preferred school: 5% • older brother/sister will be there: 5% • child's friends will be there: 4% • exam results: 4% • facilities: 3% • what school teaches/subject choices: 3% • caring approach to pupils: 2% • way school managed: 2%	• nearness/convenience: 19% • child will be happy there: 14% • child preferred school: 6% • standard of academic education: 5% • facilities: 5% • no others to choose from: 5% • school's reputation: 4% • child's friends will be there: 3.5% • exam results: 3% • caring approach to pupils: 3% • what school teaches/subject choices: 2% • older brother/sister will be there: 2% • school's head: 2%
base: 72	100	61	164	187	171

Note: The table excludes factors that were cited as most important by less than 2% of parents.

by the headteacher, and so on), the importance of family and friend-ship networks, and the school's accessibility from home. Certain factors, such as single-sex schooling, although also relevant to the issue of diversity, are not focused on in this paper as we have chosen, given limited space, to concentrate on the most widespread influencing factors.

Analysis of the pilot, qualitative interviews with parents suggested both that parental concerns and interests are complex and inter-connecting, and that certain underlying themes – academic or concerned with the child and his or her relationships, for example – might be iden-tified (Woods 1993). In line with this suggestion, certain factors are grouped with these themes in mind and presented in Table 2.3: thus it presents in aggregated form those factors that can be seen as being predominantly centred on academic concerns and those that can be seen as predominantly centred on the child's perspective and social relationships[6]. Concern with access is also shown in the table as this is the one factor, alongside certain academic- and child-centred factors noted above, which is notably influential across all the case study areas. Concentrating the main influencing factors in this way facilitates com-parisons within the surveyed parents and allows us to begin identifying broad patterns. It should be noted that it is not necessarily the resulting absolute percentages that are significant, but the variations amongst parents.

Certain patterns appear through the data approached in this way. With three of the schools (Salix Grammar, Bridgerton and Braelands), academic-centred factors are markedly more prominent. This is particu-larly the case with the grammar school: over 40 per cent indicated that standard of academic education was the most important influence on them. With Braelands, both exam results and standard of academic edu-cation are prominent as reasons. The importance of the academic-centred factors is highly variable between schools: it ranges from 53 per cent down to 4 per cent. Child's happiness is particularly prominent for St Asters, Daythorpe, Endswich and Leaside, whilst generally child-centred factors (to which we return below) are relatively more important in schools other than Salix, Bridgerton and Braelands. Concern with access is proportionally highest for Elderfield, Molehill and Dellway – the schools in semi-rural East Greenvale – where nearness to home/convenience for travel is the most frequently selected single factor. Reputation appears particularly important (13 per cent or more) for Salix Grammar, Bridgerton and Thurcleigh Hill. For Bridgerton it is the single factor indicated as most important by the highest proportion of parents; as it is with Thurcleigh Hill (alongside child's happiness and nearness to home/convenience for travel).

Table 2.3 1993 PASCI data: incidence of academic-, child- and access-centred factors as most important reason for first-preference school being preferred option, by first-preference school

	Salix	Bridgerton	Braelands	St Asters	Thurleigh Hill	Daythorpe	Endswich	Newcrest	Leaside	Elderfield	Molehill	Deltway
	academic: 53%	academic: 25%	academic: 40%	child: 21%	child: 29%	child: 23%	child: 32%	child: 34%	child: 23%	child: 24%	child: 21%	child: 27%
	child: 14%	child: 16%	child: 20.5%	access: 10%	access: 13%	access: 8%	academic: 17%	academic: 6%	academic: 21%	academic: 19%	access: 18%	access: 19%
	access: 0%	access: 10%	access: 4.5%	academic: 8%	academic: 9%	academic: 4%	access: 10%	access: 4%	access: 11.5%	access: 16%	academic: 15.5%	academic: 9%
base:	108	195	156	77	139	91	72	100	61	164	187	171

Notes: *academic-centred*: where respondent indicates 'standard of academic education', 'exam results' or 'has sixth form' as most important; *child-centred*: where respondent indicates 'child preferred school', 'child will be happy there', 'child's friends will be there', 'caring approach to pupils', as most important; *access-centred*: where respondent indicates 'near to home/convenient for travel' as most important.

All this suggests that there are differences between schools in terms of the reasons parents are drawn to see them as their first preference. Concern about access is a significant variable but, although a crucial factor to parents and children in framing the choice available, it is not a factor that in itself reveals parental concern about diversity of schooling (except in so far as for some parents localness may be a positive factor meaning more than just the school being easier and safer to travel to). The most noteworthy positive variable is the strength of the academic-centred factors. Schools with a focus on or leaning towards the academic appear to be catering for parents who particularly emphasise this. This suggests that diversity based on market specialisation – and a particular specialisation in the academic – is especially valued and likely to be successful (at least in narrow, market terms for a particular school – the wider impact, particularly where academic selection is allowed, is another matter). The desire for other forms of diversity is less strong, according to this data. For example, the proportion preferring St Asters because it is a church school is not strikingly large. Qualitative data from interviews with parents suggest that one form of structural diversity, namely whether a school is GM or LEA-maintained, has not emerged to date as a factor of any importance to parents.

Child-centred factors emerge as a relatively consistent feature amongst the reasons most important to parents: these range from 34 per cent down to 14 per cent. Thus even for a school like Braelands, where an academic-centred factor is more likely than others to be cited as the single most important influence, a fifth of parents nevertheless indicate a child-centred factor. Characteristically, where a child-centred factor is the single most important influence, it is child's happiness which is cited by the larger proportion of parents, followed by child's preference for the school – even in the case of Salix (though there the percentages are far smaller than for academic-centred factors). For Newcrest alone does caring approach to pupils overtake these other factors. The common element in these factors is the stress that they place on the child – the valuing of his or her viewpoint and a sensitivity to the impact on the child of the human context in which the child will spend a significant portion of his or her formative years[7]. This child-centredness is, evidently, a significant factor for all the schools.

In the early stages of the PASCI study it was observed that:

> In exploring family choice we are undoubtedly looking at some mixture of interest in both 'process' and 'product', to use Elliott's terms. Product or outcome is certainly important, in that parents want schools to help their children achieve in various ways, and to set them on the road for future employment. But they also value schools as a place to be, an environment for the young family

member who needs a setting where he or she can be separate from the family and develop as an individual in the company of peers.

(Glatter *et al.* 1993: 101)

The data presented here would begin to incline us to the view that the more important or fundamental values for parents tend to be child-centred (akin to 'process'). 'Product' – including emphasis on academic success – is important, but its importance appears from our data so far not so consistent, and it is not, generally, given priority above child-centred factors. The relative consistency of child-centred factors might be taken to mean that parents want – in this regard at least – not diversity, but uniformity. Most parents undoubtedly would want all schools to exhibit care and concern for the child and for the quality of his or her social environment. A 'caring, child-centred focus' might thus be conceived of as a minimum requirement as far as most parents are concerned.

All of this could incline us to the view that parents want *uniformity* in 'caring, child-centredness', *diversity* in academic focus. However, such a conclusion would be deceptively simple and premature, for at least three reasons.

First, we need to bear in mind that this paper has focused on the most widespread influential factors in our quantitative data for 1993: the significance for the issue of diversity of other data (on factors such as single-sex schooling, and findings for subsequent years, for example) will need to be brought into the frame as our analyses proceed. Second, certain forms of diversity in academic focus, in particular grammar school status, tend to provoke strong feelings, including strongly-held views on the part of many parents against academic selection. Such opposition was an important element in parents' rejection of grant-maintained status for Braelands. Third, schools *can* vary in the emphasis and form they give to child-centred policies and perception of this can be an important factor to parents (witness the weight given to caring and child-centred factors by parents whose preference was Newcrest).

A further point, already noted, is that parental views are influenced or constrained by what is actually on offer. Moreover, school managers have to consider future parental reactions to possible change, weighing in the balance varying parental views, and make decisions that *affect* (altering or preserving) what is on offer to parents. They may, for example, be concerned that a predominant caring image could clash with a school's desire to secure a reasonable proportion of academically able, middle-class children (or vice versa – Glatter 1994)[8]. Parents of these children tend to be more attractive to schools in a quasi-market and fieldwork to date has led us to hypothesise that schools are tending to show greater concern with 'traditional academic' issues in order to

(Bagley *et al.* 1996a; Woods *et al.* 1996). In this light, it is
that Newcrest, for example, is not heightening its 'caring,
1 focus', but has added a strong technology element
.ɔ appeal to such parents. Such decisions by school managers
.ificant influences on the extent and nature of differences between
schools available to parents, which in turn influence the reasons for
preferences that parents are able to express.

CONCLUSIONS AND IMPLICATIONS

Review of findings

Our focus is not on whether diversity exists in our areas but on whether
the new market-like environment has increased it. For example, while
there has long been a significant degree of diversity in Marshampton,
the only recent changes which are relevant to diversity are the wholesale
move to GM status (structural) and some curricular developments. The
consequences of these moves appear to be in the direction of greater
uniformity rather than sharper difference.

The only clear recent example in our arenas of greater differentiation
leading to diversity is the case of Newcrest with its specific emphasis on
technology. However, this has resulted not from 'consumer' pressure
but from the Government's selective dispensation of additional funds
via the Technology Schools Initiative.

We conclude therefore that the new environment has not led to an
increase in diversity in these areas. The popular schools – Salix and
Bridgerton in Marshampton, Braelands in Northern Heights and all
three in the semi-rural setting of East Greenvale – have no incentive to
differentiate further, beyond possibly (as at least Salix Grammar is
doing) enhancing their existing characteristics so as to sharpen the distinction between themselves and less successful schools. In other cases
(Molehill, Dellway and Elderfield in East Greenvale) the aim is not to
sharpen but to blunt any difference and thereby to share the mutual
benefits arising from being similar.

The schools which might be thought to have an incentive to differentiate and diversify because they are relatively unpopular (Leaside and
Newcrest in Northern Heights, St Asters, Daythorpe and Endswich in
Marshampton) would still need to regard differentiation as a route to
success. However, St Asters believes it can increase its share of the
Catholic community without differentiation, and Endswich is also pur-
suing a more conventional route in its search for acceptance. Newcrest
has taken the route of differentiation, with Government funding support.

The picture with regard to hierarchy is not characterised by dramatic movement. Clearly, it has not reduced. The grammar school in Marshampton is, if anything, drawing from a narrower élite. There seems to be some scope for schools around the middle of the 'pecking order' to take steps at least to reduce the gap with the leaders – both Thurcleigh Hill (Marshampton) and Newcrest (Northern Heights) have had some success in doing this. The remaining schools in those two areas are faced with significant barriers to transforming their position in the local hierarchy (Bagley *et al.* 1996b).

Our parental data suggest that, in terms of the main factors influencing school preference, parents varied most in the importance they attached to academic features: those parents who preferred schools which stress academic aspects tended themselves to express a high concern for these. Other factors which might provide grounds for policies on diversity, for example preferences based on religion or governance structures, were much less in evidence. Child-centred factors are cited relatively consistently among parents choosing different schools.

It is interesting to compare these findings with those of a study based on one area (Brain and Klein 1994) which concluded that there was a widespread consensus among the parents surveyed about what matters most when choosing a school – a happy atmosphere, firm discipline and a good academic reputation. The authors speculate that this consensus of parental view may explain why schools tend to stress these factors in their marketing strategies and seek to offer all things to all children ('rhetorical convergence', Brain and Klein 1994: 19). However, they also note that, while the perceived importance of a happy atmosphere did not vary according to the preferred school, that of a good academic reputation, exam results and firm discipline was greatest among parents opting for the three over-subscribed schools which put greatest stress on these features in their marketing. By contrast, parents of three under-subscribed schools serving the less affluent parts of the city attached the greatest significance to accessibility.

From our (and Brain and Klein's) findings it might be argued that, if expressions of parental preference provide any guide to the development of policy on school diversity, they suggest a case for diversity based on market – and particularly academic – specialisation, rather than on any of the other types identified in the introduction to the paper. Grammar and secondary modern schools and the specialist schools currently being promoted by the Government would fit this scenario. However, there are fundamental problems with this. Such diversity would be likely to promote further academic selection, reduce choice through enhancing over-subscription at particular schools and diminish school effectiveness overall through sharply reducing the incidence of academically balanced intakes to secondary schools (Mortimore 1995). Moreover, many parents

opposed to the introduction of grammar schools, and we do
)unds for concluding that most parents would want diversity
idemic selection. We will be undertaking much more detailed
)ur parental data – including our qualitative data – to explore
liversity of parental preferences and what significance might
be attached to differences amongst parents.

Policy considerations

The picture we are gaining from our data so far is that of a secondary
school system which is not dramatically moving in the direction of
greater diversity or reduced hierarchy, and where parental choices are
highly constrained by what is available and accessible. To promote
moves towards diversity, at least some of the following policy changes
would be required:

- A substantial further reduction in National Curriculum requirements.
- Much greater encouragement and support to potential founders
  of new schools, including religious schools other than Church of
  England, Roman Catholic and Jewish schools.
- Acceptance of a level of surplus places substantially above that
  currently recommended.
- More encouragement for innovation in schools.
- Greater public funding of home-to-school transport costs.
- High-quality information and advice services for parents.

A greater or lesser emphasis on equality of opportunity could be built
into such a policy for diversity, though the greater the emphasis in this
direction the more it would be likely to cost.

Whether more diversity is seen as important depends on the values
according to which the school system is assessed and the relevance that
diversity is considered to have to achieving goals founded in those
values. Two questions (of many) that need to be asked are: is diversity

beneficial to important educational goals (and, if so, in which forms)?;
and is diversity required in order to achieve the goal of providing schooling that parents and pupils want (and, if so, in which forms)? There are
considerations which might cast doubt on the value of further diversity
as a policy aim:

1 It is not self-evident that the schooling provided in East Greenvale,
  which for reasons of geographical location, transport facilities and
  admissions procedures is neither competitive nor diverse, is of poorer
  quality overall or less acceptable to parents and pupils than that
  offered in our other areas.

2 There may be no direct or necessary link between choice and diversity in the specific context of state education. Brain and Klein (1994) argue both that, in the city they studied where a variety of types of school was available, diversity constrained rather than extended parental choice, and also that parents might want to choose which school delivers the standard product best rather than between schools of different types.

3 Too much curricular diversity from the start of secondary school might encourage excessive specialisation – a frequent criticism of the English and Welsh secondary school system. It might then be argued that – other than perhaps for children with obviously exceptional talents in, for example, the performing arts – such diversity should be delayed until at least age 14, when it would tend to be offered within rather than across schools.

A further problem is the relationship of diversity to hierarchy. In regard to this, the cultural and historical context is a highly relevant consideration. In a paper about diversity in Canadian education, Riffel *et al.* (1994: 10) observe that 'All systems are shaped by their own histories and dynamics, and there will always be both centripetal and centrifugal forces at work'. They propose a positive (though not uncritical) approach to diversity, but the issue seems to have a very different flavour in the Canadian context of a quest to build an inclusive yet cohesive society. It is hard to conceive of diversity being reconciled with genuine parity of esteem in the English context in which, according to an OECD report, there is a 'national habit of ranking educational alternatives rather than seeing them as being of possible equal value' (OECD 1994: 65). It argues that the pluralistic attitude to education evident in some other settings will not easily take root in England.

In favour of some measure of diversity, it can be argued that some parents do attach importance to certain differences between schools. Although a minority, for example, place the highest importance on a school's denominational character, it may still be considered a crucial policy aim to provide for the aspirations of such minorities. Diversity may also assist in school improvement, by providing opportunities for developing innovative forms of schooling practice which parents, pupils and professionals may then assess and respond to. If innovations are not to be isolated attempts at change, there is a need to develop a systematic means of evaluating and disseminating such innovations. Many pilot projects and policies aimed at promoting diversity and change (for example the CTC programme) have led to specific, individual experiments in particular places with no clear 'value added' for the system as a whole. Some form of funding for innovation or demonstration projects, where evaluation and dissemination would be built into the design, could

note reflexive change, and avoid both stagnation and a pro-
lated developments.

Future research

It seems particularly important to establish more clearly whether there is
a widespread parental demand for a variety of types of school, or
whether there is a broad consensus about features of the 'ideal school'.
Such research needs to address the issue of the weight that should be
given to minorities who want different forms of schooling. Where can
and should the line be drawn? It also has to tackle the question of the
inequalities that may result from acceding to some parents' demands, if
they are given preferential access to better-resourced or more valued
forms of schooling. Such considerations also lead to research questions
concerning the extent to which inequalities may result directly from different kinds of diversity.

There is a need to monitor the specialist schools programme in terms
of its effects on the schools concerned and their students as well as on
their local competitive arenas and the wider system. The further development of CTCs should be studied, particularly because, through the
requirement upon them to recruit a wide ability profile, they represent
an attempt to move away from hierarchy based on ability. Finally, the
most effective forms and channels of support and information for
parents, particularly those with less 'cultural capital' to assist them and
their children to make successful educational choices, should be explored.

NOTES

1 The support of the ESRC is gratefully acknowledged. The study's reference
  number is R000234079.
2 From thirty-two factors listed in the questionnaire (the list was expanded to
  thirty-four in 1994 and 1995).
3 The response rate to the 1993 surveys averages 77 per cent.
4 Such as the 'menu' of options in the study of parents by Brain and Klein
  (1994).
5 Schools shown are the eleven research schools, plus Salix Grammar; the minority of parents whose first preference was another school are not shown in the
  table.
6 Care needs to be taken in grouping factors. The process is subject to researchers' own presumptions and greater prominence might be given to a grouped
  factor than it might otherwise attract if reported singly (this danger is reinforced if some are reported singly whilst others are grouped, since the prob-
  ability of the former being selected is less, all things being equal, than a
  number of factors subsequently grouped). Researcher bias in the interpretation
  of parental views on school choice is present, however, whatever approach is
  taken – whether researchers make decisions in advance of a survey by giving
  pre-coded categories for replies which are then reported without grouping, or

whether they leave questions open-ended in which case 'highly disparate and individualised parental replies have to be made more manageable by grouping them into a limited number of broad categories' (Glatter *et al.* 1993: 100).

7 It has been suggested elsewhere that these elements might be viewed as constituting a *human warmth* value perspective, distinguishable from the *rational academic* or a value perspective concerned with practical questions of travelling to and from school (Woods 1993, 1994) – a value perspective being a particular focus of parental interest or concern in relation to their child's potential school. A *rational academic* value perspective does not necessarily mean that the parent is devoid of concern for the child – value perspectives are not mutually exclusive (parents tend to hold more than one) and an academic-focused education may be an important way of meeting a particular child's needs. The development of this conceptualisation of parental concerns is continuing as analysis of the PASCI data progresses.

8 It should not be assumed, however, that any school's 'caring' and academic policies are *necessarily* antithetical: they may take different forms and be combined in varying, mutually beneficial ways.

REFERENCES

Abercrombie, N. (1994) 'Authority and consumer society', in R. Keat, N. Whiteley and N. Abercrombie (eds) *The Authority of the Consumer*, London: Routledge.

Bagley, C., Woods, P.A. and Glatter, R. (1996a) 'Scanning the market: school strategies for discovering parental perspectives', *Educational Management and Administration* 24(2): 125–138.

Bagley, C., Woods, P.A. and Glatter, R. (1996b) 'Barriers to school responsiveness in the education quasi-market', *School Organisation* 16(1): 45–48.

Ball, S. (1994) *Education Reform: A Critical and Post-Structural Approach*, Buckingham: Open University Press.

Baxter, J. (1995) 'Surplus to requirements?', *Education*, 3 February.

Blunkett, D. (1994) 'The meaning of diversity', letter to *Education*, 11 November.

Bowman, C. (1990) *The Essence of Strategic Management*, London: Prentice Hall.

Brain, J. and Klein, R. (1994) 'Parental choice: myth or reality?', Bath Social Policy Papers No. 21, Bath: University of Bath.

Carnegie Foundation (1992) *School Choice*, Princeton, NJ: The Carnegie Foundation for the Advancement of Teaching.

Dennison, W.F. (1993) 'Performance indicators and consumer choice' in M. Preedy (ed.) *Managing the Effective School*, London: Paul Chapman.

Department for Education (DfE)/Welsh Office (1992) *Choice and Diversity: A New Framework for Schools*, London: HMSO.

DfE (1994a) *Circular on the Supply of School Places*, Circular 23/94, London: Department for Education.

DfE (1994b) *Guidance to Promoters on Establishing New Grant-Maintained Schools*, London: Department for Education.

DfE (1994c) 'Specialist schools programme extended – Shephard', *Department for Education News*, 296/94, London: Department for Education.

DfE (1995) 'Language colleges – schools for international success', *Department for Education News*, 49/95, London: Department for Education.

Edwards, T., Fitz, J. and Whitty, G. (1989) *The State and Private Education: An Evaluation of the Assisted Places Scheme*, London: Falmer Press.

Fitz, J., Halpin, D. and Power, S. (1993) *Grant Maintained Schools: Education in the Market-Place*, London: Kogan Page.

Glatter, R. (1994) 'Managing dilemmas in education: the tightrope walk of strategic choice in more autonomous institutions', paper presented at the International Intervisitation Program in Educational Administration, Toronto, May 1994. To be published in: S.L. Jacobson, E. Hickcox and R. Stevenson (eds) (forthcoming) *School Administration: Persistent Dilemmas in Preparation and Practice*, Westport, CT: Greenwood Publishing Group.

Glatter, R., Johnson, D. and Woods, P.A. (1993) 'Marketing, choice and responses in education', in M. Smith (ed.) *Managing Schools in an Uncertain Environment: Resources, Marketing and Power*, Sheffield Hallam University for the British Educational Management and Administration Society (BEMAS) (first presented as a keynote paper to BEMAS Research Conference, University of Nottingham, April 1992).

Glatter, R. and Woods, P.A. (1994) 'The impact of competition and choice on parents and schools' in W. Bartlett, C. Propper, D. Wilson and J. LeGrand (eds) *Quasi-Markets in the Welfare State*, Bristol: University of Bristol, SAUS Publications.

Jobson, R. (1995) 'Week by week', *Education*, 3 February.

Maclure, S. (1992) *Education Reformed* (3rd edn), London: Hodder and Stoughton.

Mortimore, P. (1995) 'The balancing act', the *Guardian*, 28 February.

OECD. (1994), *School: A Matter of Choice*, Paris: Centre for Educational Research and Innovation (CERI), Organisation for Economic Co-operation and Development.

Richardson, E. (1975) *Authority and Organization in the Secondary School*, Schools Council Research Studies, London: Macmillan Education.

Riffel, J.A., Levin, B. and Young, J. (1994) 'Diversity in Canadian education', paper presented to the International Intervisitation Program in Educational Administration, Toronto, May 1994 (to be published in the *Journal of Education Policy*).

Simon, B. (1988) *Bending the Rules: The Baker 'Reform' of Education*, London: Lawrence and Wishart.

Walford, G. and Miller, H. (1991) *City Technology Colleges*, Buckingham: Open University Press.

Warde, A. (1994) 'Consumers, identity and belonging; reflections on some theses of Zygmunt Bauman' in R. Keat, N. Whiteley and N. Abercrombie (eds) *The Authority of the Consumer*, London: Routledge.

West, A., David, M., Hailes, J. and Ribbens, J. (1995) 'Parents and the process of choosing secondary schools: implications for schools', *Educational Management and Administration* 23(1): 28–38.

Whitty, G., Edwards, T. and Gewirtz, S. (1993) *Specialisation and Choice in Urban Education: the City Technology College Experiment*, London: Routledge.

Woods, P.A. (1993) 'Parental perspectives on choice in the UK: preliminary thoughts on meanings and realities of choice in education', paper presented at American Educational Research Association Conference, Atlanta, April 1993.

Woods, P.A. (1994) 'Parents and choice in local competitive arenas: first findings from the main phase of the PASCI study', paper presented at the Annual Meeting of the American Educational Research Association, April 1994.

Woods, P.A., Bagley, C. and Glatter, R. (1996) 'Dynamics of competition: the effects of local competitive arenas on schools', in C. Pole and R. Chawla-Duggan (eds) *Reshaping Education in the 1990s: Perspectives on Secondary Schooling*, London: Falmer Press.

3

MARKETING QUALITY

Traditional and modern versions of educational excellence

Tony Edwards and Geoff Whitty

INTRODUCTION

Private schools in England, especially those for boys, have had a natural constituency among social élites whose frame of reference so thoroughly excluded state schools that reputable private alternatives needed no marketing at all. That clientele's custom has hugely reinforced the social prestige of their 'chosen' schools, thereby creating for *arriviste* consumers the prospect of status conferred by association.

Previously the schools purveyed a strong gentry image largely un-related to academic achievement, enabling new wealth to be 'converted into cultural assets for the next generation' and then reconverted into enhanced economic opportunities' (John Scott 1991: 115). In this chapter,[1] we consider how those cultural assets have been perceived; how they have been partly transformed by being made more academic and (to a limited extent) more meritocratic; how a particular 'humanist' model of élite secondary education has been perpetuated and diffused; and how recent Conservative governments have sought simultaneously to uphold that model while promoting 'modern' alternatives within a diversified system.

CHANGING FORMS OF ÉLITE SCHOOLING

Fees in the private sector are high and have risen faster than the rate of inflation. In 1993-4 for example, they ranged from £3,300 to £8,400 for day pupils at the secondary stage and from £6,900 to £11,400 for boarders. What do those paying them believe they are buying? From inside the sector, they are seen as buying 'high academic standards, high expectations of children, a firm disciplinary framework, and smaller class sizes' (Independent Schools Information Service 1994). That is a more academically inclined answer than would have been given in the

past. The attractions of social exclusiveness, and the consequent opportunities to acquire polish and useful acquaintances, remain important.
So do the perceived benefits of placing children, especially girls, in a
'safe' environment framed by traditional values and partly insulated
from the 'perils' of the youth culture (Edwards *et al.* 1989: 184–190). But
a sector not generally noted for valuing intellectual achievement began
to do so in the 1950s, prompted initially by the need to compete successfully for university places with the state grammar schools and then by
doubts about the capacity of their comprehensive replacements to maintain traditional academic standards. The claim to a causal relationship
between independence and educational excellence therefore became
both a main argument in the political defence of private schooling and
its most obvious marketing strategy (Rae 1981; Salter and Tapper 1985).

Before examining that claim, we note how largely the image of the
entire sector has been shaped by socially exclusive boarding schools for
boys whose products have been conspicuous in various occupational
élites, and by some large, academically-orientated and highly selective
day schools. Yet in 1993–4, when the sector's 2,400 schools contained
about 7 per cent of children of compulsory school age, only one pupil in
six was a boarder and almost half the total were girls. Girls' schools
have generally been more local in their intakes, less socially exclusive,
and less orientated to élite occupations. A preoccupation with élite
formation also draws attention away from the 44 per cent of private
schools which do not have charitable status, being privately owned and
run for profit, and from the many which neither impose a searching test
of ability on would-be entrants nor could persuasively advertise their
academic results. Even from the sector's more academic segments, many
schools which applied for admission to the Government's Assisted
Places Scheme had to be rejected as inappropriate for an initiative
defended explicitly as enabling 'able children from less well-off homes'
to attend 'academically excellent schools' (Edwards *et al.* 1989: 44–45).
It remains to be seen whether doubling the number of places, as the
Prime Minister proposed at the 1995 Conservative Party Conference,
can be achieved without enlisting additional schools not credibly categorised as 'excellent'.

Those market leaders whose products are conspicuously over-
represented in various élites have thrown a halo around many less
'successful' schools. They have also caused the 'public schools question'
to be formulated largely as a question about the preservation or trans-
mission of privilege through a privileged form of schooling. Thus private
schooling is portrayed as 'the main means of transferring economic
status, social position and influence from generation to generation'
(Labour Party 1980: 10), 'a self-reinforcing virtuous circle for those who
can afford it', and an 'inside track to positions of power and influence'

(Hutton 1995: 213). Such assertions are easy to illustrate statistically. Well into the 1980s, about 75 per cent of traditional élites (senior civil servants, clerics, lawyers, officers in the armed forces, merchant bankers) had been privately educated. Even among the 'rising stars' in a less traditional range of occupations, profiled in the *Guardian* newspaper (17 October 1994), that proportion was still about a half. In the merito-cratic political regime purportedly established by Margaret Thatcher, three-quarters of her 1983 Cabinet had been to Oxford or Cambridge, slightly fewer had been privately schooled, two-thirds had followed both those privileged routes, while of her last Cabinet only she herself and one other Minister had not been to a private school (John Scott 1991: 132).

Identifying what the form and content of private schooling contributes directly to the prospects of its products is very much more difficult than such familiar facts imply. The Commission created by a Labour Govern-ment to find ways of integrating the 'public schools' into the national system regarded them as 'arbitrarily conferring advantages on an arbitra-rily selected membership who are already starting life at an advantage' (Public Schools Commission 1970: 102). For much of that membership, private schooling was a rite of passage which reflected rather than created advantage. Yet half the fathers of boys at 'leading' schools whom Irene Fox interviewed (Fox 1985) were new to private education, and half were also first-generation members of 'Class 1' in the social hierarchy. Salter and Tapper (1985: 67–69) argue that parents in the private sector 'are more interested in class reproduction than forms of schooling' and that it is the facilitating of entry to élite occupations (most obviously through attendance at Oxford and Cambridge) that con-stitutes that sector's market appeal. Fox's parents, however, expressed more individualist views of class position. They tended to see that posi-tion as needing to be justified by merit. And although character develop-ment and cultural style were included in the merit bestowed or heightened by private education, it was the prospect of excellent aca-demic results which was highlighted more often (Fox 1984: 85). That represents the significant change in the élite segment of the private sector which we mentioned earlier and now consider more closely.

In so far as private schooling had previously enabled or facilitated entry to high status occupations, its contributions had more to do with traditional expressive values than with certified academic competence. Certainly the Headmasters' Conference to which the heads of the most prestigious boys' schools belonged had long included among its tests of suitability for membership such performance indicators as examination results, size of sixth form, and entry rates to university. It is also true that some girls' schools reflected, in their foundation and their continu-ing academic orientation, the educational aspirations of their founders

(Kamm 1971). But when less than 3 per cent of the age group received a university education, as was still true for example in 1939, then graduate qualifications had little relevance even to many professional and managerial occupations. The cultural capital confirmed or bestowed by private schooling was then much more a matter of character, contacts, confidence and style. But as the growth of the 'service class' accelerated, so the market value of a degree grew. For some purposes, a private schooling might still be sufficient. But in an increasingly credentialist climate, reinforced by a democratic insistence that high positions should be deserved, the orientation of the private sector was altered by the success of the grammar schools in equipping their pupils for an increasingly competitive entry to universities and to the occupations for which a degree was now required. Evidence of boys' education across four decades indicated that grammar schools had proved increasingly effective in providing upward social mobility, so that their pupils were much less homogeneous in social origins than their privately-educated contemporaries but much more homogeneous in their occupational destinations (Halsey *et al.* 1980). The special relationship which many private schools enjoyed with Oxford and Cambridge became much less secure with the decline of Latin as an entrance test, the abolition of entrance scholarships tied to particular schools, and especially with an increasing reliance on A level performance. The response of many private schools was to participate energetically in what came to be viewed as an 'academic revolution' (Rae 1981). The Public Schools Commission had noted a recently enhanced emphasis on academic attainment. By the early 1970s this had become diffused through much of the sector, with an associated increase in the marketing of schools' academic performance.

From meritocratic perspectives the grammar schools seemed to provide a powerful curb on the inheritance of privilege, which raised doubts about weakening that curb through comprehensive reorganisation. Its effectiveness had clearly depended on offering the same kind of academic curriculum to the same standards, thereby opening up similar opportunities. The dilemma is exemplified by Tony Crosland's comments on the 'absurdity' of closing down grammar schools while leaving the bastions of inherited privilege intact (Crosland 1956), and by the acknowledgement by the editors of the first 'Black Paper' assault on the 'cult of egalitarianism' of their own debt to the grammar schools which had 'raised' them from working-class origins, and their anger that 'the fine opportunities given to them . . . are from now on to be denied to children with similar backgrounds' (Cox and Dyson 1969: 7).

The accelerating reorganisation of grammar schools, especially during Thatcher's term as Secretary of State for Education 1970–4, launched the private sector into vigorous campaigning in which associating academic excellence with independence became the obvious means of market differentiation, and maintaining an oasis of traditional academic standards an obvious defensive argument against the Labour Party's declared intention to reduce and 'eventually abolish' private education. The campaign was reinforced by the decision of most direct-grant grammar schools to become 'fully' independent when forced by the Labour Government in 1975 to choose between becoming academically non-selective or losing their public funding. Although some of these schools were ordinary grammar schools which had acquired by historical accident their special status of being funded directly by central government rather than through a local education authority (LEA), they also included many of the most academically selective and academically 'successful' schools in the country. Their complete accession to the private sector added significantly to its general reputation for preserving academic excellence against the 'progressive' and 'egalitarian' heresies which critics perceived as pervading the public sector.

In the segmentation of secondary education, this capacity of private schools to exploit their high visibility as purveyors of a traditional academic education became increasingly important (Teese 1996). Its significance is evident in the criteria cited by parents for choosing a private school, especially those parents identifiable as 'career strategists' by their forward planning of their children's futures. Much of the evidence indicates parents choosing against a form of secondary schooling they believed to have failed (Fox 1984; Johnson 1987) or, as we found in our own research, regarding a place in a private school (especially when a former direct-grant grammar school) as offering a high quality academic education of a kind no longer available in the maintained secondary schools of their locality (Edwards *et al.* 1989: Chapter 9).

That is an image of private education which has been substantially enhanced by the Assisted Places Scheme. The Scheme has been presented as creating through free and subsidised places at selected independent schools an escape route for able children whose neighbourhood comprehensive school could not provide the academic opportunities they deserved. Its public defence has therefore required that participating schools demonstrate their fitness for that purpose by meeting the entirely traditional academic criteria of high pass rates in public examinations, high entry rates to higher education, and a wide choice of academic subjects in the sixth form. For the schools themselves, especially those (almost eighty of them) allocated twenty-five or more places a year, the Scheme makes possible a more academically selective entry than reliance on fee-paying would produce. The opportunity has been seized most eagerly by former direct-grant grammar schools, for which it represented a return to a tradition of scholarships for the 'poor but able', and there are now schools with 40 per cent and more of their pupils on assisted places. But in the more academically-orientated market in which they now operate, the Scheme has enhanced many more schools' competitiveness by securing an intake more likely to 'deliver' high attainments and high levels of entry to university. Certainly the relative success of assisted place holders has been prominent in the private sector's annual reports on the Scheme, and in its more general publicity (e.g. Marks 1992).

Publicising that success has been made easier by a National Curriculum which closely resembles in structure the kind of academic, subject-based curriculum with which private schools are closely associated. Initial expectations that these schools would use their freedom from its statutory requirements to develop a more 'independent' curriculum were therefore unrealistic. Indeed, the more their marketing emphasises the successful delivery of a traditional academic curriculum, the more useful are the national and local league tables of school performance in the GCSE – which has not in practice created for private schools the potentially problematic departures from traditional provision that might have been expected (David Scott 1991) – and especially at A level. Initially, independent schools were not obliged to appear in those tables. That so many chose to do so indicates the marketing benefits of demonstrating their 'quality' – most obviously in the percentage of pupils achieving five or more 'good passes' in GCSE, and the numbers and average points score of those staying on to take the A level. In the now compulsory comparisons of school results by local authority area, reputable private schools which will often be the only (overtly) selective schools to appear in the table are likely to take the 'top' positions. Nationally, and especially as identified by A level scores, they are overwhelmingly dominant in those tables of 'the best hundred schools' which newspapers, even those as 'serious' as the *Financial Times*, present annually. The private sector has therefore often been 'the principal steward and advocate' of A level examinations which contribute so much to its marketing (Hutton 1995: 310).

Such statistics are of obvious value in the collective marketing of private education. Thus the Independent Schools Information Service (1994) reported that 75 per cent of private school pupils achieved five or more good GCSE passes compared with a national average of 38 per cent, and that 77 per cent of the sector's A level candidates achieved three or more A level passes compared with a national average of 48 per cent. It is not surprising, then, that common knowledge of such facts is apparent in interviews with parents which uncover their confidence in the 'better' education offered by private schools and the consequently better prospects which they create. But nor is it surprising that non-selective maintained schools regard such performance tables based on 'raw' results as giving a decidedly misleading impression of the relative effectiveness of highly selective fee-paying schools.

34

ALTERNATIVE VERSIONS OF 'EXCELLENCE'?

So far in this chapter we have emphasised the traditionally academic nature of the education offered by private schools. Yet from the market perspective exemplified by Chubb and Moe (1990), they should also demonstrate that freedom to experiment for which an absence of local democratic control and the compromises which it imposes is believed to be a necessary condition. David Hargreaves (1994) argues that all schools should have the freedom enjoyed by private schools to work to a single, clearly defined, set of objectives. Yet that single-mindedness has taken very similar forms, especially among the élite schools. It is true that private schools have been prominent in some curriculum innovations, most notably in relation to teaching science and mathematics to abler pupils and (more patchily) in the use of information technology. But except at the very small 'progressive' end of the sector, there is no sign of those escape routes for educational and cultural 'dissenters' which commentators elsewhere have cited in defence of private education (e.g. Devins 1989).

Rather, it is primarily for its devotion to 'traditional learning' that the sector has received strong support from the conservative Right. This pre-dominant image creates dilemmas both for market enthusiasts, and for the Government in its promotion of educational diversity. From a market perspective, public education is seen as having become homo-geneous as well as mediocre because consumer demand for greater variety was suppressed by the power of providers to go their own way. Yet those who have argued that schools should be subjected to the disci-plines of consumer preference have tended to assume that the common sense of parents would constrain them *against* wilful experimentation (Whitty 1989). It may therefore be significant that two recent books on the effects of the quasi-market produced by combining local school management and grant-maintained status with supposedly open enrol-ment contain so much on organisational 'flexibility' and so little on any consequent changes in the curriculum (Macbeth *et al*. 1995; Bridges and Husbands 1995). The main outcome of consumer common sense there-fore appears remarkably like the academic curriculum the restoration of which is urged from the conservative Right (e.g. Hillgate Group 1987 and O'Hear 1993). The effects of 'free' parental choice in English condi-tions are still being powerfully shaped by the continuing prestige of the kind of education associated with élite private schooling and by the con-sequent obstacles to securing anything like parity of esteem for conspicu-ous departures from it (Edwards and Whitty 1994).

Those obstacles have been apparent in the Government's promotion of forms of schooling adapted to the presumed needs of a modern work-force. Its first ambitious attempt, the Technical and Vocational Education

Initiative (TVEI), was intended to appeal to pupils deterred from extending their schooling by its apparent lack of direct relevance to employment, faced the traditionally low esteem accorded to vocational education, and predictably failed to attract a due share of the ablest pupils. Also predictable was the exclusion of private schools from the bidding for TVEI funds. Since that exclusion coincided with the introduction of the Assisted Places Scheme, it drew attention to the Government's promotion but 'for other people's children' of radical departures from traditional academic education (Gleeson 1988). Certainly the Scheme made no provision for those private schools with a claim to have modernised their curriculum, or to have special strengths in areas such as science and technology deemed to have particular economic relevance.

If TVEI failed to establish a modern curriculum able to compete on equal terms with the attractions of the traditional academic model, the highly targeted city technology college (CTC) programme announced at the 1986 Conservative Party Conference was an attempt to create a 'new kind of school' orientated explicitly towards an enterprise culture driven forward by high technology. Though limited to twenty even in the initial programme, and then to fifteen by the failure to obtain sufficient private sponsorship, they were intended to exemplify a new pattern of schooling. Their marketing was constrained by having to admit intakes 'representative' in ability, social class and ethnic group of the local population, a requirement dismissed from within the CTC 'movement' as illogical in times of open enrolment, but those CTCs which were new (rather than 'resurrected') schools in new buildings proved quickly successful in creating consumer demand. What it was a demand for, however, is not so easily identified.

As new competition for nearby schools, including (as Ministers hinted) those in the private sector, they were hardly assisted by a collective sales brochure which advertised them as offering 'a good education with vocational relevance' (CTC Trust 1991). The schools themselves have been far more upbeat in their publicity. The following examples, from six different CTCs, are variations on a main theme of modernity. The schools promise 'a new concept in educational thinking' and are 'designed to take advantage of latest developments in education and building design'; they offer prospective clients 'the school of the future', 'a school for tomorrow for the children of today', 'a high-tech school for the twenty-first century', and the use of 'the very latest equipment and teaching techniques' to 'meet and go beyond the challenge of tomorrow' (cited in Whitty et al. 1993). The evidence from our own and other studies indicates, however, that the CTCs' main appeal was neither an especially direct relevance to employment (even though their sponsorship by influential local employers or large national companies was stressed in their promotion) nor the unusually substantial provision for information technology, but parents' beliefs that these new schools were at least partly selective, were better resourced, and were more likely to uphold traditional values and discipline (Whitty *et al.* 1993: 82–89; Walford 1991; Gewirtz *et al.* 1991).

Although these studies were undertaken when CTCs had had little time to demonstrate as well as promise their distinctiveness, the findings indicate a market still stratified in relation to a traditionally academic model of secondary education and to the selectiveness which that is seen to entail. The parents tended to identify private and grammar schools with a better education and with 'getting on', and then to regard CTCs as offering a more accessible alternative within a similar frame of reference and as being nearer the top of the local hierarchy of schools than competing comprehensives rather than as a new choice of a new kind of school. Typical comments from our own research included – 'I think you can class the CTC, just like that, as a grammar school' and 'I couldn't believe our luck when she got in, because it's just like getting a private education' (Whitty *et al.* 1993: 87–88).

These images may have suffered from the relatively poor performance of some CTCs in the league tables of annual results, their 'representative' intakes leading some of their principals to be strong advocates of value-added measures of school effectiveness. Others may prefer to adopt new forms of selection. Walford and Miller (1991; Walford 1994) suggest that CTCs will seek to move up-market as they become established, and in doing so deviate from their intended role as 'centres of excellence' for technology. Certainly an awareness of the benefits of appealing to traditional as well as modern conceptions of excellence has produced some complex discursive positioning in the market-place. Thus one CTC claimed in its prospectus to be promoting 'values appropriate to the Christian ethos of the College within the framework of total quality management', while the appearance of another was welcomed in the local newspaper by a report which was headed 'Experimental college makes the grade with old values' and which then gave prominence to a parent's view that it offered 'a return to old-fashioned teaching standards, school as the way it was when we were young and the children love it' (cited in Whitty *et al.* 1993: 48 and 126).

DIVERSITY AND CHOICE?

Although they themselves may be caught between traditionalism and modernity, CTCs are part of a shift in policy towards forms of *un*common schooling. Their creation was identified in the 1992 Government White Paper, along with the Assisted Places Scheme, as one of the first significant steps towards an education system characterised by 'choice and diversity' (DfE 1992). Yet from a thorough-going market perspective, both steps were weak. Assisted places give (or 'restore') the choice of a traditional academic schooling to parents unfortunate enough to have low incomes but fortunate enough to have an able child and an appropriate school within reach. Conspicuously academic schools are thereby given encouragement *not* to change. CTCs are a small-scale but highly publicised attempt to create demand for a modernised curriculum in a system in which 'technical' schooling has been persistently regarded by parents as inferior to academic alternatives. Vigorously promoted and preferentially funded, they can be regarded as a direct intervention in the market, an 'interference' in the interplay of supply and demand which has not yet done much to break the mould.

Other and more extensive attempts to diversify the curriculum have followed those first moves. Extending government support for a more 'modern' curriculum, the 1991 Technology Schools Initiative gave one-off capital payments to secondary schools (including those maintained by LEAs) willing within the limits of an extensive and prescriptive National Curriculum to specialise in science, technology or mathematics. The Government's promotion of 'technology colleges' in the following year was more mixed in its objectives, since the promise to match with public funding the contributions of private sponsors to stimulate special-isation was initially restricted to voluntary aided and grant-maintained schools and so seemed to critics a blatant example of discrimination against local authorities. That restriction was removed late in 1994, so that nearly half the applications in 1995 were from maintained schools, and the scheme was extended to include specialisation in modern languages. Yet schools which are not LEA-maintained remain highly over-represented amongst these specialist schools. Individual schools are also very differently placed to attract the £100,000 of private sponsor-ship which remains the necessary condition for the special government funding.

That bids have to be made to the Specialist Schools Unit at the Department for Education and Employment illustrates the more general strategy being followed. Since 1993 encouragement has been given for secondary schools to select up to 10 per cent of their intakes on grounds of special aptitude for an area of the curriculum which the school regarded as its particular strength. In the following year, the Dearing review of the National Curriculum appeared to meet some of the persis-tent objections from the Right that its extent denied schools the scope to 'do more of what they do best' and then to market that special exper-tise (Skidelsky 1995). Whether these measures will encourage schools to pursue real diversity, or whether they will enable the more popular schools to choose specialisms (such as musical aptitude) as a cover for social and academic selection remains to be seen.

Potentially the largest move towards a market of autonomous and differentiated schools has been the creation of grant-maintained schools, 'freed' from LEA control by the exercise of a collective consumer voice in favour of self-government. Our concern here is solely with the use made of that autonomy to develop and market new versions of 'excellence'. Clearly regarded by the Government as the vanguard of diversification, they have also been suspected of providing a mechanism for restoring selection. Continuing doubts about the political acceptability of restoring selection too openly led to an initial restriction on changing the 'character' of a grant-maintained school within five years of its achieving that new status. That restriction was then removed as an inappropriate impediment to diversification. At the same time, specialisation was officially differentiated from selection; selection gives choice to schools, whereas specialisation is supposedly consumer-driven because it constitutes a response to the aspirations of parents for particular kinds of schooling (DfE 1992: 9–10).

So far, however, most grant-maintained schools have not chosen to attract custom by specialising in the ways envisaged in the White Paper. Rather, they have used their additional financial resources to market themselves more energetically. This marketing has usually been more obviously of a 'traditional' than of a 'modern' image – even in the case of some schools that have received specialist school funding. There is an obvious analogy here with the market appeal of past status as a selective school (Echols et al. 1990). It is therefore easier to see them as enhancing choice by preserving an existing option than by adding something distinctively new, nor is there evidence as yet of parents being attracted by the 'independent' status itself. There is evidence, however, that they are perceived as being 'better' because they conform more closely to traditional academic standards (Power et al. 1994). Evidence of a tendency to be more academically and socially selective in their intakes comes from the other main study of grant-maintained schools, a main conclusion of which is that they facilitate a two-tier system of chosen and unchosen schools (Bush et al. 1993). This in turn allows over-chosen schools to do the choosing, which creates market conditions very different from those intended or assumed by the advocates of diversity, especially when both parents' choice of school and schools' choice of parents remains so heavily influenced by the dominant academic model of schooling.

CONCLUSION

The current English education system combines an apparent commitment to diversity of institutional forms with a continuing adherence to an academic model of the curriculum. Despite some reduction in the extent and prescriptiveness of the National Curriculum (Dearing 1994), there is little evidence that either schools or parents have yet been persuaded that there is parity of esteem between different models of educational excellence. It is more likely therefore that privileged producers and consumers will continue to search each other out in a progressive segmentation of the market (Ranson 1994). Far from the 'free' interplay of market forces producing a system diversified horizontally in a variety of 'equal but different' forms, it is more likely to create a highly stratified system in which the élite private schools still provide the model against which other schools are judged. Recent encouragement of maintained schools to introduce vocational options from the age of 14 therefore arouses anxiety that this will merely provide new ways of separating academic 'sheep' from vocational 'goats'. That the encouragement has been accompanied by official equivocation as to whether providing vocational options would be a 'sensible choice' for all secondary schools could reinforce the traditional academic–vocational hierarchy (Blackburne 1995).

The diversifying of institutional forms while content is both centrally controlled and segmented is often portrayed as an outcome of compromise between a neo-liberal and a neo-conservative agenda in the 1988 Education Reform Act (Whitty 1989). But we have argued in this chapter that it should also be seen as deeply embedded in the history of English secondary schooling and particularly in assumptions about appropriate élite education. There are of course forces for change. Thus city technology colleges for example have been characterised as a site of struggle between 'the discourse of vocational progressivism' and the 'élitist conceptions of knowledge proselytised by the old humanists' (Ball 1990: 118), or even of a post-modern agenda vying with a modernist one. Yet what has so far remained stubbornly consistent, however those agendas are played out, is the tendency for the system as a whole to fail the already disadvantaged (Smith and Noble 1995). Connell (1993: 19) has remarked that 'justice cannot be achieved by distributing the same amount of a standard good to children of all social classes. . . . That "good" means different things to ruling class and working-class children, and will do different things for them (or to them)'. But marketing different versions of educational excellence has not proved to be a progressive alternative in a context where few parents see the alternatives as being different but equal, and where the entrenched prestige of a traditionally academic education has produced a persistent devaluing of alternatives on the part of those schools able to dominate the market.

A recent OECD (1994) study of choice in several countries concluded that demand side measures were rarely sufficient to create diversity in forms of schooling in highly stratified societies. This certainly appears to have been the case in England where, if anything, parental choice is reinforcing traditional hierarchies. Nor, to date, have the Government's limited interventions to stimulate new forms of schooling been especially effective in challenging those hierarchies. If the fostering of diversity is to be a genuine aim of English education policy, more concerted efforts to establish institutions committed to alternative conceptions of excellence will be needed. These, in turn, will only be successful if it can be demonstrated that they offer both schools and pupils better prospects than adherence to the traditional version of educational excellence.

NOTE

1 This chapter is based on a paper given in the symposium on 'Trading places: educational markets and the school response', American Educational Research Association annual meeting, San Francisco, 21 April 1995.

REFERENCES

Ball, S. (1990) *Politics and Policy Making in Education: Explorations in Policy Sociology.* London: Routledge.

Blackburne, L. (1995) '"Sensible" to shun the vocational', *Times Educational Supplement*, 31 March.

Bridges, D. and Husbands, C. (eds) (1995) *Consorting and Collaborating in the Marketplace*, London: Falmer Press.

Bush, T., Coleman, M. and Glover, D. (1993) *Managing Autonomous Schools*, London: Paul Chapman.

City Technology College Trust (1991) *A Good Education with Vocational Relevance*, London: CTC Trust.

Chubb, J. and Moe, T. (1990) *Politics, Markets and America's Schools*, Washington DC: Brookings Institution.

Connell, R.W. (1993) *Schools and Social Justice*, Toronto: Our Schools/Ourselves.

Crosland, A. (1956) *The Future of Socialism*, London: Cape.

Cox, C.B. and Dyson, A. (eds) (1969) *Crisis in Education: Black Paper 2*, London: Critical Quarterly Society.

Dearing, R. (1994) *The National Curriculum and its Assessment: A New Framework for Schools*, London: School Curriculum and Assessment Authority.

Department for Education (DfE)/Welsh Office (1992) *Choice and Diversity: A New Framework for Schools*, London: HMSO.

Devins, N. (1989) (ed.) *Public Values, Private Schools*, Lewes and Philadelphia: Falmer Press.

Echols, F., McPherson, A. and Willms, D. (1990) 'Parental choice in Scotland', *Journal of Education Policy* 5(3): 207–222.

Edwards, T. and Whitty, G. (1994), 'Inequality and inefficiency in schooling', in A. Glyn and D. Miliband (eds) *Paying for Inequality: The Economic Costs of Social Injustice*, London: Institute for Public Policy Research.

Edwards, T., Fitz, J. and Whitty, G. (1989) *The State and Private Education: An Evaluation of the Assisted Places Scheme*, Lewes: Falmer Press.

Fox, I. (1984) 'The demand for a public school education: a crisis of confidence in comprehensive schooling', in G. Walford (ed.) *British Public Schools: Policy and Practice*, Lewes: Falmer Press.

Fox, I. (1985) *Private Schools and Public Issues: the Parents' View*, London: Macmillan.

Gewirtz, S., Walford, G. and Miller, H. (1991) 'Parents' individualist and collectivist strategies', *International Studies in Sociology of Education* I(1): 173–192.

Gleeson, D. (1988) *TVEI and Secondary Education: A Critical Appraisal*, Buckingham: Open University Press.

Halsey, A., Heath, A. and Ridge, J. (1980) *Origins and Destinations: Family, Class and Education in Modern Britain*, Oxford: Clarendon Press.

Hargreaves, D. (1994) *The Mosaic of Learning: Schools and Teachers for the Next Century*, London: Demos.

Hillgate Group (1987) *The Reform of British Education*, London: Claridge Press.

Hutton, W. (1995) *The State We're In*, London: Cape.

Independent Schools Information Service (1994) *Annual Census 1994*, London: Independent Schools Information Service.

Johnson, D. (1987) *Private Schools and State Schools: Two Systems or One?*, Buckingham: Open University Press.

Kamm, J. (1971) *Indicative Past: One Hundred Years of the Girls' Public Day Schools Trust*, London: Allen and Unwin.

Labour Party (1980) *Private Schools: A Discussion Document*, London: Labour Party.

Macbeth, A., McCreath, D. and Aitcheson, J. (eds) (1995) *Collaborate or Compete? Educational Partnerships in a Market Economy*, London: Falmer Press.

Marks, J. (1992) *The Assisted Places Scheme*, London: Independent Schools Information Service.

OECD (1994) *School: A Matter of Choice*, Paris: Centre for Educational Research and Innovation (CERI), Organisation for Economic Co-operation and Development.

O'Hear, A. (1993) *An Entitlement to Knowledge*, London: Centre for Policy Studies.

Power, S., Halpin, D. and Fitz, J. (1994) 'Parents, pupils and grant-maintained schools', *British Journal of Educational Research* 20(2): 209–226.

Public Schools Commission (1970) *Second Report*, London: HMSO.

Rae, J. (1981) *The Public School Revolution: Britain's Independent Schools, 1964–79*, London: Faber and Faber.

Ranson, S. (1994) 'Towards education for democracy', in S. Tomlinson (ed.), *Educational Reform and its Consequences*, London: Institute of Public Policy Research.

Salter, B. and Tapper, T. (1985) *Power and Policy in Education: the Case of Independent Schooling*, Lewes: Falmer Press.

Scott, David (1991) 'The impact of GCSE on practice and convention in private schools', in G. Walford (ed.) *Private Schooling: Tradition, Change and Diversity*, London: Paul Chapman.

Scott, John (1991) *Who Rules Britain?*, Blackwell: Polity Press.

Skidelsky, R. (1995) 'The National Curriculum and assessment: choice or collectivism?' in S. Lawlor (ed.) *An Education Choice: Pamphlets from the Centre 1987–1994*, London: Centre for Policy Studies.

Smith, T. and Noble, M. (1995) *Education Divides: Poverty and Schooling in the 1990s*, London: Child Poverty Action Group.

Teese, R. (1996) 'Curriculum hierarchy, private schooling and the segmentation of Australian secondary education', *British Journal Sociology of Education* (in press).

Walford, G. (1991) 'Choice of school at the first city technology college', *Educational Studies* 17(10): 65–75.

Walford, G. (1994) *Choice and Equity in Education,* London: Cassell.

Walford, G. and Miller, H. (1991) *City Technology College,* Buckingham: Open University Press.

Whitty, G. (1989) 'The New Right and the national curriculum: state control or market forces?', *Journal of Education Policy* 40(4): 329–341.

Whitty, G., Edwards, T. and Gewirtz, S. (1993) *Specialisation and Choice in Urban Education: The City Technology College Experiment,* London: Routledge.

4

SCHOOL SYSTEM RESPONSES TO EXTERNAL CHANGE
Implications for parental choice of schools[1]
Benjamin Levin and J. Anthony Riffel

INTRODUCTION

This chapter provides a perspective on parental choice of schools, using work on organisational theory to locate questions of choice within a view of the way schools as organisations respond to external pressures or influences. We ask whether the assumptions of choice advocates are consistent with what we know about organisational change and in particular with our knowledge about how school systems understand and respond to external change.

Advocates of parental choice of schools believe that choice will result in schools improving the quality of education they provide in their attempt to maintain or increase enrolment. Changing the external conditions around schools, they argue, will lead to improvements in schools. The belief that schools will change to respond to so-called market forces is widely held. But is the belief justified?

We conclude that schools are poorly organised for analysing changes in their environment, that their orientation to changing external conditions is primarily one of minimising the impact on current practices, and that school systems do not have, or think much about, a strategic view of change. School systems do not have good processes for learning about and responding to changes in their environments except in a very narrow sense. These limitations are not the result of ill will or incompetence, but of long-ingrained patterns of thought and behaviour that will not be easy to change, no matter what policy makers may promulgate. All of this suggests that the responses of schools to parental and student choice are likely to be less beneficial than proponents of choice believe and, for that matter, less harmful than opponents charge.

THEORETICAL FRAMEWORK

Open systems models are still highly influential in shaping thinking about organisations. A common assumption in this literature is that

44

organisational change occurs in response to some external demand, pressure or requirement (Levin 1993; Corwin 1987; Warriner 1984). Organisations that do not change to meet changing conditions will decline or disappear. Much of the current rhetoric about school reform and its link to economic development is based, however implicitly, on this view.

Over the last twenty years or so, however, alternatives to open systems theories have multiplied in response to perceived weaknesses of the theory. To begin with, the distinction between organisations and environments is a problematic one. For most organisations it is not clear where the boundaries should be drawn, nor is it evident that organisations have single environments (Aldrich 1979; Jurkovich 1974; Pfeffer and Salancik 1978). People at different levels of the organisation may face different environments. And the concept of successful adaptation to change is also troublesome. What would it mean for schools to adapt successfully to a changing world? Is successful adaptation signalled simply by the organisation's continuing to exist?

Commentators also disagree on how organisations respond to external change. The open systems view tends to emphasise the role of human action in overcoming the challenges of external change. This approach gives primacy to the role of managers in leading their organisations to successful adaptation. Good leadership leads to success, it is argued. Again, much of the current popular literature on government, management and on educational leadership takes this perspective.

However other work emphasises the limits of human and organisational capacity to adapt (e.g. Aldrich 1979; Warriner 1984). Kaufman notes that 'organisations by and large are not capable of more than marginal changes, while the environment is so volatile that marginal changes are frequently insufficient to assure survival' (Kaufman 1985: 47). Some authors have argued that accidents or crises can also have powerful impacts on organisations, often acting as the triggers for substantive change (Corwin 1987; Dror 1986; Miller 1990). Others stress the ways in which organisations and managers fail – sometimes through oversight and sometimes deliberately – to be responsive and adaptive. The social setting of the organisation and its traditions and practices may affect its external relationships, often unknowingly (McCall and Kaplan 1985; Morgan 1986).

The empirical literature on linkages between schools and environments is scanty, but consistent with the general points raised above. Leithwood et al. (1990) show the vast and seemingly undifferentiated range of issues that school principals report as important. Wills and Peterson (1992) found that the superintendents they studied relied heavily on informal sources of knowledge, gave little prominence to research or data collection, adopted strategies that were highly consistent with existing practices, and saw increased staffing or programming as a primary means of dealing with environmental pressures. Fris and Balderson (1988: 386) concluded that few administrators, even those considered 'effective', 'scanned the environment with an anticipatory set', being much more preoccupied with internal matters and much more influenced by professional ideology. Smylie *et al.* (1993: 35) report 'a tendency for tried-and-true conventions of school administration to grow in saliency under the competing pressure of community relations reforms' in Chicago. Goldring and Rallis (1994), on the other hand, adopt a more optimistic view, arguing that many school principals they studied play an active role in adapting schools to meet changing circumstances in the community.

On the whole, the literature in educational administration has placed considerably more emphasis on the importance of human action than on the limits of our capacity to change (Fullan 1991; Ogawa 1991). But many people see schools as largely unchanged in the face of strong pressures and considerable efforts, giving reason to doubt the efficacy of various interventions. One might well take the view that the most important changes in education occur not through planned efforts of educators, but from actions of external bodies such as governments, and even more from larger social forces in the economy and society. For example, changes in youth unemployment rates have direct consequences for school enrolments; as unemployment rises so do the numbers of people staying in or returning to high school. Changing views about ethnic identity and the place of minorities have led to a great deal of conflict in schools. One could extend considerably this list of areas in which schools have been in the position of, as one respondent put it, 'scrambling to keep up' (Levin 1993).

Most commentators take the position that understanding of the environment is mediated or constructed at least to some degree by people in the organisation itself. The strongest versions of constructivism argue that people in organisations create or select their own environments, and that internal organisational processes are more important in understanding response to the environment than are characteristics of the environment itself (Hedberg 1981; Douglas 1986).

The creation of meaning in organisations is affected by a multitude of factors both inside and outside the organisation. Individual dispositions, backgrounds and interests can be important, as personality and training may predispose people to see issues in particular ways. Role and place in the organisation also shape individuals' responses to external forces (Kiesler and Sproull 1982; Nisbett and Ross, 1980). Much depends on organisational structures and processes such as policy-making and communication systems (Douglas 1986; March 1991), organisational history (March and Olsen 1989), and prevailing ideas in the organisation (Daft and Huber 1987; McCall and Kaplan 1985). Dror's work (1986) is especially insightful in illustrating many 'policy-making incapacities', both those inherent in settings or problems and those in human practices of understanding and action. Recent work in neo-institutionalism (March and Olsen 1989; Wilson 1989) shows that individual organisations are also strongly affected by long-established patterns of practice held in place by features such as professional associations, socialisation through training programmes, collective agreements, regulations set by external authorities, and other features that lie outside any particular organisation. Much educational change is influenced by actors' perceptions of what other jurisdictions are doing (Cohen 1992). Finally, ideas in the general society about a practice such as schooling can have important impacts on what institutions feel able to do. All these elements interact in complex ways to create an organisational world view, or perhaps more often multiple and competing organisational world views.

A rich body of work in organisation theory has illuminated the contextual and contingent nature of organisational functioning. Ideas of 'the garbage can' (Cohen *et al.* 1972), emergent strategy (Mintzberg and Jorgensen 1987), 'fuzzy gambling' (Dror 1986), 'the permanently failing organisation' (Meyer and Zucker 1989) and 'the logic of confidence' (Meyer and Rowan 1977) are all elements of a research tradition that emphasises the complexity, limitations and unpredictability of human behaviour in organisations. One must doubt whether the link between environmental change and organisational response is likely to be a clear or direct one.

The research reported in this paper grows from these roots. We have paid attention to issues of individual understanding and interpretation, but always within an organisational and social context. We are interested in the interplay of these factors, and the particular way in which they are worked out in schools.

THE RESEARCH

The study on which this chapter is based has two main components. One strand has involved collaborative case studies with five school districts in a Canadian province. Participating districts included an urban district with a significant inner city, a suburban district, a district that was both suburban and rural, a rural agricultural district and a self-governing aboriginal education authority on an Indian reserve.

In each district we reviewed official documents such as board and administrative minutes, and interviewed trustees, senior administrators and school principals. In total we conducted forty-three formal interviews, including fifteen school board members, seventeen central office staff and eleven principals. We have also had a number of informal meetings with individuals and groups in each of the participating districts.

The study was intended to be collaborative and useful to our co-operating districts. To this end we wrote a case study report for each district, sent this to all our respondents in the district, and had a variety of follow-up meetings to discuss our reports and the districts' responses to them, resulting in some changes to our case reports.

The second strand of the study looked at the three issues of labour force change, child poverty and information technology across a wider range of school districts in the province. We collected data on the perceptions of school trustees, school superintendents and other educators through several mechanisms, including a survey sent to all school board chairs and chief superintendents, group discussions at various meetings and educational events with school board members and with superintendents, and surveys distributed at professional development events related to our research.

In this paper findings from our study are presented in general terms. This serves to hide the important variability both within and among the districts we have studied. In fact, each of the organisations we have studied has its own history, setting, mythology, political dynamics and sets of practices. These are obscured in this paper for the sake of generalisation. It is important to try to draw more general conclusions, but just as important not to overstate the degree of convergence or to understate the differences among people and organisations.

As well, the discussion that follows is several steps removed from the actual words and beliefs of our respondents. The people we met and talked with are largely absent from this paper, although we claim to be drawing conclusions based on what they said. Some quotations from our data are included in this paper, but we realise that this is quite inadequate to represent their views fully.

Finally, we have struggled with how to present our observations and conclusions in a way that is fair to our collaborating districts and does justice to the situations in which they find themselves and the constraints facing them. We sometimes find ourselves being critical of the ways in which school systems handle issues of understanding and managing external change. We believe that schools could and should do better. At the same time, we know it is all too easy to tell others what to do and assume they can and should do it. Given the collaborative nature of our research, we have tried to find a stance that raises questions about practice, but does so sympathetically.

HOW SCHOOLS PERCEIVE A CHANGING WORLD

School administrators and policy makers feel besieged by changes which affect them but are not under their control. All educators are aware that their work is being affected in important ways by a myriad of factors – changes in families, technology, work habits, popular culture, the media, local and national economics, politics, law, demography and many other areas. Many of our colleagues are unsure of where the task of education now begins or ends, and worry about – or fear – what they see as a shift away from a traditional focus on the learning of academic subjects. Schools are seen as being asked to do more and more at the same time as their resource levels are being reduced and they are being subjected to possibly unprecedented levels of criticism from politicians and business leaders. We found deep wells of both resentment and anxiety among some educators about the pressures they feel themselves under:

> Schools already do too much. I think people in the community feel that way too. Teachers are expected to do too much, we shouldn't have to feed, we shouldn't have to clothe, kids shouldn't be sentenced to school by the justice system, we shouldn't have to do all the social aspects, but then they'll say, somebody has to do it. There's a feeling that if only those governments could figure this out so that teachers could concentrate on teaching, things would be better.

> (Urban principal)

Districts vary in their level of consensus as to which of the myriad issues are most important. In some districts most or all of those we interviewed mentioned the same issues; in other districts there was much less agreement. In no district did we find what could be described as a common world view among those we interviewed. Even when similar issues were mentioned, they were often invested with quite different meanings. For example, within the same district some respondents focused on reductions in funding as critical constraints, while others saw them as opportunities. Some respondents saw criticism from business as an opportunity to develop partnerships while others saw it as distracting schools from more important tasks.

Although our colleagues perceive many changes pressing in on them, their school systems are not very oriented towards their external environments, giving much more attention to internal matters. Much of the thinking in school systems about external pressures is casual and impressionistic. We found that issues such as changes in information technology or district demographics, though widely cited as important by our respondents, were rarely part of the formal agenda of school boards or administrator groups. We were told that in some cases these issues are discussed informally and off the record, but had a difficult time seeing how such discussions were linked to policy or practice.

School districts rely primarily on informal and experiential information sources while more formal and data-based sources may be ignored if they exist at all. Direct contact with teachers, students or parents were always rated higher as important information sources than were local surveys or research done by other organisations. People spoke most often about learning through personal processes: from discussions with staff, from attending conferences, or from interaction with parents:

> We have become aware . . . through the business community, the media, scientific and professional magazines. . . . Parents also volunteer to assist in conveying information because they are equally concerned about their kids acquiring the latest skills. . . . We have a variety of committees too, like the education committee. [T]hey take an active interest in major divisional initiatives, and interact effectively with the school board. There are also 'futurists' who have a high level of awareness about changes taking place in the society, and the future implications of these. . . . Often they do so at conferences. They keep us aware of the changes taking place, the rate of change, their projections for the future, and the need for the school system to remain responsive to changes. We hear from the news media, television, and so on. We also get briefing from the Superintendent's Office.
>
> (Suburban principal)

Professional reading was mentioned by a minority of respondents. Systematic efforts to study what was happening in their communities – for example, through regular surveys of students, parents or other community members – were rarely mentioned. People were more attuned to and more likely to remember individual stories and incidents than they were to use or recall statistical data or formal research results.

In addition to personal contacts, images of issues, often as filtered through media portrayals, can have powerful effects on people's conceptualisations of the world around them. For example, concern about increased levels of violence in schools has been fed by insatiable media interest in all such incidents. Poverty, a much more powerful influence on outcomes, receives much less attention.

Even where good information exists or is gathered, processes for analysing it are weak. Most school systems do not appear to have systematic ways of creating discussion about important changes. We have already noted that discussion of external change does not often find a place on the agendas of school boards or administrator groups. For example, our colleagues in rural districts note that large numbers of young people move away from their communities after school, either for higher education or work. Yet they acknowledge that they have done little either to help young people make this transition or to discuss with them what options the local community might provide:

50

In this area we would keep a very low percentage within the town. If they find jobs it would be in the larger centers and many of them have difficulty in finding the jobs. . . .

I do not think we are doing anything to teach them how to live in the city. A lot of kids can adjust right away, but we also find that when they go to the University some kids will drop out even if they are really good students simply because they have not adjusted to the larger University. We are not preparing them for going to a university or living in a larger city.

(Rural district administrator)

Some districts do have organised study processes, in which groups of teachers and administrators will look at an issue, examine the research, consider current practice and make recommendations for change. Almost all of this kind of activity, however, is concerned with classroom instructional issues such as co-operative learning or alternative assessment; very little of it focuses on understanding the larger context in which schools are operating:

Perhaps in some ways we are our own worst enemy because we haven't put the processes in place to develop our own focus. We don't have a mechanism that links the purpose of division with the policies and programmes, and because we lack this we are more susceptible to being distracted by other issues. . . . If we had a better framework we could know which branch to hang each issue on and be better able to work through the issues.

(Urban district administrator)

Attention in school systems, as in most other organisations, is devoted much more to immediate pressures such as government directives than to longer-term issues such as changes in demography or economic conditions. The response to policy changes made by government is particularly interesting. It seems ironic that school districts complain about how they are either pushed or circumscribed by directions from the government at the same time as they show intense interest in and sometimes rush to respond to any such directions as they appear. For example, our province has recently had a review of school district boundaries that recommended consolidating fifty-six districts into about twenty. Both during this process and since the report was released a number of districts suspended various policy development processes to await the study's outcome even though there has been considerable doubt about whether the changes would be implemented and most of them felt that their current organisation served them well.

Although many educators in our research recognise that schools will need to change, there is not yet much sense of what the changes will

51

be or how they will come about. Schools tend to rely on a limited set of practices to support change, and most of those practices imitate the current situation. For example, when new needs or issues are identified the initial response is to use existing strategies such as adding specialised staff or developing new curricula. 'Projects' are much more common than lasting changes. A particularly interesting feature of change in schools is reliance on staff who volunteer to do something new. As a result, many changes are not institutionalised and may die if key staff leave.

One reason that school systems are driven by short-term pressures and issues is that they typically lack a long-term strategy for change or development. None of the districts we have studied had a long-term strategic or development plan, though some did set and monitor annual priorities. Where goals or mission statements do exist, their link to policy and practice is often weak, largely because there is not the ongoing attention needed to move from statements of principle to changes in practice. For example, one district we studied had developed over several years a set of principles to guide the instructional pro-gramme. Yet in our interviews these were seldom mentioned, and seemed to have little prominence in the organisation's ongoing work. There is a strong orientation at all levels to dealing with immediate problems and little prioritising of organisational resources to meet the essential challenges that everyone seems to see pressing on them:

> It is haphazard because there is no overall plan. [School board members] do not see themselves as elected to change the system even if they go in . . . with this great idea, 'I am going to change what happens'. The system all of a sudden communicates, 'Things have always been done this way. Just cool it, why would you want to change that?' You are seen as the odd ball, and after a while one tires of that, just goes with the flow and does what they are doing.
>
> (Suburban principal)

All of these elements are connected and mutually reinforcing. The lack of attention to changing external conditions supports a view of change focused on immediate changes in classroom practices, which in turn moves attention away from external conditions. The focus on responding to each new government policy measure creates an increasing sense of lack of control over one's own situation, which results in more reliance on someone else – government – to define and address problems.

Many of those we interviewed were aware of these problems, as the quotations illustrate. But what to do about the barriers is less obvious, and our respondents had few specific proposals.

EXPLAINING CURRENT PRACTICES

The overall picture emerging from our research is one of school districts that are not outward looking, that do not systematically gather or analyse information about their changing situation, and that do not think carefully about what and how they need to change.

At the same time, the people we met and talked with in these studies are caring, committed and competent. They work hard and take their responsibilities seriously. They do care about students' welfare. They do want to provide the best education they can. The problems we have noted cannot be ascribed to people who are unwilling to do what they know is right. Rather, the features of these school systems are primarily the result of powerful social and institutional factors. Some aspects of school organisation that work in this direction have already been discussed, but a number of other elements that lie outside the daily life of schools are also important.

Professional background, training and socialisation

Most educators are people who liked school and were successful at it. They are not likely, then, to be oriented towards change, but towards preservation of what worked for them. Moreover, the training of teachers and administrators tends to focus on technical skills of managing the system rather than on conceptual analysis of the system or discussion of alternatives to it. Both undergraduate teacher education and graduate administrator education programmes are heavily oriented to the status quo. Perhaps this is inevitably true of all professional training programmes, but those in education labour under the additional burden that their participants do not hold them in high regard. Educators tend to believe that real wisdom is found in practice, so that the value of formal education, perhaps especially if it is unconventional, is largely dismissed.

Administrator selection and roles

If schools are organisations oriented towards the status quo, then those who are hired into administrative positions are highly likely to be similarly oriented. Promotion may depend primarily on pleasing one's superiors rather than on the demonstration of ability. If the governors are not very interested in change, then the administrators they select are unlikely to be so oriented. Empirical support for these contentions is provided by Hart (1991), who notes that the socialisation of new principals is towards fitting in and not disturbing the status quo despite the rhetoric of educational leadership. This focus may be quite antithetical to the kind of open examination of issues and options that seems necessary to deal effectively with change.

The nature of schooling

Schooling as a process also has some features that work against a more analytical and externally-oriented stance. It is, to begin with, an intensely personal activity, focused around interactions among people. In this sense it is much closer to what Lindblom and Cohen (1979) described as 'interaction' instead of 'analysis'. Where we are constantly involved with others we are less likely to step back, to try to gather data, to ask analytical questions about our work. And the activity-oriented culture of teaching and administration reflects real demands and pressures. There is a great deal to do every day just to manage the day's business.

Schooling is also an activity with multiple, sometimes inconsistent, goals and few clear outcomes. Analytical processes are hard to apply in such situations because it isn't clear what should be analysed, or from what perspective. We noted earlier the multiple and increasing pressures that educators feel. In a given day or week a principal or superintendent will confront a bewildering array of issues: teaching and learning strategies in various subjects, changing technology, physical and sexual abuse issues, youth criminal justice provisions, cultures and patterns of adaptation by immigrants, changing political practices used by various lobby groups, medical needs of multiply handicapped children, foster parenting and child welfare policies, and so on. It is inconceivable that teachers or administrators or school trustees could be knowledgeable about all the important issues facing them, since potentially – and often practically – anything and everything can turn out to be important. Yet they have somehow to cope with these issues.

Regulation

Schools exist in a highly regulated environment. Much of what they do is shaped by restrictions or requirements placed on them by external bodies – primarily governments but also professional organisations, employers, post-secondary institutions and others. In so far as governments require particular courses to be taught (and give national examinations on them), or universities require particular entrance requirements, or accreditation agencies expect certain configurations of staffing, the ability of schools to change is largely constrained. One can think of schools as caught in nets; no single strand may be especially strong, but the overall effect is to prevent anything from moving very much. Moreover, the strands of the web are not only physical, but become internalised by those in schools until they seem natural and inevitable. The limits may be more permeable than anyone imagines, but if they are not tested they remain real.

Public images of schools

Education is one of the areas in which everyone has at least some knowledge because all of us have gone to school. Public images of what schools are or should be are powerful influences on schools, and usually in a conservative direction. People's mental models of schooling, even for teachers, are largely shaped by one's own experience as a student. People may have strongly established ideas about what counts as a school, a classroom, a subject of study, an appropriate atmosphere, a disciplinary code. The power of these in maintaining the status quo can be very real.

IMPLICATIONS FOR SCHOOLS' RESPONSES TO PARENT CHOICE

In light of this discussion, we suggest that we are likely to see the following patterns in schools' responses to student and parent choice:

1 Choice and the response to it will be seen by schools as only one of many issues on the agenda, with different issues pulling in different directions.
2 Schools are unlikely to gather, and unlikely to use if they do gather, organised data about student or parent demographics or preferences. That is, schools will typically not take steps to improve their depth of understanding of the wants and needs of current and potential students. Instead, they will make decisions based on what they believe to be true of these groups, and will overestimate the importance of individual stories or instances.
3 Most schools will focus on a short-term response to what they see as the immediate implications of the policy. They will think in terms of how their enrolment will be affected in the next year or two rather than thinking of change processes that might take five or ten years.
4 Financial considerations will be uppermost. Most of the thinking about responses to choice will be driven by the presumed effects on budgets. While growth in budgets will be seen as desirable, growth in enrolment may or may not be an objective; not all schools will seek to maximise enrolment.
5 Schools will talk about many more changes than they actually make, and most of the changes made will be relatively small-scale. We can expect to see emphasis on public relations activities, changes in surface rules or procedures (e.g. discipline policies), the addition of some

courses seen to be attractive (and possibly the elimination of those seen as less attractive), or other measures that work around the margin of the organisation.

6 Most measures taken will be aimed at maintaining the status quo – largely steps to ensure that enrolment does not drop. Few schools will embark on large changes in their work. The core activities and structures of schooling will not be called into question. Competition will be in terms of the fringes rather than the core of the enterprise.

Moving authority from districts to individual school governing councils is not likely to ameliorate these trends, and may exacerbate them. There is no reason to think that parents or other community members will take a longer-term or broader view of change than do principals or teachers or district staff. The issue is not simply one of political authority, but one of the world view that informs and shapes decisions, whoever might be making them. And the incentive-based rationale for choice is only one of the factors shaping views of schooling. If we are interested in substantive and lasting change we will need not just to change a few contextual elements, but to change the way people think about what schools are and what they do.

The context for schooling is changing in important ways. The pressures that led to governments adopting programmes of choice are real and will not disappear even with changes in government. They are connected with deep-seated changes in our societies, including a better educated and more demanding public, increased cynicism about institutions, varied patterns of living and communication, a decline in the unquestioned respect for traditional authorities, and the growth of consumerist mentalities.

Educators are aware of these forces in a general sense, but do not have a good grasp of them, do not spend much time learning about them, and do not see how these changes might influence what they do each day. Changing these conditions will require dealing not only with economic incentives but with institutional factors, school cultures, and popular 'knowledge' about what schools are and do. We regard these prospects as unlikely, and given the many pressures on schools to maintain the status quo, we do not believe that providing choice of schools will result in large changes to education.

NOTE

1 The research reported in this paper was funded by grants from the University of Manitoba Social Sciences and Humanities Research Fund, the Strategic Grants Program of the Social Sciences and Humanities Research Council of Canada, the Canadian Centre for Management Development, and the General

Research Grants Program of the Social Sciences and Humanities Research Council of Canada. The opinions expressed are those of the authors only.

REFERENCES

Aldrich, H. (1979) *Organizations and Environments*, Englewood Cliffs, NJ: Prentice Hall.

Cohen, D. (1992) 'Policy and practice: the relations between governance and instruction', in G. Grant (ed.) *Review of Research in Education*, 18, Washington: American Educational Research Association.

Cohen, M., March, J. and Olson, J. (1972) 'A garbage can model of organizational choice', *Administrative Science Quarterly* 17(1): 1–25.

Corwin, R. (1987) *The Organization–Society Nexus: A Critical Review of Models and Metaphors*, New York: Greenwood Press.

Daft, R. and Huber, G. (1987) 'How organizations learn', in N. DiTomaso and S. Bacharach (eds) *Research in the Sociology of Organizations* vol. 5, Greenwich, CT: JAI Press.

Douglas, M. (1986) *How Institutions Think*, Syracuse, NY: Syracuse University Press.

Dror, Y. (1986) *Policymaking Under Adversity*, New York: Transaction Books.

Fris, J., and Balderson, J. (1988) 'Leaders' priorities and the congruity imperative', *Alberta Journal of Educational Research* 34(4): 375–389.

Fullan, M. (1991) *The New Meaning of Educational Change*, New York: Teachers College Press/ OISE Press.

Goldring, E. and Rallis, S. (1994) *Principals of Dynamic Schools: Taking Charge of Change*, Newbury Park, CA: Corwin Press, Sage.

Hart, A. (1991) 'Leader succession and socialization: a synthesis', *Review of Educational Research* 61(4): 451–474

Hedberg, B. (1981) 'How organizations learn and unlearn', in Paul Nystrom and William Starbuck (eds) *Handbook of Organizational Design*, New York: Oxford University Press.

Jurkovich, R. (1974) 'A core typology of organizational environments', *Administrative Science Quarterly* 18: 380–394.

Kaufman, H. (1985) *Time, Chance and Organizations: Natural Selection in a Perilous Environment*, Chatham, NJ: Chatham House.

Kiesler, S. and Sproull, L. (1982) 'Managerial response to changing environments: perspectives on problem sensing from social cognition', *Administrative Science Quarterly* 27: 548–570.

Leithwood, K., Cousins, B. and Smith, G. (1990) 'Principals' problem solving: types of problems encountered', *Canadian School Executive* 9(7): 9–12.

Levin, B. (1993) 'School response to a changing environment', *Journal of Educational Administration* 31(2): 4–21.

Lindblom, C. and Cohen, D. (1979) *Usable Knowledge*, New Haven: Yale University Press.

March, J. (1991) 'Exploration and exploitation in education', *Organizational Science* 2(1): 71–87.

March, J. and Olsen, J. (1989) *Rediscovering Institutions*, New York: Free Press.

McCall, M. and Kaplan, R. (1985) *Whatever It Takes: Decision Makers at Work*, Englewood Cliffs: Prentice-Hall.

Meyer, J. and Rowan, B. (1977) 'Institutionalized organizations: formal structure as myth and ceremony', *American Journal of Sociology* 83(2): 340–363.

Meyer, M., and Zucker, L. (1989) *Permanently Failing Organizations*, Beverly Hills, CA: Sage.

Miller, D. (1990) *The Icarus Paradox*, New York: Harper Collins.

Mintzberg, H. and Jorgensen, J. (1987) 'Emergent strategy for public policy', *Canadian Public Administration* 30: 214–229.

Morgan, G. (1986) *Images of Organization*, Newbury Park: Sage.

Nisbett, R. and Ross, L. (1980) *Human Inferences: Strategies and Shortcomings of Social Judgment*, Englewood Cliffs: Prentice Hall.

Ogawa, R. (1991, April) 'Implications of an institutional perspective on organizations for examining instructional leadership', paper presented to the American Educational Research Association, Chicago.

Pfeffer, J. and Salancik, G. (1978) *The External Control of Organizations: A Resource Dependence Perspective*, New York: Harper and Row.

Smylie, M., Crowson, R., Hare, V. and Levin, R. (1993, April) 'The principal and community–school connections in Chicago's radical reform', paper presented to the American Educational Research Association, Atlanta.

Starbuck, W. (1976) 'Organizations and their environments', in M. Dunnette (ed.) *Handbook of Organizational and Industrial Psychology*, Chicago: Rand McNally.

Warriner, C. (1984) *Organizations and their Environments: Essays in the Sociology of Organizations*, Greenwich, CT: JAI Press.

Wills, F. and Peterson, K. (1992) 'External pressures for reform and strategy formation at the district level: superintendents' interpretations of state demands', *Educational Evaluation and Policy Analysis* 14(3): 241–260.

Wilson, J. (1989) *Bureaucracy*, New York: Basic Books.

5

OPTING INTO THE PAST?

Grant-maintained schools and the reinvention of tradition

David Halpin, Sally Power and John Fitz

INTRODUCTION

This chapter, which is based on research carried out between 1992 and 1994, explores the impact of self-governing status on institutional continuity and change in a sample of English grant-maintained (GM) or 'opted out' secondary schools.[1,2] In particular, it assesses the extent to which the autonomy enjoyed by individual GM schools contributes to conservation and innovation in their working patterns, curriculum and educational identities.

The chapter is written in five parts. Part 1 briefly outlines the political origins of the GM schools policy and reviews the scale of opting out. Part 2 offers an account of our research objectives, theoretical concerns and fieldwork methods. Part 3 provides a summary of the overall tendencies as they relate to change and innovation. Part 4 theorises these findings in the light of Anthony Giddens' (1994a) analysis of 'fundamentalisms' within a context of 'manufactured uncertainty'. Part 5 reflects on the research implications of our work.

THE POLITICAL ORIGINS AND SCALE OF OPTING OUT

The policy of creating GM schools was promoted in the mid-1980s in England and Wales by Conservative politicians and their advisers (see Fitz, Halpin and Power 1993: 18–28) and first legislated for in the 1988 Education Reform Act. That Act enabled schools in England and Wales, following a secret ballot of parents, to opt out of their local education authorities (LEAs) and become autonomously incorporated institutions directly funded by central government.

In common with much recent educational reform, the precise objectives of the GM schools policy are complex and shifting. Nevertheless, the policy's advocates have consistently claimed that enabling schools to break free of their LEAs will bring widespread systemic benefits. Giving schools 'full control of their own destinies' (Conservative Party 1992) will, it is claimed, enhance the responsiveness of education professionals. While the bureaucratic, and allegedly often politically motivated, control of LEAs is seen to inhibit flexibility and innovation, self-governance brings teachers the freedom to experiment and transform. This, in turn, enables GM schools to overcome the dull uniformity which, it is argued, characterises LEA-maintained provision. In short, GM schools will use their autonomy to become 'leading edge' institutions or 'beacons of excellence' that make a difference by offering something which is both distinctive and exemplary.

At the time of writing just over 1,000 primary and secondary schools in England have opted out of LEA control. This represents slightly more than 4 per cent of all state-maintained schools in England, or 2 per cent of primaries and just under 16 per cent of secondaries, and involves approximately 10 per cent of the school age population. Although these figures do not amount to a radical transformation in state schooling, the policy's impact should not be underestimated. Certainly, few LEAs in England remain untouched in one way or another by the policy. Moreover, while the pace of opting out has certainly slowed, the experience of the early GM schools is important for both policy makers and researchers. While policy makers may uphold the 'GM experience' as the blueprint for future reform, policy researchers can use it to explore the relationship between institutional autonomy and educational continuity and change.

RESEARCH DESIGN

The concerns addressed in this paper derive from the second of two investigations into the GM schools policy. The first project looked at the ways in which the policy was implemented and its early impact on education authorities and education markets. The second project shifted focus to concentrate on the changes which opting out has wrought *within* schools. Our chief research aim was to explore how the form of self-governance arising from the GM schools legislation impacts on the organisational features, management structures and educational identities of schools. This aim arose initially out of two theoretical preoccupations. The first was associated with the conceptualisation of the relationship between any discernible changes in the division of labour within self-governing GM secondary schools and the degree of institutional autonomy experienced by such schools. The second related to the extent to which increased differentiation of local systems of school provision promoted by the GM schools policy assists in the creation of distinctive identities within and between schools. In this connection, there was an underlying concern to examine the degree to which the magnification of organizational diversity within local school systems helps to reproduce or modify prevailing conceptions of what counts as a 'good' education. We considered it axiomatic that as the British Government pursues a market policy for education based on diversity and choice, schools as institutions and pupils as individuals will be subject to parallel processes of reorientation and re-identification.

In order to explore the connections between institutional autonomy, innovation and educational identity, in-depth fieldwork was undertaken in seventeen secondary schools, nine of which are grant-maintained, seven LEA-maintained, and one privately funded. Six of the nine GM schools featured in our earlier study of opting out (see Fitz, Halpin and Power 1993), as did the private school and four of the LEA schools. Indeed, the research reported on here involved us returning to three localities in each of which the GM schools in our sample were in direct competition with schools from both the private and LEA-maintained sectors.

The relationship between institutional autonomy and changes in the distribution of power and control was investigated through a question-naire survey of teachers working in each of the six previously researched GM schools, all of the LEA schools and the private school. Issues sur-rounding whether institutional autonomy enjoyed by self-governing GM secondary schools helps them to be innovative and in ways that either 'break the mould' of, or significantly depart from, conventional notions of 'good' schooling were explored through semi-structured (audio-recorded) interviews with the headteachers of all seventeen schools in our sample. These were supplemented by further interviews of a similar nature with a range of governors. The extent to which institutional autonomy fosters diversity of pupil experience of schooling and contri-butes to differentiated and stratified educational identities was researched in two ways: first, through the use of a questionnaire survey of Year 7 pupils drawn from the six previously researched GM schools, six of the LEA-maintained schools and the private school; and, second, by con-ducting semi-structured (notebook-recorded) interviews with Year 9, 10 and 11 pupils, all of whom had taken part in our first study of the GM schools policy.

Clearly, only a fraction of the issues which these data raise can be con-sidered here. In the following section, we will consider some of the key findings as they relate to continuity and change at the level of manage-ment, curriculum and pupil experience. Where individual schools are mentioned, they have been given pseudonyms.

MANAGEMENT, CURRICULUM AND PUPIL EXPERIENCE

Management

All of the GM schools in our sample can be considered to have success-fully absorbed the extra responsibilities of self-governing status inasmuch as staff are paid, resources provided and the curriculum delivered. How-ever, the costs, measured in the committed time and effort required of headteachers and governors in this process, have been substantial. Indeed, our clear impression is that GM school autonomy comes with a high price tag. Moreover, it is headteachers and senior management teams who bear most of the brunt of the increased responsibilities – a finding which is also reflected in research on headteachers in LEA-maintained schools operating under the local management of schools (LMS) policy (Bullock and Thomas 1994). However, while headteachers are often keen to stress the extra work which self-governance entails, they frequently neglect to mention the enhanced opportunities it affords them as managers.

There is little doubt that the acquisition of GM status is followed by a noticeable shift in power and control upwards to headteachers who are located at the centre of all flows of information, advice and policy direc-tives coming into the school. In this sense GM heads are well placed to 'manage' both staff and governors. Thus, despite the extra responsibilities which governing bodies in GM schools carry, they are rarely involved in determining matters of whole school policy on central issues relating to, for instance, the curriculum. It is headteachers who force most of the pace and shape most of the key decisions. Similarly, for all the GM schools in our study, autonomy has not as yet been translated into a dif-ferent, more extended, notion of teacher professionalism and empower-ment. In this connection, we have no data to suggest that the advent of GM status results in classroom teachers having a greater material control over educational activities such as determining whole school priorities and other policies such as those affecting pupil grouping, discipline and intake, although an increased number of middle managers (mostly sub-ject heads of department) are now significant budget-holders in their own right and thus more involved in financial decision-making. Although other work (e.g. Maychell 1994) suggests that similar processes are taking place in schools operating under LMS, our data suggest that the concentration of power within the hands of the headteacher is more pronounced in schools which have opted out. Our questionnaire survey of teachers in LEA and GM schools indicates that staff in GM schools are *less* likely to be involved in decision-making. Nearly one-half of teacher respondents claimed not to have been engaged in consultations on matters of whole school policy with their headteacher during the week preceding the survey. This was the case for less than one-third of the teachers in our LMS sample. Conversely, while nearly two-fifths of respondents in LMS schools had been consulted on policy issues at least twice that week, only one-quarter of staff in opted-out schools had. In some schools, opting out had made the headteacher more distant from the body of staff. Teachers reported that the headteacher 'seems more remote', 'acts far more as an accountant now – less visible to staff and kids', being generally 'less accessible'.

Of course, negative comments about headteachers are by no means confined to GM schools. Teachers in schools operating under LMS could also be critical – though the claim that heads are preoccupied with finance and reputation featured less. Similarly, staff in some GM schools were extremely positive about their heads. Indeed, where the process of opting out had been bitter and protracted, staff spoke of closer relationships than hitherto. We comment elsewhere (Power, Halpin and Fitz 1996) that consistent patterns are hard to find. One of the key findings of the project has been the extent to which opting out has *localised* the provision of education. This has led to the personality and priorities of the GM headteacher being writ large throughout the school in highly visible and pervasive ways. Thus whether the headteacher was seen to be autocratic, charismatic or even, and exceptionally, democratic, there was little ambiguity over who set the tone.

We are in no position to pronounce judgement about the significance of this outcome. We are certainly not able to conclude whether the leadership styles adopted by some GM heads and the consolidation of power and control at the top of their institutions are good or bad things. For while Hargreaves (1994) argues that a stricter division of labour between those who mostly 'manage' and those who mostly teach may be a more efficient and therefore more effective way of running schools, other analyses would suggest differently. Indeed, there is general agreement by researchers in the area that teacher empowerment is a necessary condition for greater school effectiveness.

Either way, there can be little doubt that the autonomy of the kind afforded by opting out has no inevitable implications for the development of innovative practice. GM schools are more likely to have additional administrative posts and more teacher support than adjacent locally managed LEA institutions. But these developments are not associated with an organizational structure that departs from that found in most schools – indeed, our data would suggest that it is more hierarchical and traditional than that found in many LEA-maintained schools.

Curriculum

Similarly, curricular change within the GM schools in our sample was limited, but not unknown. Greenbank, for instance, serves a largely

Asian community and has sought to reflect aspects of its cultural heritage within the curriculum. The school has introduced Bengali and Urdu as GCSE modern languages and has Islamic Studies as an option choice. A level Urdu will soon be introduced into the new sixth form. Northwood, a girls' comprehensive, emphasizes and invests in its science and technology curriculum in order to provide its students with opportunities hitherto monopolised by boys.

However, these innovations are exceptional. While the picture is somewhat obscured by the introduction of the National Curriculum, few of the schools in our sample have embarked upon significant curriculum reform. Most of the changes mentioned by GM headteachers in interview represent either glosses on the National Curriculum (notably in technology) or revivals of academic selectivity and traditional modes of education generally. Even where, as above, there have been attempts to 'modernise' the curriculum, these are surrounded by a proliferation of traditional values and symbols. For instance, Greenbank also emphasises the traditionalism of the English academic curriculum, where *'old* standards . . . are cherished and upheld'. Northwood, despite its 'high tech' image, requires that the girls use fountain rather than ballpoint pens. Bellevue, an ex-grammar school, represents the most extreme case of 'opting into the past'. The school is busy delineating behaviours and installing 'props' to augment its legacy. For instance, £10,000 has been spent providing a pipe organ for assemblies. Pupils may no longer call the place where they have lunch a 'canteen' but must refer to it instead as the 'dining hall'. And again, while we would not want to argue that this trend is unique to GM schools, the extra money and flexibility of GM schools just means that they can take it further than other maintained schools.

Pupil experience

Associating GM status with being 'more' and 'better' than other schools has been an emergent feature of our pupil interview data. Whereas in our first study of opting out many GM pupils had ambivalent feelings about or were ignorant of the implications or meaning of GM status, there is now a greater tendency for older GM pupils to identify differences between the character of their own and adjacent locally managed LEA schools. An increasing number are aware of the relatively elevated status of their particular school. In many cases, this is connected with the new resources with which the school has been invested. However, frequent reference was also made to the enhanced nature of the school's local reputation. Many students have an increased sense of 'being different' from their counterparts in LEA-maintained schools. A few spoke, often with resentment, of the imposed responsibility of being 'flag-bearers' not just of their school but of a school movement. Usually, however, this feeling of 'otherness' was rarely articulated in terms of opting out. Rather, it seemed to be based upon an appreciation that certain traditional 'rules' and 'routines' commonsensically contribute to a well run school. For example, in assessing their own and other schools' reputations, students made connections between the strictness of the uniform and the level of discipline and learning. These associations were by no means unproblematic, however. For while students made these connections in a commonsensical way, they were often aware of the gap between the image of their own school and its reality. They were not only often conscious of the superficiality of rules and routines as indicators of discipline and learning, but were also less than enthusiastic about their having any value for their own educational development.

This mismatch between commonsensical perceptions of schooling and their own experience as pupils is important because it indicates a lack of coherence between what is held up as 'good' schooling and visions of what might be a useful and appropriate education. Moreover, this lack of coherence is likely to be reinforced by a growing disjuncture between the world of the school and worlds outside. If the concept of the 'information superhighway' provides an appropriate metaphor for the ways in which students will communicate in home and work settings, the 'GM experience' promotes the equivalence of a stroll down memory lane.

TRADITIONALISM AND THE UNCERTAINTIES OF THE EDUCATION MARKET PLACE

So, how can we understand the many ways in which schools are 'opting into the past'? Some explanations might focus on the political complexion of central government, the public pronouncements of which are clearly underlain by a preference for old-fashioned values. However, no matter what the Government's implicit and often explicit perception of what counts as 'real' schooling, there is nothing within the terms of the GM legislation which prevents GM schools from being more innovative. Indeed, the 1992 White Paper (DfE 1992) and 1993 Education Act expressly encourage diversification. It might, therefore, be more appropriate to explain GM schools' conservatism in terms of the English context in which 'educational innovation has persistently failed when it has diverged too sharply from the academic model' (Edwards and Whitty 1992: 113). In this light, it is possible to argue that GM schools represent the latest manifestation of 'a constant tendency to revert to a bipartite or tripartite division across very different formal structures' (Johnson 1989: 95).

We would not want to suggest that the experience of GM schools dis-confirms this trend. And we would certainly not claim that opting out is likely to interrupt the associated patterns of social class differentiation and educational opportunity. On the other hand, we wonder whether the reinvigorated traditionalism of GM schools represents something more than continuity. In this connection, what at first sight appears to be an anachronistic legacy might be recently manufactured. Bellevue's reinvented traditionalism is more thoroughgoing than any it experienced as a grammar school with a strong academic reputation. While it may draw on this powerful legacy, the school's pipe organ and retitled 'dining room' are newer than its computer suite. Bellevue's traditionalism is certainly more recent than the continued allegiance to the ideals of the progressive comprehensive school evident in the LEA-maintained sector.

The organizational orthodoxies and curriculum and pedagogical con-servatisms to which reference has been made might represent a response to the 'manufactured uncertainties' of the education market place. Anthony Giddens characterises 'manufactured uncertainties' as 'global-ised forms of risk', the damage resulting from which is impossible to compensate for because 'their long-term consequences are unknown and cannot be properly evaluated'. He identifies four global 'bads' that provide the main contexts in which manufactured uncertainty is experi-enced: the negative impact of modern social development on the world's ecosystems; the polarising effect that global capitalist markets exert on world-wide distributions of wealth and income; the widespread existence of weapons of mass destruction; and the large-scale repression of demo-cratic rights (Giddens 1994a: 97–100).

To suggest that such profound forms of globalised risk articulate straightforwardly with the potentially unsettling consequences of the education market place lays us open to the charge of overstretching, even trivialising, Giddens' analysis. But our starting point is the assump-tion that the education market place is a distributive mechanism pre-mised on capitalistic economic principles. As such, it creates its own set of uncertainties which, like Giddens' 'global bads', willy-nilly interpene-trate people's everyday lives, especially teachers', parents' and children's, whose experience of the education service takes on a greater degree of indeterminacy than hitherto. What they previously regarded as a rela-tively stable and enduring service is now experienced as fallible and obdurately imperfectable. Thus headteachers can no longer assume a steady and ready supply of pupils to fill their schools; teachers no longer feel that permanency is written into their informal working condi-tions and they feel undermined professionally; parents can no longer be confident that they will get the school of their choice or the education they want for their children; and pupils, faced with uncertain futures of their own, no longer accord schools the moral authority which in a previous age could mostly be taken for granted. Moreover, 'manufactured uncertainties' do not impact only through the means by which education is distributed – they are likely to threaten the legitimacy of the entire enterprise. Education as a national resource is at the centre of the enlightenment project.

Confronted by this wave of uncertainty, schools can respond, broadly speaking, in either one of two ways: they can imitate a particular version of the past in order to protect against chronic contingency, or they can engage with and anticipate change through innovation and risk-taking. In our sample of schools, it is the former rather than the latter strategy to which headteachers are more attracted. They seek comfort in reproducing the past, an approach they 'justify' in terms that take for granted its 'traditional' qualities. Indeed, their interpretation of 'tradition' in education is that of an a priori 'good', which they use to celebrate an unchangeable past and to defend the status quo, including their 'rights' as managers to manage and the subordinate role of pupils. However, as we stress, what they draw on in this process is assumed rather than made available to discursive justification. This gives rise to a form of educational 'fundamentalism' (Giddens 1994a: 84–86) in which certain 'rules', 'routines' and 'rituals' are 'reinvented' and defended in a traditional way. Defending tradition in the traditional way means asserting its 'formulaic truth without regard to consequences' (Giddens 1994b: 100). This entails a disengagement from the requirement to justify one's position using reasons. In our sample of GM schools, the assertion of formulaic truth amounts to an unargued-for reconsolidation of educational values which prioritises academic achievement and assumes an unproblematic interpretation of the role of authority. Through assemblies, systems of rewards and punishments and rigorously enforced dress codes, the schools reproduce without argument a 'traditional' education based on conventionally understood notions of rigour and discipline. In their literature – prospectuses, mission statements, etc. – they reiterate the self-evident 'truth' that a 'traditional' education is by definition a better education.

This is profoundly paradoxical. In a society whose members are routinely caught up in 'everyday experiments' (Giddens 1994a: 93 and 1994b: 59–60) involving 'a multiplicity of changes and adaptations in daily life', 'deciding "how to be" in respect of the body . . . what one's "sexuality" is, as well as grasp what "relationships" are and how they might best be constructed' (Giddens 1994a: 82–83), and which therefore require them 'to choose among alternatives', we have here a group of schools which deny, without serious reflection, the possibility and utility of other ways of doing things. Instead, they are uncomplicatedly wedded to the past; they inherit old rather than create new working patterns. They reinforce, even actively promote, a growing disjuncture between the world of the school and worlds outside.

But why are these schools so risk-aversive? Why, given their high degree of relative autonomy from external constraint, do they swing towards traditionalism? It could be said that this trend is nothing more than superficial gloss or a cynical marketing ploy designed to manufacture associations between 'good' education and high status models of schooling with the aim of attracting gullible or frightened parents. But this account doesn't explain why educational conservatism is presently so appealing nor, relatedly, why alternative value systems are so unreassuring and therefore unattractive. We need, then, an account which articulates current swings towards traditionalism in education with wider social transformations. Giddens' analysis certainly helps here, but only, we think, up to a point. For while Giddens enables us to appreciate better the links between traditionalism in education and fundamentalism generally, his account does not explain the current salience of this phenomenon. Stuart Hall's (1988: 138–147) discussion of the nature of the emergence of what he terms 'authoritarian populism', on the other hand, may. Briefly, Hall argues that the power of the Right in recent times to redefine significant fields of public discourse – around popular morality, 'law and order' and 'welfare' – derives in large part from its capacity to exploit successfully particular fissures in modern British society, most notably the weakening political base of social democracy. The context here is a crisis of political representation in which old allegiances and visions appear to be breaking down (witness the emergence of New Labour and the abandonment by both socialists and Tories of class politics in favour of appeals to 'middle Englanders'). Traditionalism successfully fills this vacuum through its wide (populist) appeal and its 'common touch'; its ability to condense moral, philosophical and social themes; and its capacity to make reaction radical. On this understanding, the current fashion for traditionalism in education (and traditionalism in discourse around the family and elsewhere) articulates with conditions of radical social upheaval that (after Giddens) create sets of new uncertainties. What it does, at a time when people are chronically unsure of which way to turn, is produce a new, but familiar, kind of common sense which makes the conditions of their lives intelligible because it addresses what are perceived to be 'real problems, real and lived experiences, real contradictions' (Hall 1988: 56).

SUMMARY AND IDEAS FOR FURTHER RESEARCH

To summarise: GM schools enjoy a regulated autonomy and exhibit a tendency towards managerial orthodoxy. The form of self-governance entailed in the GM schools policy has been translated broadly into a segmented hierarchy of power and control in which headteachers have increased capacity to manage staff and governors. There is no evidence that institutional autonomy is transforming the work of classroom teachers. Moreover, in local competitive settings, GM schools consolidate and recreate existing institutional identities and eschew radically redefining their purpose or attempting new, mould-breaking forms of curriculum development or delivery.

On the other hand, pupils being educated in a GM school are frequently very aware of their schools' relatively elevated status and of their responsibility to uphold its local reputation. While such pupils mostly hold on to a conventional conception of 'good' schooling, they are often either ambivalent about, or hostile to, the manner in which this is interpreted, particularly in relation to dress codes and traditional rules and routines. Paradoxically, it is frequently along traditional lines of this sort that such pupils distinguish positively their school from others in the same locality.

NOTES

1 The research reported here was funded for two years (1992–4) by the Economic and Social Research Council, the support of which we gratefully acknowledge.
2 A longer version of this chapter, which includes two case studies, was presented at the 'Trading places: education markets and the school response' Symposium, Annual Meeting of the American Educational Research Association, San Francisco, 21 April 1995.

REFERENCES

Bullock, A. and Thomas, H. (1994) 'Context, complexity and the impact of local management', paper presented at the Annual Conference of the British Educational Research Association, St Anne's College, Oxford, 8–11 September.

Conservative Party (1992) *Better Schools – Better Standards*, London: Conservative and Unionist Central Office.

Department for Education (DfE)/Welsh Office (1992) *Choice and Diversity: A New Framework for Schools*, London: HMSO.

Edwards, T. and Whitty, G. (1992) 'Parental choice and educational reform in Britain and the United States', *British Journal of Educational Studies* 40(2): 101–117.

Fitz, J., Halpin, D. and Power, S. (1993) *Grant Maintained Schools: Education in the Market Place*, London: Kogan Page.

Giddens, A. (1994a) *Beyond Left and Right: The Future of Radical Politics*, Cambridge: Polity Press.

Giddens, A. (1994b) 'Living in a post-traditional society', in U. Beck, A. Giddens and S. Lash (eds) *Reflexive Modernisation: Politics, Tradition and Aesthetics in the Modern Social Order*, Cambridge: Polity Press.

Hall, S. (1988) *The Hard Road to Renewal: Thatcherism and the Crisis of the Left*, London: Verso.

Hargreaves, D. (1994) *The Mosaic of Learning: Schools and Teachers for the Next Century*, Cambridge: Demos.

Johnson, R. (1989) 'Thatcherism and English education: breaking the mould or confirming a pattern?', *History of Education* 18(2): 91–121.

Maychell, K. (1994) *Counting the Cost: The Impact of LMS on Schools' Patterns of Spending*, Windsor: National Foundation for Educational Research.

Power, S., Halpin, D. and Fitz, J. (1996) 'School autonomy and grant-maintained status: the English experience', in C. Pole and R. Chawla-Duggan (eds) *Reshaping Education in the 1990s: Perspectives on Secondary Schooling*, Lewes: Falmer Press.

Walford, G. (1993) *Choice and Equity in Education*, London: Cassell.

6

SCHOOLS' RESPONSIVENESS TO PARENTS' VIEWS AT KEY STAGE ONE

Martin Hughes

INTRODUCTION

One central feature of the recent educational reforms in England and Wales is the explicit encouragement of an educational 'market' (e.g. DfE 1992). In such a market, schools are seen primarily as 'producers' (or traders), while parents are cast in the role of 'consumers' (or customers). The operation of this market assumes, amongst other things, that schools will be aware of the preferences of their parents, and that they will take active steps to change their practice in accordance with these preferences. In other words, it is assumed that the external pressures of the market will lead to internal changes in the functioning of schools (Bagley *et al.* 1996).

This chapter[1] will present findings which cast some doubt on these assumptions. In particular, the chapter will raise questions about the extent to which schools are aware of their parents' views, and about the extent to which they will change their practice to accommodate these views. The chapter will argue that other forces operating within schools – such as teachers' sense of their own professionalism and their deeply-held views about the role of parents – present a substantial barrier to the development of an educational market.

THE PAKSO PROJECT

The findings reported in this chapter are drawn from the work of an ESRC-funded project on 'Parents and Assessment at Key Stage One' (the PAKSO project). This project was part of a larger ESRC programme on 'Innovation and Change in Education', which has been examining the quality of teaching and learning in the context of the recent educational reforms. The PAKSO project ran from 1991 to 1994, while the programme on 'Innovation and Change' started in 1991 and is due to finish in 1996. Further information about PAKSO can be found in Holden *et al.*

(1993, 1996) and Desforges *et al.* (1994a, 1994b, 1995), while the work of the larger programme is described in Hughes (1995).

The PAKSO project looked at the relationship between parents and schools in the context of the standardised assessment procedures introduced for seven-year-old children at Key Stage One. Such assessment procedures are seen as having a particular prominence within the market model, in that they supposedly provide parents, in their role as customers, with product information calibrated to national standards. The project focused on Key Stage One as this was the phase of schooling where many of the educational reforms were first introduced (see Pollard *et al.* 1994; Plewis and Veltman 1995 for other accounts of the effects of the reforms on Key Stage One).

The conceptual framework underlying the PAKSO project is shown in Figure 6.1. Although this model is necessarily a simplification of complex social processes, it nevertheless depicts some of the core processes implicit in the thinking behind the 1988 Education Reform Act. The arrows in the diagram indicate the assumed direction of influences if these core processes are to operate in practice. These processes are seen as operating over a period of time, represented by the horizontal axis of the diagram. For the purposes of the PAKSO project, the time period consists of a few months either side of the standardised assessment procedures operating at Key Stage One.

The model attempts to explain how parents' views might influence classroom practice, and vice versa. Parents' initial views are represented

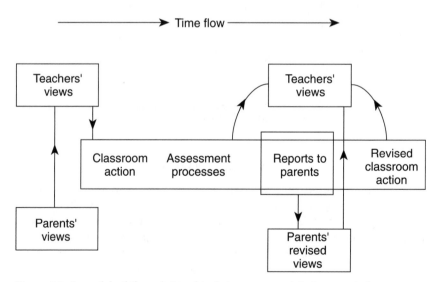

Figure 6.1 A model of the relationship between parents' views and classroom practice.

by the box on the lower left-hand side of the figure. It is assumed that, if parents' views are to influence classroom practice, then they must do so by first influencing teachers' views (the box on the upper left-hand side of the figure). In other words, if teachers are to be responsive to parents' views, then they must have at least some awareness of what these views are. Similarly, there must be opportunities for teachers to amend their classroom practice in the light of parents' views. Within the model, a central role is given to the procedures for collecting and reporting assessment information. The model assumes that these procedures present crucial opportunities for parents and teachers to refine their views, in the light of the supposedly objective evidence presented by the assessments. For parents, possible revisions to their views will come primarily from the reporting process. For teachers, revision can come both from their direct involvement in the assessment process and from their subsequent discussion of assessment results with parents.

The PAKSO project consisted of two separate studies, both of which will be drawn on here. Study One was a large-scale descriptive study which followed two cohorts of children through the 1991 and 1992 assessment procedures. Interviews were carried out with the children's teachers and parents, both before and after the assessments, and observations were made in the children's classrooms. Study Two was a small-scale action research project based in three schools. These schools all committed themselves to finding out more about their parents' views, and to developing their practice accordingly. Further details of Study One can be found in Holden *et al.* (1993) and Desforges *et al.* (1994a, 1994b), while further details of Study Two can be found in Holden *et al.* (1996).

STUDY ONE

Methods

Two cohorts of around 120 seven-year-old children were followed through the 1991 and 1992 assessment procedures. Each cohort was drawn from around twenty schools in London, Bristol and the South West, chosen to represent a range of classroom settings (infant/combined, large/small, urban/rural, working class/middle class, white/ethnic minority). In each school, six children were chosen on the basis of gender and attainment (three boys and three girls; two high attainers, two medium attainers and two low attainers). The parents and teachers of all children were interviewed before and after the assessments took place, and the children were also observed in their classrooms. Findings reported here are from the 1992 cohort; the pattern of findings for 1991 was similar.

Two main methodological approaches were developed for evaluating the extent to which teachers were aware of parents' views. The first approach was to ask teachers about parents' views *in general* (e.g. 'do you think that parents in general are in favour of the formal assessment of seven-year-olds?'). Their responses could then be compared with the views actually expressed by the whole sample of parents. The second approach was to ask teachers about the views of the six *target parents* in their class (e.g. 'do you think Mr/Mrs X are in favour of the formal assessment of seven-year-olds?'). Their responses could then be compared at the individual level with the views actually expressed by these target parents.

In this chapter, findings will be reported based on both these methods and will draw from three sets of interviews with the 1992 cohort: initial parent interviews, initial teacher interviews and final teacher interviews. Findings from the first two sets of interviews will be reported in considering teachers' awareness of parents' views. Findings from the latter two sets will be reported in considering the extent to which teachers' practice was affected by parents' views.

Findings (1): teachers' awareness of parents' views

Findings on teachers' awareness of parents' views will be considered within three areas: *satisfaction, knowledge* and *assessment*. Parents' views in each area will first be summarised, and then data will be presented on the extent to which teachers were aware of these views.

Parents' satisfaction with the school

The parents were generally satisfied with their children's schools. Over two-thirds of the parents (70 per cent) said they were 'happy' with the school, and a further 18 per cent were 'happy with reservations': only 6 per cent of parents said they were 'not happy'. Over three-quarters (79 per cent) of the parents felt they had a 'good' or 'reasonable' relationship with their child's teacher, and virtually all parents (96 per cent) said they felt either 'fairly welcome' or 'very welcome' in the school.

The teachers considered that parents were generally satisfied with their children's schools. All twenty-two teachers thought their parents were 'happy' with the school, and most teachers thought that parents felt 'welcome' in the school. However, teachers were less sure about how parents saw their relationship with the teacher: several teachers would go no further than 'hoping' that parents saw the relationship in positive terms.

While teachers were mostly correct in their judgement of parents' happiness, their judgements did not seem to be based on any systematic attempts to measure parental satisfaction. Rather, happiness was usually inferred from a lack of parental complaints, as the following comments suggest:

They're invited to come in anytime if they're not happy, but they don't – so we assume they are happy.

They do have the opportunity to complain at governors' meetings, but they don't take it up. We get a very small turnout, which proves that they are reasonably happy.

Similarly, parents' feelings of being welcome in the school were inferred from the fact that parents did in fact visit the school: as one teacher commented, 'if they didn't feel welcome, they wouldn't come in'.

Parents' knowledge about the school

One area in which parents felt less than fully satisfied was in their knowledge of what was going on at school. Nearly two-thirds of the parents (64 per cent) felt they did not know enough about what was happening to their child at school, compared with just over a third (36 per cent) who did. Parents wanted to know more about the curriculum, about their child's daily routine, about the teaching methods, and about their child's strengths and weaknesses. In addition, almost all the parents (90 per cent) said they wanted to know more about the assessment procedures which their children would shortly be experiencing.

The teachers were for the most part unaware of parents' desire for more knowledge. Parents were generally seen as having little interest in educational matters (including assessment), and it was sometimes considered that additional knowledge would be of little use to them anyway:

They don't know much about educational issues . . . and I don't think they want to know much more either. As long as their child is happy, and I'm saying reasonably positive things, they're happy.

They wouldn't benefit from knowing more.

As before, the level of parents' interest in educational matters was inferred rather than based on any kind of survey. Low attendance at parents' evenings was the main reason cited for lack of interest amongst parents.

Parents' views on assessment

Parents' attitudes towards assessment were slightly more positive than negative. 49 per cent of parents either 'approved' or 'approved with reservations', compared with 38 per cent of parents who 'disapproved' of assessment. The main arguments put forward by parents in favour of assessment were that it would help in the early diagnosis of children's strengths and weaknesses, and that it would provide useful information for parents. The main arguments put forward against formal assessment were that continuous assessment was more appropriate at this age, and that it might have adverse effects on children. In addition, nearly half the parents (43 per cent) wanted to be involved in some way in the assessment process – for example, by preparing their children at home beforehand, or by providing the school with additional information about their children's interests and achievements at home.

When asked in general terms about parents' attitude towards assessment, teachers tended to underestimate parents' support for it. Thus only five teachers thought parents were in favour of assessment, whereas eight teachers thought that parents were against it. However, the picture was somewhat different when teachers were asked about the views of individually named parents. Teachers were accurate with their judgement for 32 per cent of parents, underestimated parents' support for assessment for 15 per cent of parents, and overestimated parents' support for 12 per cent of parents. For a third of the parents (33 per cent), teachers did not know what the parents' views were.

The teachers' comments give some insight into the criteria underlying their responses. Several teachers appeared to use the child's ability as the basis for their judgement: for these teachers, parents of high-attaining children were considered more likely to favour assessment than parents of medium or low attainers. One teacher, for example, commented of two sets of parents in her class:

> Yes, definitely. They want to know how their children are doing. They also want to be told that their child is better than others. They want to compete with their neighbours.
> [One parent was actually in favour while the other was against.]

Another teacher appeared to base her judgement on the amount of contact she had with each parent. Those parents whom she saw a lot were considered not to be in favour of assessment, while those whom she did not see were regarded as being in favour:

> No, she doesn't need it. I keep her well informed and she knows he's getting on well. It won't tell her anything.
> [Parent actually in favour.]

Other teachers appeared to see parents' views on assessment as being akin to a vote of confidence in themselves:

No, she's against it. She has faith in me as a teacher, so she'll see it as unnecessary.
[Parent actually had mixed feelings.]

The teachers also underestimated the extent to which parents wanted to be involved in assessment, with only four teachers thinking that parents wanted to be involved. In fact, most of the teachers felt that it was inappropriate for parents to be involved in the assessment process. Their reasons were both ideological and practical:

I wouldn't want parents to coach up their children.

I've got enough to do already without organising parents.

Findings (2): the effect of parents' views on teachers' practice

We were interested here in the extent to which the teachers' perceptions of particular parents influenced the way they approached the tasks of assessing children and/or preparing reports. We raised this issue in both sets of interviews with teachers.

In the pre-SATs (standard assessment tasks) interviews, teachers were asked whether the parents' expectations had influenced the way they monitored or assessed their children (as the SATs had not started, the focus here was on teacher assessment). In almost all cases (95 per cent), the teachers said they had not been influenced in any way by parental expectations. However, there were a few cases where teachers said they had been influenced in this way. One of these parents was also a classroom assistant in her child's class, and the teacher commented that the parent therefore had a different perspective on the child from that of other parents. For a further two parents the teachers said they took particular care to keep their records up to date, as the parents were always likely to enquire how their child was getting on. For the remaining three parents, the teachers explained that they monitored the children particularly carefully because of differences of opinion between teacher and parent about the child's ability. One teacher explained in some detail what she meant:

Yes, I want to show that she's better than what mum expects. Mum knows she's bright as well, but she doesn't expect that much of her. Mum's quite complacent about it now – 'well, G's not achieving, never mind' – but I really wanted to give G that bit extra, particularly on the English side, just to find out what she does know. She's one of those children who suddenly surprises you – comes out with a gem. I'm doing that more for G than for G's mum. I'm desperately trying to build up this child's self-esteem.

The issue was also raised in the final interview. Here the teachers were asked, for each target parent, whether their knowledge of that parent had affected the way they wrote the report. For the majority of parents (68 per cent), the teachers said they had not been influenced 'at all' by their perception of parents. However, on a quarter of occasions (25 per cent) they said they had been influenced 'in a general way' (e.g. the parent might have influenced their general tone or choice of terminology), while in a small number of cases (6 per cent) they felt they had been influenced 'in a specific way'. For example:

> I needed to be very positive because I am aware that Dad might be a little physically violent if he wasn't happy with the report. If you think a child might really suffer, you tend to be very careful what you write.

STUDY TWO

In view of the findings emerging from Study One, we set up a small-scale action-research study to look at how schools might work more closely with parents. In particular, we wanted to find out how schools might develop a closer understanding of their parents' views, and how this information might be incorporated into the school's practice. As with Study One, the focus was on assessment issues at Key Stage One.

Methods

Three contrasting schools known to be sympathetic to parental involvement were invited to join the project, and all three agreed. School A was a small primary school situated in a fairly affluent village a few miles outside the city. School B was a large first school (5–8 years) serving an economically deprived area within the city. School C was another large first school in the city, but with a mixed catchment area. In each school the headteacher and at least one Year 2 teacher were involved in the project.

The project team did not suggest or prescribe specific ways of working with parents. Instead, the three schools were given a summary of the main findings emerging from Study One, and asked to address two key questions:

1 What methods can schools use to develop a closer understanding of their parents' views, particularly in regard to the productive use of assessment?
2 How can this information about parents' views be used to develop partnerships with parents aimed at promoting pupils' learning?

Each school was asked to develop its own programme of activities, appropriate for the school, which would address these questions. Teachers involved in the project were given a few days' supply cover to work on the project and meet teachers from the other project schools. A meeting was held each term for all the participating schools and the research team, at which the project aims were reviewed, ideas exchanged and progress discussed. The project ran for a full school year.

The work of the schools was supported, monitored and evaluated by one member of the project team, who kept in almost weekly contact with each school. This project member interviewed the participating teachers and headteachers at the start of, during and at the end of the project, interviewed a sample of parents from each school at the end of the project, attended events (such as parents' evenings) during the year and collected other documentary evidence relevant to the project. Each participating teacher also kept a project diary. Follow-up interviews were carried out in each school a year after the project had formally ended.

School A

The staff at this small village school held an evening meeting (with wine and cheese) to discuss the project with parents. About 30 per cent of families attended. The parents made a number of suggestions for improving home–school relationships: these included more accurate information about their children's progress, home visits by teachers, more information about assessment, an opportunity to see their children at work in the classroom, and guidance on how to help older children with homework.

The school rejected some suggestions on the grounds that they did not fit with current school policy. For example, helping with homework was not encouraged as it did not fit with the school's policy on encouraging independent learning. However, the school agreed to implement three specific suggestions. These were:

- parents invited into school to 'shadow' their child in class;
- programme of home visits instigated;
- meeting held with Year 2 parents to discuss SATs.

The project evaluation revealed that parents and teachers had different perceptions concerning the success of these innovations. The 'shadowing' innovation, for example, was greatly appreciated by those parents who had made use of it. However, the staff did not feel that the parents had gained much from the innovation. In contrast, the teachers felt they had learned a great deal from the home visits, but the parents did not think it had been of much use. The SATs meeting drew a mixed reaction from both parents and teachers – some felt it had been useful, others did not.

The follow-up interviews conducted a year after the project ended revealed that none of the innovatory practices had been continued. Ironically, one reason for this was that the school had undergone an OFSTED inspection during the year, in which it had been highly praised for its relationships with parents. However other areas had been criticised, and the school had reacted by switching time and resources away from their work with parents. No adverse reaction from parents had been reported to this decision.

School B

The staff in this large inner-city first school decided to concentrate on one particular Year 2 class as a 'pilot' for work elsewhere in the school. The parents in this class were invited to attend one of three short meetings, at the beginning or end of the school day. The three meetings together attracted nineteen out of a possible thirty families. At the meetings, the teacher explained the aims of the project and then grouped the parents in twos or threes to generate ideas. The parents suggested a number of innovations, including a diary/folder which could travel with the child between home and school and contain information and examples of work, longer and more frequent parent interviews, more information about the curriculum and how parents could help, and more information about assessment.

As in School A, some suggestions were rejected while others were put into effect. Thus the request for longer and more frequent parent interviews was turned down on the grounds that this would be too demanding on teachers' time. The suggestions which were implemented included the following:

- diaries/folders to convey work/information between home and school;
- information to parents about each term's topic and suggestions about activities they could undertake at home;
- a simplified guide to the English Attainment Targets (in 'Childspeak') written by teachers for parents.

The evaluation showed that these innovations had experienced mixed fortunes. Of the three, the simplified guide to the attainment targets was the most appreciated by parents. Parents also appreciated the information about each term's topics, but few took up the suggested activities. The diaries/folders never really took off, mainly because the class teacher did not actually use them for conveying information about school to the parents.

The follow-up evaluation revealed that some of the new practices were still in place a year after the project had ended, although they had usually been streamlined to reduce the demands on teachers. All the classes in the school were now providing parents with information about the term's topic, together with suggestions for related activities. However, the plan to write simplified guides for other attainment targets had proved too daunting.

School C

This large first school adopted an approach slightly different from that of the other two schools. While the school was keen to develop better relationships with parents, there was a history of parents having little contact with the school. The headteacher and three Year 2 teachers involved in the project felt that one problem lay in the old and unwelcoming school buildings; as a first step, they instigated regular (termly) coffee mornings in order to improve communication between parents and teachers. Other innovations introduced by the school included:

- open meetings to discuss SAT procedures and materials;
- information on topics sent home at the start of each term;
- longer parent–teacher interviews to discuss children's progress.

As with the other two schools, these innovations were viewed with varying degrees of enthusiasm by parents and teachers. There was general agreement that the extended parent–teacher interviews were valuable, and the SAT meetings and information sheets were also seen as useful. However, there was a mixed response to the 'coffee mornings'. Many parents were unable to attend, and some who did felt that the atmosphere was 'a bit strained'.

The follow-up interviews revealed that – unlike the other two schools – all these innovations were still in place one year after the project had finished. The coffee mornings had been extended to all the classes in the school, and were used primarily to provide information to parents about the term's work. The SAT meetings and extended parent–teacher interviews had also been sustained.

DISCUSSION

The PAKSO project set out to examine some of the assumptions underlying the development of an educational market. Specifically, the project looked at how far schools are aware of their parents' views, and how far they are prepared to change their practice to take account of these views. Two studies were carried out, based around the assessment procedures introduced in 1991 and 1992 at Key Stage One. The main findings were as follows.

The teachers in Study One were only partially aware of the views of their parents. While they accurately judged that parents were generally satisfied with the school, they seriously underestimated parents' desire for more knowledge and for more involvement. There was no sign that any of the schools in Study One had made any systematic attempt to discover the views of parents. Instead, teachers' judgements were frequently based on inference (e.g. from non-attendance at parents' evenings) or from stereotypical assumptions about parents in general and individual parents in particular.

There was also little evidence from Study One that teachers' practice had been significantly influenced by their knowledge of parents' views. In the few cases where this occurred, teachers appeared to be acting in what they perceived to be the best interests of the child, rather than responding to market forces. The most clear-cut illustration of this was provided by the teacher who went out of her way to write a positive report about a child, on the grounds that her father might be physically violent to the child if he was not happy with the report.

The three schools in Study Two explicitly set out to increase their knowledge of parents' views, and to change their practice accordingly. Our evaluations suggested that this had only happened to a limited extent. All three schools had consulted their parents, but all three had been selective in implementing suggestions arising from this consultation. The most successful innovations were those which increased parents' knowledge about what was going on at school, either by sending more information home or by allowing parents to observe their children in the classroom. However, there was little indication that the teachers had become more knowledgeable about parents' views, or that the teachers had either sought or obtained from parents information about their children which could have been used productively in school. In addition, few of the innovations had continued after the project team had withdrawn its support.

Clearly, care must be taken in generalising from a single project, based primarily in one part of the country and focusing on one particular age group. Nevertheless, a number of implications can still be drawn from the findings reported here.

First, it is useful to revisit the model shown in Figure 6.1 in the light of these findings. This model, which provided the conceptual framework for the PAKSO project, is an attempt to specify some of the processes which are assumed to be operating if parents' views are to have a significant influence on classroom practice. The model assumes both that teachers are aware of parents' views, and that they are likely to modify their classroom practice in the light of this awareness. In fact, the findings from the PAKSO project provide little support for either assumption. Teachers have only a hazy awareness of parents' views and this awareness has little influence on their classroom practice. Instead, the major influences on teachers' views and practice appear to lie in factors not shown in the model. These factors, which might be loosely termed 'producer interests', include teachers' sense of themselves as professional educators and teachers' perception that their primary responsibility is to children, not to parents. Such factors are likely to provide major barriers to the development of an educational market.

Our research also indicates that many schools do not routinely seek information concerning parents' views, nor do they have appropriate mechanisms for translating this information into practice. None of the schools involved in Study One had made any systematic attempt to obtain parents' views by means of standard market research techniques, such as postal questionnaires, opportunity interviews or telephone surveys. Even in Study Two, where the schools had committed themselves to discovering more about parents' views, the techniques were limited to calling parents' meetings (sometimes at inconvenient times of day) and asking for suggestions. If schools are to become genuinely responsive to parents' views, then teachers will need to develop new skills for the collection and analysis of data, and to introduce new internal procedures for acting on the information so obtained. Such changes are in fact required, in a limited way, by the new inspection procedures recently introduced by OFSTED for schools in England and Wales: as part of their periodic inspection, schools are required to survey parents' opinions of the school, and to call a meeting with parents to discuss any issues they might want to raise. The effect of these requirements on schools remains to be seen.

Even if teachers and schools had the skills and procedures for routinely obtaining and acting upon the views of parents, it is by no means clear how far they would actually use them. The PAKSO project unearthed no major desire on the part of schools to seek out the views of parents and to incorporate suggestions from parents in their practice. Even the schools in Study Two, which explicitly set out to do this, were modest in what they achieved, despite a substantial degree of additional support and encouragement from the research team. Moreover, only one school continued its work with parents to any significant degree when this external support was no longer forthcoming.

It might be argued that being responsive to parents whose children are already in the school is not the most effective strategy for operating in an educational market. Instead, it could be argued that schools are better advised to direct their efforts towards attracting new parents to the school, through the use of promotional materials, videos and other marketing techniques. Indeed, given the high levels of parental satisfaction reported both here and elsewhere (e.g. Hughes *et al*. 1994), it might well be argued that there is little to be gained (in purely market terms, that is) from investing further in parents who are already at the school.

This argument, while superficially attractive, rests on a somewhat limited view of what it means to be a 'consumer' in an educational market – or indeed, in any other kind of market. As Woods (1995) has convincingly argued, there are many facets to being a consumer, of which the initial activity of 'choosing' is only one. Other facets, for example, include checking that the service is meeting the consumer's needs, carrying out quality assurance, and attempting to influence the decision-making process. We have reported elsewhere (Hughes *et al*. 1994) that for many parents the notion of being a 'consumer of education' extends well beyond the initial choice of school: it is just as much about the ongoing relationship between parents and school once that choice has been made. A crucial element in this relationship is the feeling that parents are being listened to by the school, and that their views have some influence on everyday practice. Schools which fail to provide this kind of relationship may find that parents are indeed taking their custom elsewhere.

In conclusion, the work of the PAKSO project suggests that many schools at Key Stage One may not be providing the kind of relationship which parents appear to value. Instead, the picture of schools which emerges from this research is of institutions which are conservative, inward-looking and resistant to external change. Indeed, our work strongly supports the conclusion drawn by Levin and Riffel, based on evidence from North America, that:

> School systems do not have good processes for learning about and responding to changes in their environments except in a very narrow sense. These limitations are not the result of ill will or incompetence, but of long-ingrained patterns of thought and behaviour which will not be easy to change, no matter what policy makers may promulgate.
>
> (Chapter 4, p. 44, this volume)

NOTE

1 This chapter is based on the work of the ESRC-funded project 'Parents and assessment at Key Stage One' (reference number X208252007), co-directed by Charles Desforges and Martin Hughes. We are very grateful to Cathie Holden, Christabel Owens, Caroline Smith and Tricia Nash for their substantial contributions to the research reported here. The project was part of the ESRC programme on 'Innovation and change in education: the quality of teaching and learning'.

REFERENCES

Bagley, C., Woods, P.A. and Glatter, R. (1996) 'Scanning the market: school strategies for discovering parental perspectives', *Educational Management and Administration* 24(2): 125–138.

Department for Education (DfE)/Welsh Office (1992) *Choice and Diversity: A New Framework for Schools*, London: HMSO.

Desforges, C., Hughes, M. and Holden, C. (1994a) 'Parents' and teachers' perceptions of assessment at Key Stage One', in M. Hughes (ed.) *Perceptions of Teaching and Learning*, Clevedon: Multilingual Matters.

Desforges, C., Hughes, M. and Holden, C. (1994b) 'Assessment at Key Stage One: its effects on parents, teachers and classroom practice', *Research Papers in Education* 9: 133–158.

Desforges, C., Hughes, M. and Holden, C. (1995) 'Parents, teachers and assessment at Key Stage One', in M. Hughes (ed.) *Teaching and Learning in Changing Times*, Oxford: Blackwell.

Holden, C., Hughes, M. and Desforges, C. (1993) 'What do parents want from assessment?' *Education 3–13* 21: 3–7.

Holden, C., Hughes, M. and Desforges, C. (1996) '"I just want to know what he does all day": action research with parents and schools', *Education 3–13* 24: 42–50.

Hughes, M., Wikeley, F. and Nash, P. (1994) *Parents and their Children's Schools*, Oxford: Blackwell.

Hughes, M. (1995) *Teaching and Learning in Changing Times*, Oxford: Blackwell.

Levin, B. and Riffel, A. (1996) Chapter 4, this volume.

Plewis, I. and Veltman, M. (1995) 'Changes in the classroom experiences of inner London infant pupils, 1984–1993', in M. Hughes (ed.) *Teaching and Learning in Changing Times*, Oxford: Blackwell.

Pollard, A., Broadfoot, P., Croll, P., Osborn, M. and Abbot, D. (1994) *Changing English Primary Schools? The Impact of the Education Reform Act at Key Stage One*, London: Cassell.

Woods, P. (1995) 'Parents as consumer-citizens: an investigation into parent governors', unpublished PhD thesis, Open University.

7

PARENTAL INVOLVEMENT AND SCHOOL CHOICE

Israel and the United States

Ellen B. Goldring

INTRODUCTION

The ways in which parents and schools interact have strong implications for the types of educational opportunities experienced by children. Effective schools provide opportunities for parents to both support and participate in their children's education (Smith and O'Day 1991). The research on parental involvement in schools also indicates a relationship between student achievement and certain types of involvement (Epstein 1992; Henderson 1987). Thus parental involvement is an important component of providing students with opportunities to learn.

Many proponents of school choice argue that parental choice will result in greater parental involvement, satisfaction, empowerment and sense of community (Bryk and Driscoll 1988; Smrekar 1993). Choice may increase communication between home and school and promote parent commitment to that school. These are elements which are crucial in developing a stronger sense of community and communal opportunities to learn (Cookson 1993).

The purpose of this chapter is to explore parental involvement and school choice. This chapter offers data in a comparative context between the United States and the State of Israel and then focuses on three central questions:

1 To what extent are schools of choice segregated by social class?
2 Why are parents choosing outside their neighbourhood attendance zone?
3 What is the nature of parental involvement in schools of choice?[1]

School choice and parental involvement are integral parts of many school reform efforts. Many countries are considering parent and community empowerment as mechanisms for school improvement. The results reported in this chapter in a comparative context should help inform discussions about how families can be better consumers of education and how schools can be more effective in responding to parents. By examining school choice contexts in two countries from an empirical base, this chapter offers an international perspective for complex educational policy issues.

PARENTS, CHOICE AND INVOLVEMENT

Discussions concerning schools of choice have focused on interrelationships between parent's social class, reasons for choice and parental involvement (Maddaus 1990). Advocates of school choice argue that public schools of choice (Blank 1989):

1 attract pupils of different racial and socio-economic backgrounds with similar educational interests so as to create racially heterogeneous schools;
2 provide unique sets of learning opportunities; and
3 encourage innovation.

Critics of choice programmes charge that schools of choice can exacerbate existing class or socio-economic differences, especially when they are academically selective and few in number. They assert that middle-class parents are more motivated and more informed regarding the availability of educational options, while lower income parents opt for or 'end up' in zone schools with no specialised offerings and fewer resources.

Expanding parental involvement is viewed as an important goal of public schools of choice in light of the assumption that parental involvement helps promote achievement (Seeley 1984; Henderson 1981). Proponents of school choice predict that it would encourage educators to be more open to parental involvement and would build parental support for schools (Nathan 1985; Watt 1983). This support can then be translated into a higher sense of satisfaction. Furthermore, debates surrounding school choice have drawn attention to the importance of the place of parents in a shared mission or shared sense of community in promoting school effectiveness.

This chapter focuses on whole-school magnet schools as one type of public school of choice. Research has suggested that schools of choice, such as Catholic schools and single-focus magnet schools, that have a unified mission and curricular focus, appear better able to provide opportunities for parental involvement and effective communication between school and home (Bauch and Goldring 1995; Bryk and Lee 1992). These findings are explained in terms of a communitarian model of school organisation. The communitarian school organisation, in contrast to a bureaucratic one, fosters a greater sense of social cohesiveness among students, parents and school professionals. '[P]arents are bound by a perception of shared interests and mutual goals embodied in the act of public choice' (Smrekar 1993). These schools, it is suggested, unlike schools with a geographic community, can develop a joint system of identity and belonging amongst all school members: parents, students and professionals. This chapter explores these issues by focusing on schools of choice – specialty or single-focus magnet schools – in Israel and Cincinnati, Ohio.

THE CASE OF ISRAEL

Israel presents a unique opportunity to study parental choice because schools of choice are part of the public school system where there are no private school alternatives.[2] Parental choice is being promoted to move the highly centralised system away from uniformity towards more local school autonomy in an attempt to meet the diverse needs of parents and students.

All of the specialty schools are responsible to the Director General of the Ministry of Education as part of the state school system and are publicly funded as are all other schools in Israel. Their attendance zones go beyond the notion of neighbourhood schools, and often encompass more than one municipality. Parents pay a monthly fee to cover transportation and enrichment activities. The schools have also raised additional funds through independent fund-raising activities. Thus, schools of choice in Israel are not viewed as private schools in terms of financing. However, they are alternatives to the regular school system in terms of their self-sustaining ethos (Goldring 1992; James 1989). Parental investment in choosing the alternative specialty schools is quite high in that children lose the neighbourhood social network which is extremely important in Israeli society. Furthermore, they invest in transportation time, sometimes more than an hour each way, and in paying ancillary fees to support the school (Goldring 1992).[3] The specialty schools are usually of three types:

1 schools with a unique ideological orientation;
2 schools with a special content; and
3 schools with a distinctive educational philosophy.

Data sources

This chapter presents the results of a synthesis of secondary data analyses of two data bases from Israel (see Shapira and Goldring 1990; Goldring 1991 for complete details). The first data set is based upon a comprehensive study of parents who send their children to specialty schools, in a central metropolitan region of Israel. An anonymous questionnaire, developed for the study of parental involvement in schools of choice, was administered to a random sample of parents from one class of each first to eighth grade levels (out of two classes) at each of the six elementary schools.[4] The schools were selected to participate in this study because they each have a unique specialty or theme. Three are specialty schools, and three are neighbourhood schools accepting attendance zone children only.

The second data base is a study of parents who chose to send their children to specialty religious schools throughout Israel.[5] Each school distributed an anonymous questionnaire to all parents.

Results

To what extent are specialty schools segregated by social class?

Debates regarding choice often focus on issues of self-selection and the so-called 'creaming effect'. That is, opponents of school choice programmes claim that 'choice parents' are of higher social classes and are more motivated than those who do not choose. In this section we review the question of whether the enrolment of children in public schools of choice sorts students along socio-economic lines and/or by race.

The data suggest that schools of choice in Israel are segregated by social class. However, the nature of this segregation differs according to the specific specialty and the geographic location of the schools.

The results of the comprehensive study of six schools in the central region of Israel, three specialty schools and three neighbourhood schools, indicate that parents in the specialty schools have significantly higher levels of education than their counterparts in neighbourhood schools (Shapira and Goldring 1990). In addition, in a related study of parents in specialty schools in that same region, data show that 57 per cent of the respondents have more than a high school education, compared to 35 per cent of the total Jewish adult population who have some type of higher education (Statistical Abstracts of Israel 1987).

The study of specialty religious schools, all of which are schools of choice, indicates that they do have an ethnic mix of students, as defined by country of origin. However, there is social class bias in these schools. Using the level of education indicator, parents from traditionally lower social classes in Israel, from African-Asian origins, are more highly educated than those from similar origins in the population at large (Goldring 1991). Five per cent of the Israeli population from African-Asian origin have higher education degrees, while of those who returned the questionnaires from the schools of choice system, 52 per cent have higher education (Statistical Abstracts of Israel 1987).

Why are parents choosing outside their neighbourhood attendance zones?

Parents in Israel seem to be choosing specialty schools for a variety of reasons. Some parents consider their neighbourhood schools 'not as good as an average school' (Menachem *et al.* 1993). Other parents (82 per cent) who indicate favourable opinions of their neighbourhood schools explain their choice in terms of the school's unique programme. Less than half of those who expressed a low opinion of their neighbourhood school suggest they chose their school because of the unique programme. Forty-one per cent of these parents explained their choice in terms of good quality rather than its unique programme. In fact, the parents in specialty schools rate their neighbourhood schools significantly lower than their counterparts in neighbourhood schools (Shapira and Goldring 1990).

Other research examining reasons for choice of the specialty religious schools supports the finding that parents are choosing because of unique programmes. In this study, parents indicate they chose the schools due to the special religious/ideological mission of the schools. Those parents whose personal religious practices are most congruent with those of the school are the most likely to indicate that they chose the school because of its ideology (Goldring 1991).

What is the nature of parental involvement in specialty schools?

Parental involvement and empowerment are two ways parents express their sense of ownership and commitment to their schools. Empowerment refers to parents' role in exercising influence within a school, typically through decision-making, while involvement refers to participation or input into a school without influence (Saxe 1975).

Overall, the majority of parents indicate that they are not involved. Those parents who do participate are involved mostly in the ancillary aspects of schooling, such as bazaars (64.1 per cent), while the least amount of involvement is around the formal curricula (19.7 per cent) and in developing the ideological values (19.1 per cent) of the school.

When levels of parental involvement are compared in specialty schools and neighbourhood schools, the analyses indicate that there are no meaningful differences except in one area: neighbourhood school parents are more involved in the educational areas than specialty school parents. In the specialty schools there are also differences depending on the specialty or theme of the school. Parents are more involved in those areas that are directly related to the specialty of the school. Thus, for example, in the ideological schools, parents have a higher tendency to be involved in educational policy, in the value/ideological and curricula

areas. A low but significant negative correlation exists between involvement and socio-economic status for all types of specialty schools
($r = -.15$). Parents of lower status are more involved, perhaps because
they have more time.

Another area of parental involvement is the extent to which parents
perceive they can influence or take part in decision-making processes
(Woods 1993a). We term this parental empowerment (Goldring and
Shapira 1993). We asked parents to indicate on a four-point scale the
general level of parental input and influence in decision-making in their
school:

1 no partnership – school staff make decisions;
2 final decisions are made by the school staff – parents can try to
  influence;
3 school staff weigh parents' views and confer with them when making
  decisions; and
4 full partnership – parents and school staff are equal partners in
  decision-making processes.

The sample of specialty school parents indicate that there is a moderate
level of empowerment. Furthermore, there is a low, negative, significant
correlation between empowerment and social class ($r = -.13$). Higher
social class parents perceive less empowerment in their specialty schools.

Comparing parents' perceptions of levels of empowerment in specialty
schools and neighbourhood schools, the data indicate moderate differences. The neighbourhood school parents (26.0 per cent) say their
schools offer more opportunities for full partnerships in contrast to
specialty school parents (17.5 per cent). Approximately the same percentage of neighbourhood (46.1 per cent) and specialty school parents
(44.1 per cent) indicated that the school staff weigh parents' views and
confer with them when making decisions.

THE CASE OF CINCINNATI, OHIO

Magnet schools are used in Cincinnati, as in many other urban school
districts in the United States, as a primary tool for achieving desegregation goals and encouraging innovation. Magnet school enrolment is
regulated to ensure that attendance is racially balanced.

During the 1993–4 school year, the Cincinnati Public School District
operated sixty-one elementary schools, eight junior high/middle schools,
ten secondary schools, and seven special schools. Magnet (or what the
Cincinnati system calls alternative) programme choices were offered to
students at all grade levels (K-12). The system operated a total of fifty-
one alternative programmes in 1993–4, including twenty-six separate
programme themes at forty-four different school sites. In the Cincinnati

91

system, magnet programmes are differentiated by curriculum or special interest areas, as well as by instructional approach (e.g. Montessori, Paideia).

Acceptance into magnet programmes is based primarily on the application date (first-come, first-served) and race. Transportation is provided for students in grades K-8 who live more than a mile from their alternative school. Transportation assistance is provided for all students in grades 9–12.

The system enrolled 46 per cent of its students in magnet programmes in the 1993–4 school year. Of those enrolled in magnets, 61.7 per cent were African-American. Over 43 per cent of the district's African-American students were enrolled in magnet programmes in 1993–4. Total district enrolment in 1993–4 was approximately 51,000 (66 per cent African-American, 32 per cent white, 2 per cent other).

Data sources

A comprehensive sample of ten magnet schools participated in this study. This sample includes two Montessori magnets, two Paideia magnets, three schools with a foreign language theme, one 'fundamental academy' (emphasising traditional curricular themes and instructional approaches), and one school having a mathematics and science curricular emphasis.

Ten non-magnet zone schools were selected for the final study sample by pair-matching them with the ten selected Cincinnati magnet schools on the basis of the racial composition of the student body.

Data collection

An anonymous questionnaire was distributed to all fifth grade parents ($N = 736$) and to all non-administrative certified staff ($N = 417$) in each school in the sample. Members of the research team visited each school and delivered questionnaires to a designated school contact person, who then distributed the parent questionnaires to the students through their fifth grade homeroom teachers. Teacher questionnaires were distributed either in their school mailboxes or during a faculty meeting.

The response rate for the parent data in Cincinnati is 62.1 per cent. There are equal percentages of responses from African-American and white parents from zone and magnet schools; however, across both types of schools, there is response bias for white parents. That is, white parents are over-represented in the sample when compared to the district.

Results

To what extent are magnet schools segregated by social class?

There is little difference between the percentage of minority parents in magnet and zone schools, due to the apparently successful implementation of enrolment guidelines contained in the district's desegregation settlement. As noted above, 66 per cent of the district's 1993–4 total enrolment is African-American. The district's magnet population is composed of 61.7 per cent African-American students, while African-Americans constitute 69.7 per cent of the district's zone school enrolment.

However, parents in magnet schools are of a significantly higher social class than are their counterparts in zone schools. This is the case across all racial groups. Magnet school parents, across all racial groups, have significantly higher income levels than do parents in zone schools. Twenty-five per cent of magnet school parents have a household income below $15,000, compared to 44 per cent of zone school parents. Similarly, 34 per cent of magnet school parents have incomes totalling above $50,000, as compared to 18 per cent of zone school parents. Information obtained from principals about their schools indicates that, on average, 49.4 per cent of students enrolled in magnet schools receive free or reduced price lunch, compared to 79.7 per cent of students in zone schools.

For minority parents in magnet schools, 34 per cent have income levels below $15,000, compared to 54 per cent of minority parents in zone schools. Twenty-nine per cent of minority parents in magnet schools have incomes above $50,000, compared to 11 per cent of minority parents in zone schools. Similar trends are evident for white parents. Seventeen per cent of white parents in magnet schools have incomes below $15,000, compared with 33.3 per cent of white parents in zone schools, while 35.5 per cent of white parents in magnet schools have incomes above $50,000, compared with 22.7 per cent in zone schools.

In summary, although there is a racial balance and ethnic mix in the magnet schools in Cincinatti, it is very clear that magnet schools enrol students whose parents have higher socio-economic status. These differences are consistent for all racial groups.[6]

Why are parents choosing outside their neighbourhood attendance zones?

We asked parents to identify the issues that were important to them in selecting a school. The most prevalent reasons reported from all parents are the academic reputation of the school (72.0 per cent), teaching style (64.7 per cent), and availability of transportation (50.7 per cent).

Social class seems to influence parents' reasons for choosing a magnet school. Higher income parents are significantly more likely to choose schools because of the academic reputation of the school. Similarly, higher income parents are more likely to choose because of the schools' values and beliefs, and because of the principal. In contrast, lower income parents are significantly more likely to choose on the basis of the availability of special services, individual help and transportation.

Race also influences some reasons for choice. Both white and minority parents are equally likely to choose magnet schools because of academic reputation. White parents in magnet schools, however, are significantly more likely to choose a magnet school because it is located near their home (50.7 per cent white, compared to 15 per cent minority). White parents are also significantly more likely than minority parents to indicate they chose a magnet school because of the teaching style, parental involvement, the child's friends, teachers, and the principal. In contrast, minority parents in magnet schools are more likely to indicate that they chose a magnet school because of the availability of more individual help for their child, the racial mix of the school and availability of transportation.

Parents in magnet schools generally give their schools better 'grades' than do parents of zone schools. Specifically, 42.2 per cent of magnet school parents, compared to 23.5 per cent of zone parents give their schools a grade of 'A'. This holds true for all racial groups and all income levels, although whites in magnet schools have a slight tendency to give higher grades to their schools than do minority parents in magnet schools.

Magnet school parents are significantly more likely than zone school parents to give their schools a higher grade than public schools in the community. For example, 59.3 per cent of zone school parents give the same grade to their own school and the other schools in the community, compared to 32.0 per cent of magnet school parents. In contrast, 20.7 per cent of magnet school parents, compared to only 9.0 per cent of zone school parents, report that their present schools are better than the public school in the community. These findings underscore the perception of magnet school parents that they got a 'good deal' when they enrolled their child in a magnet school. Magnet school parents may be choosing alternatives because of a sense that their neighbourhood schools were not adequate.

What is the nature of parental involvement in magnet schools?

There are relatively low levels of parental involvement in all Cincinnati schools. Parents in both magnet and zone schools report that they are rarely involved in school activities, have very little influence in school decision-making and rarely have contact with other parents. Parents also report that they rarely receive information about the school, and have only occasional communications from their children's teachers.

Despite the low levels of parental involvement in all schools, analyses indicate differences in magnet and zone schools in Cincinnati. Controlling for income level of parents, the primary area that differentiates magnet and zone schools is the extent to which parents sense there is a supportive, caring climate that welcomes parental involvement. Magnet school parents report a more supportive school climate than do zone school parents. This finding supports the idea that parents who choose a school often perceive that they are a part of a school community with unity of purpose and social cohesion (Smrekar 1993).

It should be noted that sceptics may suggest that these results point to a self-fulfilling prophecy. This argument points out that when there is an investment associated with making a choice, whether it be time, energy or other ancillary issues, parents tend to report higher levels of satisfaction:

> It is generally assumed parents who invest in their child's education by actively making a choice will view their schools favorably. Even if there are no visible reasons for the choice to lead to satisfaction, many parents may justify their choice and investment by indicating satisfaction with the school and viewing it through 'rose colored glasses'.
>
> (Goldring and Shapira 1993: 399)

Other important differences occur between zone and magnet schools in the levels of parental involvement and amount of school information to parents. Magnet school parents are significantly more likely to indicate that they are involved in their children's school and that they receive more frequent information about the school than do zone school parents. Magnet school parents are most likely to attend teacher conferences, especially when there is a problem, and attend performances and other social events.

Other areas where there are differences between magnet and zone schools are levels of teacher communication with parents and frequency of parent–parent interactions. Zone school parents report more frequent communications with other parents, and more frequent communication with their children's teachers than do magnet school parents. Levels of parental influence in decision-making do not distinguish between magnet and zone schools.

Thus, in the area of teacher communication with the home and parent networking, zone schools 'do it better' than magnet schools. These two areas may be linked to the geographic community. When parents live in close proximity to one another, they have more opportunities to interact with each other on an ongoing, informal basis. These face-to-face interactions between parents provide crucial opportunities for informal networking and the sharing of information that can contribute to expanding the school community to include parents (Smrekar, in press).

CONCLUSION

Reviewing these two different cases, with extremely different contexts and types of students, we may draw three broad conclusions:

1 There does seem to be a 'creaming effect' in specialty/magnet schools. In both the Israeli and American context there is strong indication that upper social class students are more likely to be enrolled in the magnet schools across all ethnic groups.
2 Parents report that they are choosing alternatives to their neighbourhood schools because of special programmes and high academic quality. Parents seem to be looking for alternatives to their neighbourhood schools, often due to dissatisfaction.
3 Parental involvement is at relatively low levels in specialty/magnet schools.

In both Israel and Cincinnati, the socio-economic level of the parents in specialty schools is higher than that of parents in neighbourhood schools. Although in both cases there seemed to be ethnic and racial integration, this does not translate into social class integration. This has been referred to as the 'new improved sorting machine' (Moore and Davenport 1989). Students who are considered at risk in terms of their previous achievement, behaviour or attendance are often left out of choice options.

This finding has strong policy implications. There has been widespread emphasis on ethnic integration and racial balance in promoting magnet schools as an alternative to mandatory busing in the United States, but policy makers and educators are not taking into account the wide disparity of social classes within ethnic groups. Our data suggest that schools are being sorted along socio-economic lines.

One explanation for this finding could be that magnet schools have broad discretion to determine admission procedures. This is true in the cases in Israel, but not in Cincinnati. The specialty schools studied in Israel have widespread discretion over who they admit. Admission decisions are not controlled in any central manner, and some of the schools have selective admission criteria. In the Cincinnati case, however, admission policies are centralised through the district office. Racial balance is ensured. However, there are many informal mechanisms that may explain the social class bias. For example, students are given their first choice of schools on a first-come, first-served basis. Some parents are unable to take the time to stand in long lines or arrange transportation to get to the places where they need to submit their applications. In addition, informal conversations with parents and educators suggest that there are mechanisms by which people get 'bumped up' in their place on the list based on informal networks and connections.

A second explanation is that for some parents the unique ideology or philosophy of the school may not correspond with their own values. Thus, in the case of the specialty religious schools in Israel, the ideology does *not* typically correspond to that of the lower social status groups. This is a case of segmentation according to religious preference, which is highly correlated with social class. The relationship between a school's special theme and preference for parents of different social classes and ethnic groups has been documented in the United States as well (Rossell 1990).

A third explanation is to consider social class creaming in schools in relation to patterns of residential segregation (Menachem *et al.* 1993). Parents who are satisfied with many aspects of their residence but are dissatisfied with local schools, may be the most likely to choose specialty schools especially if their occupational and educational status is high compared to the average status of their neighbourhood. In one of the ideological/philosophical schools in Israel, for example, there is an over-representation of educated families from low and medium socio-economic status neighbourhoods. Thus it supports the view that the school is used by some well-educated parents, living in areas of low status, as a solution to the dilemma of sending their children to a neigh-bourhood school or relocating because there are no private school options.

In Israel, we found that some parents who are dissatisfied with their neighbourhood schools, would relocate to other neighbourhoods if the option of the specialty schools was not available. These responses are more prevalent among parents whose status is high relative to the neigh-bourhoods in which they live.

Transportation is a major issue that could explain social class bias in magnet schools. However, in Cincinnati there is an elaborate system of free school transportation for all children. In Israel, public transportation is relatively easy to access and is safe. From a very young age, children are accustomed to riding on public transportation by themselves. In the case of Israel, availability of transportation may not explain social class bias in choice.

It has been suggested that one way to help reduce the 'creaming' effect is to have a complete system of information dissemination to encourage parents to exercise choice. Cincinnati does have an official process of dis-seminating information. However, our data indicate that parents do not use it. Parents indicate that they rely on their own social networks and conversations with teachers and principals to make decisions rather than on the formal dissemination of information through newspapers, official mailings and radio announcements.

This introduces a whole new set of issues that needs further clarification. For example, are certain students and parents being counselled informally by school personnel that they are 'inappropriate' for the magnet schools? Are certain students being 'mentored' towards magnet school enrolment by school personnel? Are parents denied access to certain types of information if they are not part of the social networks of parents that consider alternative school choices as part of their culture? Is the admissions process so complex that certain families are at a disadvantage?

These questions allude to a competitive market model where parents respond to information provided, school claims, and responsiveness of schools to parents' need (Woods 1993b). As consumers, parents of lower social classes seem to be choosing schools for their academic quality. They articulate this in terms of meeting the individual special needs of their children. Higher social class parents are the most likely to say their neighbourhood schools are not 'up to par', perhaps explaining why upper social class parents are the most likely to exercise choice. Both sets of parents are responding to a product. This model offers insights for schools, parents and policy makers for creating a maximum opportunity for parental involvement in schools.

In Cincinnati, the data suggest that there is more parental involvement in some aspects of the magnet schools than in zone schools. Research has suggested that schools that share a unity of purpose and a common agenda for all participants are better able to promote and support higher levels of parental involvement (Coleman and Hoffer 1987; Bauch and Goldring 1995). Parents who choose a school often perceive that they are part of a school community and are more likely to become involved (Smrekar 1993). It is disappointing, however, that despite this finding, the overall level of authentic participation is quite low in magnet/specialty schools in Cincinnati and Israel. There are few opportunities for participation in decision-making and little communication between home and school. For some parents, this is due to lack of transportation and for others it is because of their work schedules.

It is clear that choice in and of itself does not inherently lead to closer relations between home and school. Research suggests that deliberate planning and strategising on the part of school personnel about how a school might involve parents more effectively can lead to closer home–school relationships (Bauch and Goldring 1995). However, schools that have a well-focused curriculum based on voluntary participation, such as magnet schools, may be able to promote this type of effective involvement more readily than schools with mandatory assignment. Bryk and Lee (1992) suggest that schools that function as voluntary communal organisations based on a shared set of beliefs, values and expectations, can evoke high levels of commitment and participation.

The research in both Israel and Cincinnati points to the increasing complexity of designing choice plans that promote meaningful parental involvement and social class diversity. At the onset of designing choice plans, policy makers learned that three things would be crucial for addressing equity: transportation, information and centralised selection processes (Moore and Davenport 1989). These, perhaps, are only the minimal criteria for beginning to implement choice plans and are controlled at the centre, the school district level or the municipality level. The research presented in this chapter suggests that we must look beyond these criteria to learn how individual schools can interact with parents so that all parents will want to consider alternative schools and participate in them.

NOTES

1 Parts of the research in this chapter were supported by a grant from the Spencer Foundation. The opinions are those of the author and do not necessarily reflect the views of the granting agency.

2 This section refers to elementary schools only. The secondary school system in Israel is highly diverse, offering numerous alternatives and choices.

3 Recently the municipality of Tel Aviv has embarked on a school choice programme that is aimed at ethnic integration. This plan follows the idea behind controlled choice plans in the United States and not all schools have single-focus special themes.

4 A 40 per cent response rate was achieved. The extent to which the parents who responded to the questionnaires over-represent certain groups of parents in the same school can be assessed by referring to the 'disadvantaged index' of each school (Dar and Resh 1988). This is an index provided for each school by the Ministry of Education indicating the percentage of families in that school who are considered to be at risk. This index is based upon a composite score consisting of such measures as ethnicity, parents' level of education and household income. Comparing the background characteristics of the respondents on a school-by-school basis, to each school's disadvantaged index, we estimate a fairly low level of bias.

5 Four hundred and ten were returned to the researchers (50 per cent rate). There is no separation of church and state in Israel. These specialty religious schools are part of the public school system.

6 Similar trends are evident with regard to educational level and employment status of parents. Parents in magnet schools, across all racial groups, are more likely to have higher educational levels than their counterparts. They are also more likely to be employed than parents in zone schools.

REFERENCES

Bauch, P.A. and Goldring, E.B. (1995) 'Parent involvement and school responsiveness: facilitating the home–school connection in schools of choice', *Education and Evaluation Policy Analysis* 17(1): 1–22.

Blank, R. (1989) 'Educational effects of magnet high schools', paper presented at the Conference on choice and control in American Education, University of Wisconsin, Madison, WI.

Bryk, A.S. and Driscoll, M.E. (1988) *The High School as Community: Contextual Influences and Consequences for Students and Teachers*, Madison: National Center for Effective Secondary Schools.

Bryk, A.S. and Lee, V.E. (1992) 'Lessons from Catholic high schools on renewing our educational institutions', in S. Plank, K. Schiller, B. Schneider and J. Coleman (eds) *Choice: What Role in American Education?*, Washington, DC: Economic Policy Institute.

Coleman, J.S. and Hoffer, T. (1987) *Public and Private High Schools: The Impact of Communities*, New York: Basic Books.

Cookson, P.W., Jr (1993) 'School choice and the creation of community', paper presented at workshop, 'Theory and practice in school autonomy and choice: bringing the community and the school back in', Tel Aviv University, Israel.

Dar, Y. and Resh, N. (1988) 'Educational integration and academic achievement: a review of the research in Israel', *Megamot* 31: 55–67 (Hebrew).

Epstein, J.L. (1992) *School and Family Partnerships*, Baltimore: The Johns Hopkins University Center on Families, Communities, Schools and Children's Learning.

Goldring, E.B. (1991) 'Parents' motives for choosing a privatised public school system: an Israeli example', *Educational Policy* 5: 412–426.

Goldring, E.B. (1992) 'System-wide diversity in Israel: principals as transformational and environmental leaders', *Journal of Educational Administration* 30: 49–62.

Goldring, E.B. and Shapira, R. (1993) 'Choice, empowerment and involvement: what satisfies parents?', *Educational Evaluation and Policy Analysis* 15: 396–409.

Henderson, A. (ed.) (1981) *Parent Participation – Student Achievement: The Evidence Grows*, Columbia, MD: National Committee for Citizens in Education.

Henderson, A. (1987) *The Evidence Continues to Grow: Parent Involvement Improves Student Achievement*, Columbia, MD: National Committee for Citizens in Education.

James, E. (1989) 'Public and private education in international perspective', in W. Boyd and J.G. Cibulka (eds) *Private Schools and Public Policy*, New York: Falmer Press.

Maddaus, J. (1990) 'Parental choice of school: what parents think and do', in C.B. Cazden (ed.) *Review of Research in Education 16*, Washington, DC: AERA.

Menachem, G., Spiro, S., Goldring, E. and Shapira, R. (1993) 'Parental choice and residential segregation', *Urban Education* 28: 30–48.

Moore, D.R. and Davenport, S. (1989) 'High school choice and students at risk', *Equity and Choice* 5(1): 5.

Nathan, J. (1985) 'The rhetoric and the reality of expanding educational choice', *Phi Delta Kappan* 66: 476–481.

Pitsch, M. (1994, September 21) 'States seek Goals 2000 aid for existing efforts', *Education Week* 17: 19.

Rossell, C. (1990) *The Carrot or the Stick*, Philadelphia, PA: Temple University.

Saxe, R. (1975) *School–Community Interaction*, Berkeley: McCutchan.

Seeley, D. (1984) 'Home–school partnership', *Phi Delta Kappan* 65: 383–393.

Shapira, R. and Goldring, E. (1990) *Parental Involvement in Specialised Schools*, Tel Aviv: Unit of Sociology of Education and the Community, School of Education, Tel Aviv University (Hebrew).

Smrekar, C. (1993) 'Building community: the influence of school organisation and management', in S.B. Bacharach and R.T. Ogawa (eds) *Advances in Research and Theories of School Management and Educational Policy* 2, Greenwich, CT: JAI Press.

Smrekar, C. (in press) *The Impact of School Choice and Community: In the Interest of Families and Schools*, Albany, NY: SUNY.

Smith, M.S. and O'Day, J. (1991) 'School system reform', in S.H. Furhman and B. Malen (eds) *The Politics of Curriculum and Testing, 1990 Yearbook of the Politics of Education Association*, New York: Falmer Press.

Statistical Abstracts of Israel (1987) Jerusalem: Central Bureau of Statistics, Government Printing Office.

Watt, D.G. (1983) 'Some thoughts on educational reform and renewal', *American Education* 19: 2–5.

Woods, P.A. (1993a) 'Responding to the consumer: parental choice and school effectiveness', *School Effectiveness and School Improvement* 4(3): 205–229.

Woods, P.A. (1993b) 'Parents as consumer-citizens', in R. Merttens, D. Mayers, A. Brown and J. Vass (eds) *Ruling the Margins: Problematising Parental Involvement*, London: University of North London Press.

8

PARENTAL CHOICE AND SPECIAL EDUCATION

Jennifer Evans and Carol Vincent

INTRODUCTION

Our main intention in this chapter is to explore the impact of the quasi-market currently operating within the state education system on the ability of parents to exercise choice if their children are experiencing difficulties in learning. We propose to concentrate in particular on an analysis of the values, beliefs and assumptions which define the role and responsibilities of a parent both in relation to a market-oriented education system, and also in relation to the special education system.

We want to start by first justifying our concentration on special education. Foucault (1967) argues that confinement, segregation, stigmatisation and exclusion are all ways in which societies at different stages in their history have reacted to those construed as 'other', different and abnormal. Who is categorised in this way, on what grounds, and what happens to them is dependent upon the cultural and economic influences manifest in particular spatial and historical moments[1]. Just as the ways in which society treats its 'deviants' give us an insight into that society, we suggest that special education can be a particularly informative 'lens' through which to examine the changes occurring in the education system as a whole. As Thomas Skrtic notes:

> Because social institutions are best understood . . . from the perspective of institutional practices that emerge to contain their failures (Foucault 1983), special education is a particularly insightful vantage point for deconstructing twentieth century public education.
>
> (Skrtic 1991: 153)

Therefore we suggest that special education should be considered, not as something closed off and apart from the rest of the education system, but rather as a critical case. A study of the special education system highlights fundamental issues relevant to all aspects of education: namely, the organisation of teaching and learning, patterns of selection, exclusion and categorisation, and relationships between professionals and parents.

The special education system is based on the identification and 'treatment' of *individual* pupils who are perceived to deviate from the norm. In this chapter, we ask whether these pupils and their parents are potentially weak players within a market system that is dominated by another form of individualism: that of parents making individual choices to obtain the best possible advantage for their children within the educational market place. First, we examine how the discourse of normality plays out in relation to the special education system. Second, we look at how this discourse shapes parents' role as consumers. Third, we argue that the norms operating around both consumerism and special education are pervaded by social class differentials. Thus, in relation to special education, a child's social class background is a factor informing the definitions of learning difficulty and the constructions of 'need' which are then attached to that child. Fourth, we consider how schools respond and contribute to the increasing stratification of the school system, through fear of the possibly detrimental effects on their recruitment if they are labelled as 'good at' special education.

THE DISCOURSE OF NORMALITY

Foucault famously describes discourses as: 'practices that systematically form the objects of which they speak. Discourses are not about objects; they do not identify objects, they constitute them and in the practice of doing so they conceal their own invention' (1977b: 49 quoted in Ball 1990a). The processes by which human beings are 'made subjects', Foucault calls 'dividing practices'. Kenway suggests that Foucault has demonstrated that 'dividing practices' interconnect with the growth of state provision and control of welfare services and that they relate historically to 'humanitarian rhetoric on reform and progress' (Kenway 1990: 174). Similarly, Ball argues that these dividing practices are 'clearly central to the organisational processes of education in our society. . . . Through the creation of remedial and advanced groups, the separation of the educationally sub-normal or those with special educational needs, abilities are stigmatised and normalised' (Ball 1990b: 4).

This is illustrated by Richardson who argues that, in the United States, asylums, schools for the deaf, and reformatories were all established *before* schooling was made compulsory. Thus '(t)he reform movements to segregate and yet "educate" the worlds of the delinquent and special were critical antecedents to the formalisation of the common school' (Richardson 1994: 715). He does not see the formal development of special education as a 'progressive maturation, tied to the growth of public education itself'. Rather, the conflation of the 'delinquent' with the 'special' and the incorporation of these statuses within the framework of schooling has led to the creation of 'categories' which separate and divide 'exceptional students' and provide for their 'special' instruction within the public school system. Just as Gillian Fulcher (1989) has noted the tendency in England to deem up to 20 per cent of the school population as 'special', so in the USA around 10 per cent of students have been given individual education programmes which differentiate them from their peers.

With regard to the present day, Skrtic (1991) argues that 'special education' is an artefact of the bureaucratic organisation of schools and that recent 'managerialist' reforms in education have standardised the educational process to such an extent that there is very little room left for teachers to exercise discretion in their work, or to adapt standardised programmes to the needs of their students. Therefore, he argues, more and more children's needs will fall outside the narrowing range of what schools will cope with. Moreover, Skrtic contends, since the numbers of children which can be dealt with by the special education system are limited, there will be a greater number of students who will fall outside the education system altogether. Although Skrtic is writing about the American system, his analysis could well apply to the current situation in England following the 1988 Education Reform Act which imposed the National Curriculum and permitted a move towards a more selective education system.

Notions of selection and segregation derive from a discourse of 'normalisation'. Julie Allen (1994) has used a Foucauldian approach to analyse mainstreaming policies in Scotland. She argues that children experiencing difficulties in learning are defined in relation to normality, yet the boundaries of normality are not themselves well defined. Techniques of examination and surveillance (the 'gaze') are used so that individual children may be 'described, judged, measured, compared with others' (Foucault 1977a: 191). Thus the individual characteristics of children are used to justify offering them a different education to that offered to the majority. Thus, research (Goacher *et al.* 1988) suggests that, when choices are offered to parents of children with special needs, these choices are likely to be limited, perhaps to a special school, or to a less popular mainstream school (see below).

However, the concept of normalisation, as used by Foucault, applies to *every* area of human activity. Therefore, the behaviour of parents, as well as children, is subject to surveillance and examination. In the next section we examine the conception of 'normality' as it applies to parents' roles as consumers. A 'good' parent is defined by the various charters, codes and circulars as one who operates effectively within a consumerist framework for education. We discuss whether having a child experiencing learning difficulties is likely to be seen as affecting the competence of parents to be effective consumers.

CONSUMING EDUCATION AND SPECIAL EDUCATION

The 1988 Education Reform Act and the 1993 Education Act have set up an education system in which parents are expected to view schooling as a commodity and to compete with each other to gain places in favoured schools (i.e. schools which are perceived to confer on their children certain advantages *vis-à-vis* other children – Jonathan 1989, 1993). These moves make explicit a tendency which has always been present within the British system (parents with particular financial and social resources have always been able to buy an apparently superior education for their children at prestigious independent schools). The idea of the 'voucher' which had a cash value was conceived to enable all parents to operate in this way (Ball 1990a; Sexton 1987). The present system could be described as a 'crypto-voucher' system within which parents with particular social resources and attitudes towards education can use their 'voucher' (child) to 'buy' an education at the most sought-after state schools.

An apparent prescription for parental behaviour within a consumerist framework is contained within the Parent's Charter (DES 1991; DfE 1994a). The original version states in the introduction: 'This is your Charter. It will give new rights to you as an individual parent, and give you personally new responsibilities and choices' (DfE 1991: 2). The emphasis here is on the *individual* parent, and not on parents as a group. Parents are encouraged to see themselves as *individually* responsible for choosing their child's school. The discourse throughout the text construes parents as individual consumers who are able, by using the rights offered in the Charter, to exercise control over the product by making an informed choice about which school to send their child to. However, the 'good' parent is not only the effective consumer, but also the responsible parent, prepared to offer whole-hearted support to the school and conform to its priorities and values. Once the initial consumer choice of school is made, the parental role, for the majority of parents, is marked by subordination to the school. Parental 'voice' only impinges upon the margins of the school's operation as an educational institution. Under the heading of 'Partnership in education' the revised Parent's Charter describes a parent's role once their child is in school:

> It is true that discipline begins at home. Children learn a great deal in their earliest years. This means that parents, relatives and friends have a big responsibility. . . . Children can be very quick to copy an example whether good or bad. When your child starts school you

can play your part in many ways. By law you are responsible for making sure that he or she goes to school regularly and on time. But you can do a lot more than that. For instance, by supporting the school's policy on homework and behaviour you can help the school to run efficiently and to develop pupils' full potential.

(DfE 1994a: 25)

This emphasis on parents' contribution to, indeed responsibility for, their children's behaviour is also a major theme within a set of circulars, *Pupils with Problems*,[2] which were published in 1994, and to which we return later in this paper.

Individualism, consumerism and special education

The discourse of consumerism is clearly a strongly individualistic one, a key element in a wide-ranging and largely successful attempt by the new right to centralise social welfare policy away from a collective orientation and towards an individual one. Consumers employ their particular resources in an effort to secure the type of provision or product which they have chosen. Thus consumerism denies the effect of class, 'race' and gender stratifications and maintains that everyone has an equal chance to succeed, and that responsibility for that success (or failure) is their own. Consumerism derives from a libertarian ideal of society whereby 'a collection of atomistic individuals each seeks for herself increased private advantage' (Jonathan 1989: 332). Meanwhile, the location of education as a social and a positional good is therefore overlooked.

The field of special education is also essentially defined by and located within an individualistic framework. Several commentators have argued that our definitions of disability are often shaped by medical and clinical ways of 'seeing', which view disabilities as individual problems rather than social creations (Oliver 1988; Mason 1992). Such influences are pervasive, affecting the ways in which problems are defined and solutions formulated in educational spheres. Thus an 'identity of difference' (Fulcher 1990: 351) is constructed, which results in individual students being perceived as lacking or inadequate in some way. The process of statutory assessment reflects the individualism inherent in special education, as the student is identified and assessed in a way which marks him/her out as different from the peer group. It is a common criticism that the nature of the statementing procedure focuses attention on within-child 'deficiencies' rather than on the child's context and the relationship between the two (Goacher *et al.* 1988; Roaf and Bines 1989; Ainscow 1991).[3]

This emphasis on *individuals* atomises and at the same time totalises parents and children. To use Foucault's terms, individuals are subject to surveillance and examination which renders them 'subjects', and by a process of 'normalisation' presents them as a totality – 'parents' and 'pupils' who are expected to act in certain narrowly defined ways. Those who do not are categorised and labelled and are subject to forms of discipline which restrict their competence to operate within the dominant discursive form: the quasi-market in schooling.

Social class, consumerism and special education

We have suggested in the previous section that competence as a consumer is heavily affected by social factors such as class, 'race' and disability. In order for a parent to operate effectively as a consumer, he or she needs to be in possession of particular social, cultural and financial resources, most frequently associated with membership of the professional middle class (Ball *et al.* 1995). Thus the introduction of the quasi-market in education stratifies and segregates children on the basis of their social class position. As Ranson notes:

> The market is formally neutral, yet substantively interested. . . . Yet of course the market masks its social bias. It elides but also reproduces the inequalities which consumers bring to the market place. Under the guise of neutrality, the institution of the market actively confirms and reinforces the pre-existing social order of wealth, privilege and prejudice. The market, let it be clear, is a crude mechanism of social selection and is intended as such.
>
> (Ranson 1992: 72)

It is therefore likely that, given their children's departure from the 'norm', parents of children experiencing difficulties in learning might be automatically positioned as less effective, less powerful consumers (Goacher *et al.* 1988). 'Here, unlike most other markets, who the client is matters: quality and reputation are related to the clientele themselves and not solely to the service' (Ball 1994: 110). This would appear to be verified by the discrepancy in parents' 'rights' to choose a school. For most parents their increased powers of choice (however qualified in practice) were granted by the 1988 Education Reform Act. Parents with children who have gone through the statutory assessment process, however, had to wait until the 1993 Education Act for similar concessions. This Act does strengthen their right to choose the school which is named on their child's statement, but that right remains qualified and subject to professional verification.

The 1993 Act also attempts to intervene in the market by providing additional resources (through statements) to 'compensate' schools for accepting pupils with special needs. It also provides a separate mechanism (the Special Education Tribunal) to enable parents to challenge decisions by local education authorities (LEAs) which restrict or deny their choices. There is also a recognition (through the provision of a 'named person' to give parents independent advice) that most parents will have some degree of difficulty in effectively challenging the LEA. However, there is no comparable independent forum to enable parents to challenge the decision of a *school* not to admit a pupil with 'special needs', or to exclude such a pupil. Thus, in the competition for places at the most popular schools, the market is still operating in its more undiluted form, and the attributes of individual children and families are crucial.

However, the primacy we have given in our analysis to personal, cultural and financial resources, leads us to emphasise not within-child factors as affecting choice, but the variations that are embedded in social class. That is, parents of children experiencing difficulties in learning, like any other group of parents, vary in their command of such resources. Thus some families are socially positioned in such a way that they can, to refer back to the terms we used earlier, challenge the 'gaze', and by doing so shape the process of state intervention to their own desired ends. This conception of social relations is supported by a Foucauldian view of power. For although Foucault argued for a view of power as having diverse sources and being heterogeneous in its manifestations, he also reminds us that 'certainly everyone doesn't occupy the same position; certain positions predominate and permit an effect of supremacy to be produced' (Foucault 1980: 156).

The way in which family and social class background affects definitions of need is apparent in the current system of special education. Highly subjective categories, such as emotional/behavioural difficulties (EBD) or mild learning difficulties (MLD), are applied unevenly throughout the population. In the early 1980s, Sally Tomlinson noted the preponderance of working class, especially African-Caribbean male students in segregated provision (Tomlinson 1982). Today, the largest group of pupils excluded from school consists of African-Caribbean males (Gillborn 1995). Barton and Tomlinson (1984) further comment that the EBD and MLD labels describe two of the largest categories of 'special educational need' and are still used as if they were descriptors of an objective state rather than being highly context-bound. The professional status of doctors, teachers and psychologists allows them a position as 'legitimate labellers' (Gibson and Jackson 1974) which consequently gives their judgements the appearance of objectivity and hence validity (see also Foucault 1977a).

Professional attitudes towards pupils' parents, as well as towards pupils themselves, are also influenced by social class. Consider, for example, these two views of parents from two government documents published in the same year:

> Children's progress will be diminished if their parents are not seen as partners in the educational process with unique knowledge and information to impart. Professional help can seldom be wholly effective unless it builds upon parents' capacity to be involved and unless parents consider that professionals take account of what they say and treat their views and anxieties as intrinsically important.
>
> (DfE 1994b: para 2.28)

> Schools should take what steps they can to encourage parents to understand the importance of ensuring that their children take their school work seriously, that homework is properly completed on time, and that parents actively encourage and reward progress. *Some parents may be unwilling to engage constructively with the school, but schools can use prospectuses and other communications to convey and reinforce the nature of parental responsibility and the notion of home–school partnership.*
>
> (DfE 1994c: para 45, our emphasis)

The first quotation is from the Code of Practice; its emphasis is on the importance of involving parents, although the nature of the 'partnership' offered is rather unclear. The Code maintains that the parents' perspective should be considered by the school, and acknowledges that this might involve making changes in school procedures to accommodate parents' wishes (see also DfE 1994b: para 2.33).

However, apparently not all families are perceived as suitable candidates for 'partnership'. Families of disaffected pupils are often seen as irresponsible themselves, a point illustrated by the second quotation, which is from the 'six-pack', the package of circulars entitled *Pupils with Problems*. It presents a skewed notion of 'partnership', one where the balance, the equality, normally expected between partners, is replaced by parents submitting entirely to the school's agenda. Here, there is no room for the concept that some parents may be justified in challenging the school's priorities for their children or its way of dealing with a problem. These two differing views of parents suggest that parents of disaffected children are more likely to be seen as 'irresponsible' parents than parents of those children who respond to their schooling in less challenging ways. Furthermore, the notion of the irresponsible parent feeds into wider moral panic about the behaviour and morality of the 'underclass' (David 1993; see also DfE 1992).

A particularly interesting example of social class affecting the ways in which difficulties in learning are conceived and defined, is that of children with specific learning difficulties (dyslexia). The existence of dyslexia is often the subject of dispute. Supporters argue that it can be objectively defined and measured and that it requires separate specialist provision. However, opponents argue that the label is highly subjective, and represents little more than middle-class parents attempting to differentiate their children from those experiencing more general learning difficulties, in order to win extra resources for them without the stigma of an 'MLD' categorisation. Sheila Riddell and her colleagues, drawing on their research with families with children with specific learning difficulties argue that the majority of their sample group were middle-class parents who had the ability to act as 'critical consumers' (Riddell *et al.* 1994: 341).

Their findings are supported by evidence that we collected during a recent research project examining the effects of local management of schools (LMS) on special educational provision.[4] Although relationships between parents, schools and the LEA were not the major focus of the study, we discovered that in five of our ten case study authorities, groups organising around specific learning difficulties had a high profile. Officers had a tendency to perceive these parents as middle-class professionals who were able to 'work the system' effectively. As a result, by winning sometimes significant resources for their child, these parents were seen as interfering with the officers' attempts to distribute limited resources evenly across the entire special education field (see also Wright 1994):

> It does [cause us problems] in that we don't always feel that the children have needs which merit the huge cost of providing residential education at a cost of £15,000 to £20,000 a year; their needs could be met within the resources provided by the borough. We see [the dyslexia lobby] as a sort of corrupt Dickensian group of people who recommend friends who run schools that deal with dyslexia and carry out their own assessments.
>
> (Officer, 'Jaston' LEA)

> Another thing that bothers me about the current system in Coal Valley is this lack in equity. . . . I think we've got a strong [local] dyslexia lobby, and that's the most unjust thing. I'm not commenting on dyslexia as such. I'm saying the lobby is particularly powerful. To me it's like the health service which identifies a whole range of illnesses, and all these people are ill, but it also has to make choices. That's what I mean by equity. The authority should perhaps further spell out what its range of priorities are.
>
> (Officer, 'Coal Valley' LEA)

The absence, as well as the presence, of claims around specific learning difficulties can have a corresponding effect upon an LEA's position:

I've not encountered a situation where I've been minded to press the point that the authority should go to an appeal contrary to the parents' view, and I think that's because this authority by virtue of its socio-economic make-up, has not really been exposed to the dyslexia lobby.

(Officer, 'Tate' LEA)

Another example of this particular group's ability to act as 'critical consumers' concerns the new Special Education Tribunal system. When proposals for this body were first mooted, fears were expressed that it would provide a formal, legalistic environment which may be off-putting to some parents, and therefore, as we noted above, a source of support for parents in the form of a named person should be available. However, at this early stage it seems clear that the Tribunal is being used by parents who are already able to and experienced in challenging the LEA, getting support from voluntary groups and so on. More than half the appeals are around specific learning difficulties (*Times Educational Supplement* 27 January 1995; Aldridge 1995).

SCHOOL RESPONSES

There is a growing body of evidence which suggests that schools are responding more pro-actively to this stratification of the parent body. Whilst social segregation, usually reflecting patterns of residential segregation, was far from unknown across and between local school systems, the 1988 Act and related legislation have increased this effect by 'providing a way for the middle classes to reassert their reproduction advantages in education which had been threatened by the increasing social democratic de-differentiation of schools' (Ball 1994: 123).

Schools are therefore responding by 'pricing' children, some children being more highly valued customers than others. This is what the Association of Metropolitan Authorities refers to when it comments that 'schools seem more inclined to reject students who are difficult to provide for, and for whom schools are not able to gain extra or sufficient resources outside the funding formula' (AMA 1995: 15). However, whilst over-subscribed schools may be able to choose their pupils, under-subscribed schools are in a far less secure position. The experience of one of the case study schools from our research referred to above, illustrates these points.

Waldergrave is situated in a county town in Kingsley LEA. The school had experienced a drop in the number of pupils coming in to the school at 11, since open enrolment had been in force. This situation meant that it was financially very vulnerable. In terms of the local education

111

market, it was described by one teacher as 'the poor relation' of the other local schools. Most of its nearest competitors were near the top of the authority's league tables, whilst Waldergrave was near the bottom. The school had a reputation for being 'good at' special needs, and as they explain below, staff and governors felt that a change in the school's image was needed, if it was to recruit more widely:

> We're seen as a school of low achievers, there's no doubt about that.
>
> (Chair of governors)

> We would very much like a wider range of ability from several of our intake schools. We don't [get that]. What we do get is one or two who are directed to us, because we're 'good at' special needs.
>
> (Headteacher)

In the past, the school had maintained a commitment to the values of an inclusive, comprehensive system. For example, Waldergrave had mixed attainment classes in its first three years. Support for children experiencing learning difficulties was mainly provided in-class, rather than through withdrawal, and the head asserted that the school tried to avoid either excluding or statementing children. The school had a good record of integrating children with physical disabilities. It was these values that were now under pressure from the combined effects of open enrolment, league tables and local management of schools.

This is not intended to romanticise the school in its pre-1988 Education Reform Act days. Low teacher expectations were identified as a widespread and entrenched problem by some staff, for example. However, the need to compete for pupils risks focusing schools' attention on marketing strategies which do not directly address existing problems with teacher expectations and assumptions. The temptation for the school would then be to concentrate on the *packaging* of its product and not the product's *intrinsic* quality. To a great extent Waldergrave resisted this temptation, although other research has shown that some secondary schools have not (Gewirtz *et al.* 1993). However, there *were* signs that Waldergrave was modifying its commitment to its position as the local neighbourhood school. To cope with its recruitment problems staff and governors took a number of steps. The school had previously shared the name of the surrounding housing estate, but had been renamed in order to disassociate it from its surroundings and give it a new image. In 1993, mixed ability teaching was abandoned as setting was reintroduced throughout the school. Attempts to expand the intake provided recurring themes in governing body discussions. The fragility of Waldergrave's financial position was a great source of pressure. In response to this, there was a growing perception from staff and governors that the 'desirable' pupils, the ones the school needed to attract, were not those that made up its present population.

CONCLUSION

We have argued that social class differentials affect not only the positioning of parents as competent/incompetent consumers or desirable/undesirable customers, but also have a further impact for families with children experiencing difficulties in learning, as class-based inequalities affect the way in which children's readiness and willingness to learn is constructed and defined.

Thus, in conclusion, we return to our opening point, that special education can be considered a critical case, a lens through which to view the education system. An analysis of the special education system starkly reveals how normative discourses of the 'good' parent and 'good' pupil pervade the education system and function as regulatory devices. Therefore parents' own social, cultural and financial resources are crucial in determining the nature of educational provision received by their children. Whilst this has been the case in special education since the 1981 Education Act and before, the positioning of parents as consumers since the 1988 Education Reform Act has meant that this now applies to all parents.

A future research agenda needs to take account of the key issues of the effects of social factors (including the complex interaction of class, race, gender and disability) on school choice and the provision of schooling. Recent research indicates that these factors will be crucial determinants of a more socially stratified education system. Current and proposed policies of both the Labour and Conservative parties do not indicate a change in direction for education policy. It is important, therefore, to evaluate the impact of current policies on the educational outcomes for all schools and all children.

NOTES

1 For example, in *Madness and Civilization* (1967: 46) Foucault points out that, in the seventeenth century, not only those who were mentally ill, but also the unemployed, sick and aged were liable to be subject to confinement. Foucault explains such treatment as an authoritarian state response designed to maintain social order in the face of a legitimation crisis caused by economic upheavals.
2 *Pupils with Problems*: Circulars 8/94 – *Pupil Behaviour and Discipline*, 9/94 – *The Education of Children with Emotional and Behavioural Difficulties*, 10/94 – *Exclusions from School*, 11/94 – *The Education by LEAs of Children Otherwise than at School*, 12/94 – *The Education of Sick Children*, 13/94 – *The Education of Children being looked after by Local Authorities*.

3 It is interesting to note that the title of the 'six-pack', as it became known – *Pupils with Problems* – suggests that the 'problems' reside with the pupils and not with the system set up to serve them.
4 The project was funded by the ESRC, grant number R0002335876.

REFERENCES

Ainscow, M. (1991) 'Effective schools for all: an alternative approach to special needs in education', *Cambridge Journal of Education* 21(3): 293–303.

Aldridge, T. (1995) 'Appeal in Progress', *Education* 185(18): 14.

Allen, J. (1994) 'Foucault and special educational needs: developing a framework for analysing children's experiences of mainstreaming', paper given at BERA Conference, Oxford, 9 September 1994.

AMA (1995) *Reviewing Special Educational Needs*, London: Association of Metropolitan Authorities.

Ball, S. (1990a) *Politics and Policy Making in Education*, London: Routledge.

Ball, S. (ed.) (1990b) *Foucault and Education. Disciplines and Knowledge*, London: Routledge.

Ball, S. (1994) *Education Reform*, Buckingham: Open University Press.

Ball, S., Bowe, R. and Gewirtz, S. (1995) 'Circuits of schooling: a sociological exploration of parental choice in social class contexts', *Sociological Review* 43(1): 52–78.

Barton, L. and Tomlinson, S. (eds) (1984) *Special Education and Social Interests*, London: Croom Helm.

Citizen's Charter (1991) London: HMSO.

David, M. (1993) *Parents, Gender and Educational Reform*, London: Polity Press.

Department of Education and Science (DES) (1991) *The Parent's Charter. You and Your Child's Education*, London: HMSO.

DfE/Welsh Office (1992) *Choice and Diversity: A New Framework for Schools*, London: HMSO.

DfE (1994a) *Our Children's Education. The Up-dated Parent's Charter*, London: HMSO.

DfE (1994b) *A Code of Practice on the Identification and Assessment of Special Educational Needs*, London: HMSO.

DfE (1994c) *Pupil Behaviour and Discipline* (Circular 8/94), in *Pupils with Problems*, London: HMSO.

Foucault, M. (1967) *Madness and Civilisation*, London: Tavistock.

Foucault, M. (1977a) *Discipline and Punish: The Birth of the Prison*, Harmondsworth: Penguin.

Foucault, M. (1977b) *The Archeology of Knowledge*, London: Tavistock.

Foucault, M. (1980) *Power/Knowledge: Selected Interviews and Other Writings 1972–1977*, edited by C. Gordon, New York: Pantheon.

Foucault, M. (1983) 'The subject and power', in H.L. Dreyfus and P. Rabinow (eds) *Michel Foucault: Beyond Structuralism and Hermeneutics*, Chicago: University of Chicago Press.

Fulcher, G. (1989) *Disabling Policies? A Comparative Approach to Education Policy and Disability*, London: Falmer Press.

Fulcher, G. (1990) 'Students with special needs: lessons from comparisons', *Journal of Education Policy* 5(4): 347–358.

Gewirtz, S., Ball, S. and Bowe, R. (1993) 'Values and ethics in the education market place: the case of Northwark Park', *International Studies in Sociology of Education* 3(2): 233–254.

Gibson, D. and Jackson, R. (1974) 'Some sociological perspectives on mental retardation', *Educational Review* 27(1): 16–25.

Gillborn, D. (1995) *Racism and Antiracism in Real Schools*, Buckingham: Open University Press.

Goacher, B., Evans, J., Welton, J. and Wedell, K. (1988) *Policy and Provision for Special Educational Needs*, London: Cassell.

Jonathan, R. (1989) 'Choice and control in education: parental rights, individual liberties and social justice', *British Journal of Educational Studies* 27(4): 321–338.

Jonathan, R. (1993) 'Parental rights in schooling', in P. Munn (ed.) *Parents and Schools: Customers, Managers or Partners*, London: Routledge.

Kenway, J. (1990) 'Education and the right's discursive politics: private versus state schooling', in S. Ball (ed.) *Foucault and Education: Disciplines and Knowledge*, London: Routledge.

Mason, M. (1992) 'The integration alliance: background and manifesto', in: T. Booth, Will Swann and Mary Masterson (eds) *Policies for Diversity in Education*, London: Routledge.

Oliver, M. (1988) 'The social and political control of educational policy', in L. Barton (ed.) *The Politics of Special Educational Needs*, London: Falmer Press.

Ranson, S. (1992) 'Towards the learning society', *Educational Management and Administration* 20(2): 68–79.

Richardson, J. (1994) 'Common, delinquent and special. On the formalization of common schooling in the American States', *American Educational Research Journal* 31(4): 695–723.

Riddell, S., Brown, S. and Duffield, J. (1994) 'Parental power and special educational needs: the case of specific learning difficulties', *British Educational Research Journal* 20(3): 327–344.

Roaf, C. and Bines H. (1989) *Needs, Rights and Opportunities in Special Education*, London: Falmer Press.

Sexton, S. (1987) *Our Schools: A Radical Policy*, Warlingham: Institute of Economic Affairs.

Skrtic, T. (1991) *Behind Special Education. A Critical Analysis of Professional Culture and School Organisation*, Denver, Colorado: Love Publishing Company.

Tomlinson, S. (1982) *A Sociology of Special Education*, London: Routledge and Kegan Paul.

Wright, J. (1994) 'Crumbs! Is that all?', *Special Children* 73: 9–10.

9

THE IMPACT OF COMPETITION ON SECONDARY SCHOOLS

Jason Hardman and Rosalind Levačić

INTRODUCTION

The 1988 Education Reform Act heralded a fundamental change in the way in which pupils and resources are allocated to schools in England and Wales. Prior to this a local education authority (LEA) was mainly concerned with ensuring that each of its schools received enough pupils to offer a full range of curriculum activities and to attempt to balance the social and academic mix of pupils in comprehensive schools. Under such circumstances the overall distribution of pupils was perceived to be more important than matching particular children to given schools. The Education Reform Act reversed these priorities, supplanting a centrally managed school admissions system with the mechanism of parental choice. Through more open enrolment combined with delegated school budgets, primarily determined according to the number of pupils on roll, the Government has attempted to fashion what has been called a 'quasi-market' (see Le Grand and Bartlett 1993; Levačić 1994). According to the rhetoric, parents will take account of published information such as 'league tables' of examination results and truancy rates when choosing a school, thereby creating a dynamic under which resources will be channelled into 'good quality' schools and away from their 'poor quality' rivals. Furthermore, schools are expected to respond to this consumer pressure by raising their 'standards' and hence improving their competitive edge.

Critics of the reforms have questioned the extent to which this consumer pressure, and hence its intended benefits, will actually emerge given the local nature of schooling, arguing that in cases where parents have only one realistic choice, the school in question has no competitive incentive to improve. However, in conceiving of parents as an homogeneous group, such an argument ignores their demographic distribution in relation to a particular school or schools. Thus while a school may indeed serve some individuals who have no other realistic alternative, it is likely to be the subject of deliberation by others. A much more tenacious criticism is concerned with the issue of inequality of opportunity.

116

Ball (1993: 3), for example, argues that 'markets in education provide the possibility for the pursuit of class advantage and generate a differentiated and stratified system of schooling'. He sees the uneven distribution of the cultural capital required to implement parental choice as systematically disadvantaging working-class families. Moreover he goes on to claim that it is the schools of working-class communities who will suffer as funding follows those who have exercised their prerogative to 'exit'.

This paper investigates whether these changes to the delivery of education have promoted competition between secondary schools and/or increased differentiation between schools. Starting from the year when formula funding and delegated financial management were introduced, we have tracked over time the changes to the pupil recruitment and financing of a large sample of secondary schools and assessed these changes in relation to certain measurable characteristics of those schools.

RESEARCH DESIGN

The data base

The study employs a longitudinal quantitative methodology which utilises LEA administrative data relating to individual secondary schools. Data have been collected from six English LEAs providing a database of over 300 schools (schools from one of the authorities (LEA5) are not included in this analysis). The over-riding strategy for selection of participating authorities has been to assemble a representative sample that will provide an adequate basis for the generalisation of results. As shown in Table 9.1 the sample includes county and metropolitan LEAs to give a spread of rural and urban schools and a diversity of socio-economic backgrounds and school systems (i.e. to include a selective system and a high proportion of grant-maintained (GM) schools).

Table 9.1 Characteristics of the six participating LEAs

Authority type	Number of secondary schools 1993–4	School system	Educational need index 1994–5	No. (%) of GM schools 1993–4	
1 County	35	comprehensive	0.74	0	(0)
2 Metropolitan	32	comprehensive	1.31	2	(6)
3 Metropolitan	79	some selection	1.82	15	(19)
4 County	41	comprehensive	0.84	10	(24)
5 County	44	mainly selective	0.82	8	(18)
6 County	103	some selection	0.86	69	(67)

Note: The educational need index figures are as used in the standard spending assessment.

117

The data base currently comprises the following school-level information (where available) for each year from 1989–90 through to that which
is most recent: numbers of applications and appeals; rolls and intakes
(from form 7 returns); standard intake numbers; aggregate GCSE and
A level examination results; budget shares (from section 42 statements);
measures of the socio-economic and ethnic background of pupils (e.g.
proportion of pupils eligible for free school meals; proportion of pupils
with English as a second language); number of final year pupils (form 7)
at primary schools. Specific measures depend upon availability.

Analytical framework

In considering the issues addressed here it is important to bear in mind
the local nature of schooling and the limits this places on parental
choice. In this paper schools are organised within what are termed
'regions of competition'. These analytical devices group together closely
located and therefore potentially competing schools. They are based on
the administrative divisions employed by LEAs and are thus only loose
approximations to the theoretical ideal of a closed system of schools
within which each school competes with every other (i.e. wherein all
schools draw from a common population of pupils).

Turning to the substantive research questions, the first of these asks
whether the structure of the school system enables the exercise of parental choice to have an impact on school rolls and hence provide the proposed incentive for competitive responses from individual schools. The
paper focuses on the expression of parental choice that occurs when
children transfer between primary and secondary school (or in some
cases middle and upper school) and thus, for any particular academic
year, discussion of pupil recruitment relates to this 'intake cohort'. In
general terms, if a market fails to allow consumers to exercise choice
between suppliers providing goods which are reasonable substitutes
then it will not be competitive. In the school context, the incentive for
competition, as defined here, would *not* arise if a particular region was
served by only a single school, or by a group of schools amongst which
there was no surplus intake capacity (i.e. a situation where the number
of transferring pupils was greater than the number of available places).
In the former case, the lack of alternatives means that the school in question can rely on the whole cohort of available pupils year after year, while
in the latter each school is guaranteed to fill all of its available intake
places. The second scenario is slightly different, however, in that the
amount of surplus capacity amongst a group of schools varies from year
to year. The question of whether or not individual schools are potentially
subject to competition is explored within the framework of regions of
competition.

The introduction of more open enrolment would be anticipated to bring about a change over time in the distribution of each successive cohort of transferring pupils amongst any particular group of competing secondary schools, which reflects the relative popularity of those schools. The extent and direction of this change would, however, seem to depend on two key factors – the limits on the number of pupils able to be admitted to schools, and the temporal stability of school popularity. For example, if it is assumed that a school's popularity remains consistent over time, a position of equilibrium would quickly be reached whereupon the most popular schools would fill all of their intake places year after year, leaving only that portion of the cohort with the weakest claim to a place in those schools (according to the authority's over-subscription criteria) in the less popular establishments. A comparison over time of individual schools' recruitment success will provide the basis for an exploration of how competition is in fact impacting on school intakes. Furthermore, as it was the intention that the exercise of parental choice should determine the distribution of each LEA's school budget, a comparison of schools in terms of their success in both recruiting pupils and attracting financial resources will reveal the extent to which this particular competitive pressure is being brought to bear.

Finally the association between schools' market success and two key school characteristics are investigated. The first of these characteristics relates to educational performance, a multifaceted concept which is notoriously difficult to assess and for which reliable information is not widely available. Thus, rather than attempting to establish whether or not truly effective schools are succeeding, this study set out to test the Government's assertion that schools which exhibit market success will be those with the best 'raw' examination results. Such an analysis would, however, be incomplete without considering the relationship between exam results and pupil background. Thus, as a check on the fully expounded Government declaration, namely that the gains from the competitive ratcheting of standards will be enjoyed by 'all pupils of all abilities' (DfE 1992: para. 2.1), market success is also analysed in relation to the socio-economic status (SES) of pupils within each school. The emergence of a positive association here would do nothing to calm the fears of critics who claim that parental choice will serve to stratify the school system along social class lines.

RESULTS

Does the potential for inter-school competition for pupils exist?

A list of each of the regions of competition (indicated by the LEA number and a suffix) detailing the number of secondary schools in each

Table 9.2 Regions of competition across the sample

Region of competition	No. of secondary schools	% of spare capacity over the period 1990–1 to 1993–4	
		minimum	*maximum*
LEA1a	7	12	21
LEA1b	6	14	30
LEA1c	6	6	11
LEA1d	9	27	31
LEA1e	7	4	12
LEA2	32	5	16
LEA3i	7	4	15
LEA3_11+	74	4	9
LEA4a	9	8	24
LEA4b	10	13	18
LEA4c	12	2	8
LEA4d	12	9	15
LEA6a	19	20	24
LEA6b	17	14	18
LEA6c	12	3	8
LEA6d	23	19	23
LEA6e	21	12	15
LEA6f	11	16	20
All schools	294	14	19

is given in Table 9.2. Also given in this table is the range, over the period 1990–1 to 1993–4, of the percentage of spare capacity available in each region of competition. This figure is arrived at by comparing the combined intakes of all the secondary schools in a particular region with their combined standard numbers. The resulting proportion is the number of intake places filled for any particular year. Spare capacity is simply the percentage of remaining places. As can be seen there are, for the four years examined, more intake places available than there are transferring students in each region, although there is considerable variation over the period both within and across regions. On this basis it is evident that for each of the four academic years studied there did exist the potential for parental choice to change the annual distribution of intake pupils amongst the schools in each region of competition. Thus for this sample of schools the structure of the school system can be said to have been competitive over this period. However the large and fairly arbitrary nature of the regions of competition almost certainly overstates the extent to which particular schools are potential competitors. Thus it may be the case that within any particular defined region of competition there exist several smaller groups of schools each of which serve a particular subset of the region's population. Additionally the analytical framework ignores the possible existence of school 'systems' which comprise a single school. Some attempt will be made to address these limitations in the following section.

Are schools beginning to experience differential success in the market place?

Whether or not a particular school will be subject to the competition that arises from parental choice is dependent upon both geographical and temporal factors. The local nature of schooling (see Glatter and Woods 1994: 57–60 for a discussion of this) leaves individual families with only a relatively small number of alternative schools from which to choose. Moreover as people tend to live in communities, the same alternatives can apply to particular populations of parents. Thus for any particular academic year (i.e. for a particular pupil transfer exercise) it is possible to conceptualise a national network of fairly small and self-contained regional school systems, the boundaries of which are defined by the constraints on parental choice. In this paper an attempt has been made to incorporate this notion of local school systems through the use of the analytical devices we have called regions of competition. However as this framework was arbitrarily imposed on the data rather than derived from it, it has been recognised that this will tend to group together schools which may in fact form separate systems. A particular consequence of this is that schools which are not in fact subject to competition[1] may have been presumed to be so. Thus before we explore the impact of competition on schools in the data base we must first attempt to distinguish between competitive and non-competitive local school systems.

A competitive school, as defined here, is one which is affected by parental choice. In other words if, for a particular academic year, the pupil transfer exercise has the potential to impact on a school's recruitment such that the number of pupils admitted may deviate from the number available in its local constituency, then the school is said to be competitive. In contrast, the annual intake of a non-competitive school will be subject only to fluctuations in local demography – it will always recruit the entire intake cohort of pupils in the local population. This differential impact on annual intake between competitive and non-competitive schools can be utilised to distinguish between the two as well as to reveal the relative recruitment success of competitive schools.

In terms of the available data structure, the number of final year pupils in the primary schools of each school's catchment area was taken as an estimate of the size of the local intake cohort. Catchment areas, defined

121

here as those conurbations in close proximity to a secondary school, were created to be non-overlapping and in most cases were based on the catchment system employed by the LEA. This estimate of the number of locally available pupils was contrasted with the actual number of pupils in the intake year of each school to give a ratio of actual intake/local cohort size. This ratio is referred to as the recruitment 'market success indicator' or MSI. The year by year change, from 1990–1 to 1993–4, in the recruitment MSI was then examined. If this change was consistently between 0.95 and 1.05[2] *and* the school was not recruiting at or near capacity over this period then it was categorised as 'non-competitive'. Only five such schools were identified (1.8 per cent of the sample). The fact that all of these were recruiting below capacity ruled out the possibility that they were competitive schools that were merely full. No schools were identified that met the first but not the second part of the above conditional and so the remainder of the sample was classified as 'competitive'.

The change over time in the recruitment MSI of 'competitive' schools was then examined for the emergence of any particular trends. A simple categorisation system was developed with schools classified as either 'improving/full', 'middling', or 'declining/plateau'. The 'middling' category is a catch all that includes all those schools which do not meet the criteria for entry into the other categories. It is recognised that the classification procedure, the rules for which are summarised in Table 9.3, needs refining in order to further delineate these schools.

Table 9.3 Rules for classifying competitive schools according to trend in recruitment MSI

Category	Rule(s)
Improving recruitment yield/full	• Recruitment MSI increases year on year apart from when the school is full to capacity, *or* • school is consistently full to capacity
Declining recruitment yield/below capacity plateau	• School is not consistently full to capacity and: (a) recruitment MSI decreases year on year, *or* (b) recruitment MSI decreases until a plateau is reached, whereupon the recruitment MSI remains consistent (within a two-way 5% margin for error)
Middling	• All competing schools *not* falling into the above categories

Note: 'Full to capacity' means that the annual intake/capacity (as defined by the standard number) ratio of a school is higher than 0.95.

From a total of 276 competing secondary schools for which valid data was available, 100 were classified as 'improving/full', thirty-one were classified as 'declining/plateau', and 145 were classified as 'middling'. Figures 9.1 and 9.2 reveal how this classification breaks down according to region of competition. In all regions there emerges a proportion of schools that can be categorised as either 'improving/full' or 'declining/plateau' and in all but four of these both categories of school are present. These figures demonstrate that most schools are experiencing fluctuations in their annual intake that are consistent with competition. Moreover the emergence of the particular trends identified suggests that the redistribution of the annual intake cohort amongst groups of competing schools reflects the differential popularity of those schools which would appear to be related to some fairly stable school characteristics. However, further work needs to be done on delineating the trends, if any, that are emerging amongst the large group of schools classified as 'middling'.

The differential market success of schools was also explored in financial terms. Between the academic years 1990–1 and 1993–4, the year-by-year change in each school's budget, expressed as a proportion of the overall LEA budget, was examined thus enabling changes in the distribution of the overall budget to be tracked. This measure, referred to as the financial MSI, was constructed so as not to be affected by changes in the level of the LEA's aggregated schools budget. From the 255 schools for which consistent data was available, forty-nine schools showed a 'consistent gain' in the proportion of the overall budget share delegated to them, forty-one showed a 'consistent loss', and 165 showed 'no consistent change'. This divergence in financial success also emerged at the regional level although not all three categories of school were present in each region of competition.

The relationship between schools' financial success and their recruitment success, as defined here, is revealed in the cross-tabulation in Table 9.4. The total number of schools in this analysis is 252.

The overall proportion of schools classified as 'improving/full' (34.1 per cent) is over three times greater than the number categorised as 'declining/plateau' (11.1 per cent). Of the schools falling into the former category, only 22.1 per cent demonstrate a 'consistent gain' in financial terms. Thus, it appears that many 'improving/full' schools are not making immediate fiscal gains. Similarly the financial penalty for losing parental support does not appear, over the short term, to be applied consistently. In accordance with this only 39.3 per cent of schools classified as 'declining/plateau' have shown a 'consistent loss' in the proportion of the overall budget share delegated to them. As may be expected schools falling into the catch all 'middling' category (53.2 per cent of all schools) are represented in all categories of financial success, although the majority (61.2 per cent) show 'no consistent change'.

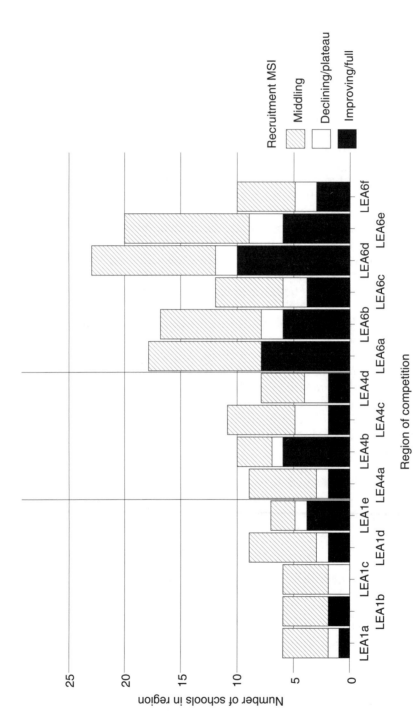

Figure 9.1 Recruitment success trends of competitive schools by region over the period 1990–1 to 1993–4 (county authorities)

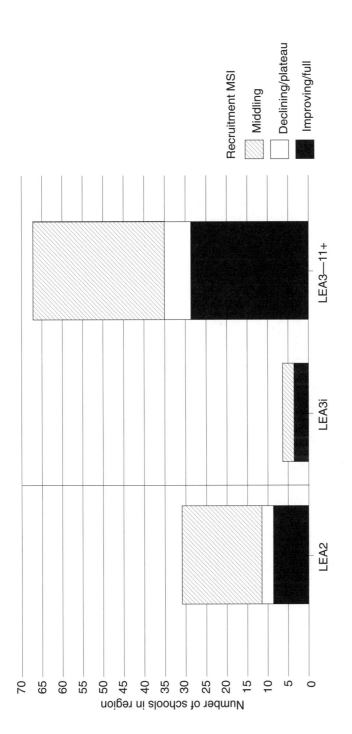

Figure 9.2 Recruitment success trends of competitive schools by region over the period 1990–1 to 1993–4 (metropolitan authorities)

Table 9.4 Cross-tabulation of market success indicators

Recruitment success 1990–1 to 1993–4		Financial success 1990–1 to 1993–4			Row total
		Consistent loss	No consistent change	Consistent gain	
Improving/full	(a)	3	64	19	86
	(b)	(3.5)	(74.4)	(22.1)	(34.1)
	(c)	(6.4)	(38.8)	(47.5)	
Middling	(a)	33	82	19	134
	(b)	(24.6)	(61.2)	(14.2)	(53.2)
	(c)	(70.2)	(49.7)	(47.5)	
Declining/plateau	(a)	11	16	1	28
	(b)	(39.3)	(57.1)	(3.6)	(11.1)
	(c)	(23.4)	(9.7)	(2.5)	
Non-competitive	(a)		3	1	4
	(b)		(75.0)	(25.0)	(1.6)
	(c)		(1.8)	(2.5)	
Column total	(a)	47	165	40	252
	(b)	(18.7)	(65.5)	(15.9)	(100)

Key: (a) Frequency
(b) (Row percentage)
(c) (Column percentage)

The overall number of schools categorised as 'consistent losers' (18.7 per cent) and 'consistent gainers' (15.9 per cent) do not correspond to the overall proportions of 'improving/full' and 'declining/plateau' schools. Thus, considering that many more schools lose in financial rather than recruitment terms, one would perhaps expect more 'declining/plateau' schools to show a 'consistent loss' than actually do. On a similar basis, the proportion of 'improving/full' schools which turn out to be 'consistent gainers' in financial terms does not seem so low when we discover that in the overall sample the former outnumber the latter by a factor of two.

The association between market success, examination results, and pupil socio-economic status.

In the final analysis the introduction of competition into the school system must be judged in educational terms. Has it improved the quality of teaching and learning? Has it raised 'the standards achieved in schools by all pupils of all abilities' (DfE 1992: para. 2.1)? These are, however,

126

complex questions. How do we define 'quality of teaching and learning'? What is meant by 'standards'? And even if some agreement can be reached here, it is no easy task to isolate, and hence evaluate, the part that competition may have played in bringing about any improvements. There are other issues. Who is benefiting from the change to a system which places individual rights before collective goals? More broadly, whom is education for? What is it for? Ultimately, advocacy or criticism of competition is tied in with fundamental differences in ideals and values and any purely empirical evaluation of competition will in itself be insufficient. With this in mind it must be conceded that the most this paper can hope to do is describe the current 'state of play' and leave the readers to make up their own minds about the political significance of the findings.

It is apparent in the policy literature that for the present Government standards are synonymous with examination results. The publication of 'league tables' of schools' aggregate performance is intended to inform parental choice – to be the guide by which schools are compared. From this it can be hypothesised that schools which exhibit market success will be those with the higher proportions of GCSE passes and vice versa. An idea of the overall levels of and trends in GCSE performance of schools with diverging recruitment success can be gleaned from a comparison of means for each of these groups. Table 9.5 provides such an analysis for schools in the sample. For each year from 1989–90 through to 1993–4, variation in recruitment success of schools is found to be associated with different levels of GCSE performance such that 'improving/full' schools tend to have a higher percentage of their pupils achieving five or more A–C grade GCSEs than 'middling' schools, which in turn tend to have a higher percentage of such pupils than 'declining/plateau' schools[3]. Analysis of variance reveals significant mean differences for each academic year. Following a Scheffe test (alpha level = .01) these were found to lie between 'improving/full' and 'middling' schools and between 'improving/full' and 'declining/plateau' schools. There is no significant difference in the GCSE results of 'middling' and 'declining/plateau' schools. A further interesting and potentially significant aspect of the results in Table 9.5 is the rate of improvement over time in the GCSE performance of the different categories of school. It seems that although all schools are improving their results, 'middling' and 'declining plateau' schools are doing so at a much faster rate than 'improving/full' schools.

Schools exhibiting differential recruitment success were also examined for differences in the proportion of children on roll who were eligible for free school meals. Unfortunately a lack of data limits this analysis to a single year, 1992–3, and to the schools of only three authorities – LEA1, LEA2 and LEA3. Moreover, the usefulness of a sample-wide statistic

Table 9.5 Mean GCSE performance of schools with differential recruitment success

Recruitment success 1990–1 to 1993–4		% of year group with five or more A–C grades					% change over the period 1989–90 to 1993–4
		1989–90	*1990–1*	*1991–2*	*1992–3*	*1993–4*	
Improving/full	(a)	42.04	42.84	45.13	48.42	50.22	+19.5%
	(b)	(n = 90)	(n = 100)	(n = 100)	(n = 100)	(n = 100)	
Middling	(a)	23.92	24.74	27.77	29.01	31.25	+30.6%
	(b)	(n = 125)	(n = 144)	(n = 145)	(n = 145)	(n = 145)	
Declining/plateau	(a)	22.62	24.02	27.26	30.30	31.11	+37.5%
	(b)	(n = 29)	(n = 31)	(n = 31)	(n = 31)	(n = 31)	
Non-competitive	(a)	27.56	29.34	39.63	34.32	40.64	+47.5%
	(b)	(n = 5)	(n = 5)	(n = 4)	(n = 5)	(n = 5)	

Key: (a) Mean
(b) (Valid cases)

(such as the mean) to explore group differences on this measure is limited as there is a wide variation between schools on the pupil socio-economic status (SES) measure. Overall mean values do not adequately represent this variation and so a breakdown by region of competition is presented in Figures 9.3 and 9.4.

In LEA1 there is little SES variation in absolute terms between many of the schools, regardless of recruitment success. This is particularly so in the regions LEA1c, LEA1d, and LEA1e. In the regions where inter-school SES differences are greatest (i.e. LEA1a and LEA1b) it is apparent from Figure 9.3 that 'improving/full' schools tend to have lower proportions of pupils eligible for free school meals than 'middling' schools although the relative position of 'declining/plateau' schools is unclear as there are so few of them (only one in LEA1a and none in LEA1b). The greater number of schools in the metropolitan authorities along with the much wider variability in school SES makes comparisons between the groups of differentially successful schools easier. It seems that there is a tendency across each of the three identified regions for 'improving/full' schools to have lower proportions of low SES pupils than both 'middling' and 'declining/plateau' schools. However, on the basis of this data there is no such clear difference between 'declining/plateau' and 'middle' schools. Overall, the only consistent difference in pupil SES that emerges between differentially successful schools is that the most successful

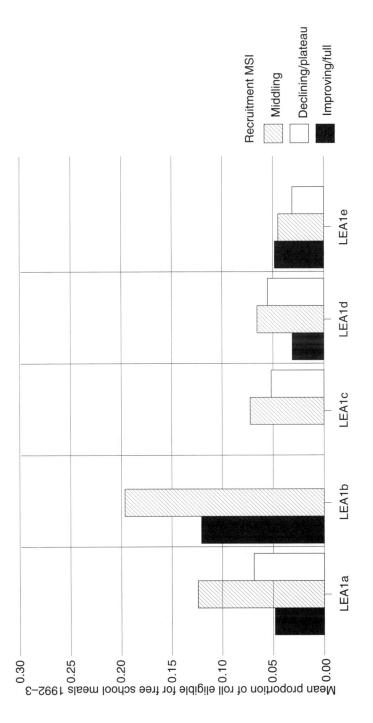

Figure 9.3 Pupil socio-economic status amongst groups of schools with differential recruitment success: LEA1

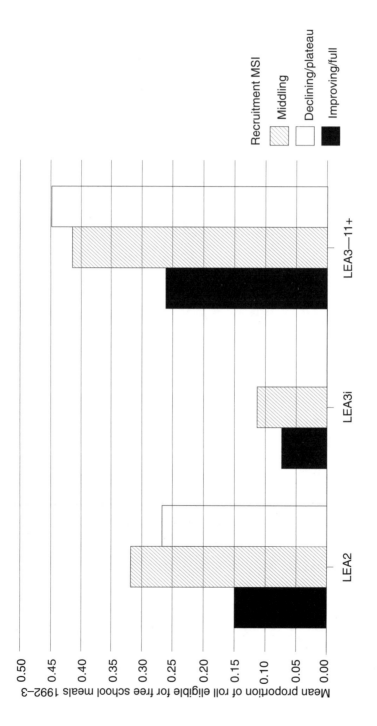

Figure 9.4 Pupil socio-economic status amongst groups of schools with differential recruitment success: LEA2 and LEA3

(i.e. 'improving/full') tend to have lower proportions of pupils qualifying for free school meals than their competitors.

A key result that emerges from the above analyses is the positive association between schools' market success and their raw GCSE performance, such that those schools classified as 'improving/full' tend to have greater proportions of pupils attaining higher grade GCSE results, and vice versa.

A more tentative, though nonetheless interesting, finding is the association between recruitment success and pupil socio-economic status. However, both of these results based as they are on mean differences are in need of validation. Several questions need to be addressed before their typicality can be established. As an initial inquiry, the characteristics of those individual schools which did not 'fit' into the emerging model of successful and unsuccessful schools were examined although missing data prevented a thorough analysis of schools in LEA4 and LEA6.

Bearing in mind that different classifications on the recruitment MSI tend to be associated with different levels of GCSE performance and pupil SES, schools' adherence to this model was evaluated by comparing individual schools' GCSE performance (for the year 1993–4) and the proportion of pupils eligible for free meals (for the year 1992–3) to the authority averages for these measures. For example, a 'declining/plateau' school would be expected to show a below average GCSE score and have on roll a greater than average number of 'low SES' pupils – a deviation from this pattern indicates that the school does not 'fit' the general trend. The results suggest that the classification of most schools in terms of the recruitment MSI is in line with the overall pattern of association between these two characteristics. In LEA2, for example, all thirty-two schools comply with the model. Amongst the other authorities there are, however, several noteworthy exceptions. In LEA3 one-half of all the schools categorised as 'improving/full' have a lower than average GCSE score or a higher than average proportion of low SES pupils and, in some cases, both. This seems to suggest that in this authority a factor other than those considered may be important in accounting for differential market success. Indeed such an explanation may be related to the fact that, compared to the other authorities in the study, LEA3 has a relatively large ethnic minority population. However, it seems more likely that the large number of schools in LEA3 makes evaluation of individual performance in relation to authority averages unsuitable, given the local nature of schooling and the emphasis this places on the *relative* virtues of neighbouring schools. In the light of this, schools' performance in this authority was evaluated against ward level (a smaller geographical unit based on the administrative districts employed for representative elections) as opposed to authority level means. After taking into account this evaluation, the number of 'improving/full' schools in LEA3 which deviate from the model is reduced to four. Amongst the schools of LEA1, three 'declining/plateau' schools demonstrate an incongruent pattern of examination performance and pupil SES. Interestingly each of these schools demonstrated a plateau in recruitment success rather than a decline which leaves open the possibility that these schools are in fact 'non-competitive'. This finding points up the necessity for further methodological development.

CONCLUSIONS AND POLICY IMPLICATIONS

The existence of surplus capacity along with evidence of the annual redistribution of the incoming pupil cohort amongst groups of closely located schools together indicate that competition between schools as a result of parental choice can and does arise. Thus across each of the authorities in the sample, there is a sufficient level of provision to allow most parents some degree of choice between schools. Moreover, almost all schools in the sample (98.2 per cent) demonstrate recruitment changes that are consistent with the presence of competition. Initial inspection of year-by-year trends in recruitment suggests that many parents rate schools, by whatever criteria, in the same way and that school popularity is relatively stable over time spans of a few years.

In tandem with these developments, the distribution of the annual LEA budget amongst the schools within each authority is changing over time and trends are emerging which further indicate that competitive pressures are being brought to bear. However, the overlap between recruitment success and financial success is not as great as might be anticipated. For example, only 15.9 per cent of schools in the sample manage consistently to increase their relative share of the overall budget, compared to the 34.1 per cent of schools that are proving to be popular with parents. Thus in contrast to the simple platitudes offered by the Government, it does not appear to be the case that parental choice and financial reward are straightforwardly linked. This dissonance will, in part, be due to methodological factors. For example, the variables employed to measure the impact of competition on school rolls and budgets are only indicators and need refining. However there are also procedural reasons why the groups defined by the MSIs do not directly map onto one another. The link between choice and the distribution of resources is made via a funding formula that is applied to all schools within a particular LEA, the major element of which is based on pupil numbers – the more pupils a school attracts the more money it receives. However, it is apparent that there is a limit to the number of pupils that a particular school can accept and thus a limit to the proportion of budget to which it can aspire. In the case of the analysis presented here about 80 per cent of schools classified as successful on the recruitment MSI are so classified because they are consistently full to capacity. Consequently the intake of these schools will be more-or-less consistent from year to year which no doubt explains the relative lack of correspondence with the schools classified as successful on the financial MSI. Another possible reason for this discord relates to the fact that there is a 'time-lag' inherent in the school resourcing mechanism. Thus, whereas choice impacts on only the intake cohort of pupils, the per capita funding formula takes into account the number of pupils in every year group of the school. Moreover, the formula is weighted in favour of older pupils which means the influence of the intake year will be proportionally less than that of other years (this will be especially so for schools which have sixth forms). Consequently, sustained parental support for a particular school will take several years to be translated into financial reward.

Although the connection between choice and financial gain is not clear cut, there is one particular factor which marks out successful schools from their less fortunate rivals. Thus it tends to be the case that quasi-market success is coupled with a relatively high level of GCSE performance. This result is found to hold at both the overall sample level and more locally within regions of competition and implies that parental choice and the school resourcing mechanism are tending to favour schools in line with Government expectation. More specifically it suggests that the most popular schools are those with the higher proportion of GCSE passes. However this does not necessarily imply that competition, *per se*, will lead to a raising of 'standards'. Moreover other results inform potentially conflicting perspectives on this issue. Thus, for example, the lack of a significant difference in the mean GCSE performance of 'middling' and 'declining plateau' schools suggests that examination results may not be a key reason for parents avoiding particular schools, and consequently the role that exam results play in informing choice and acting as the dynamic of competition is unclear. In contrast to this, the differential rate of improvement in the proportion of pupils with GCSE passes, and particularly the observation that over the period 1989–90 to 1993–4 'declining/plateau' and 'middling' schools improved much more quickly than 'improving/full' schools, could be interpreted as indicating that competition has given these schools a greater spur to improve.

Improvements in examination performance cannot be divorced from the potential of pupils and this potential is related to pupil background. Thus, although the association between market success and exam results is consistent with the hypothesis that competition stimulates schools to improve educational outputs, this conclusion depends on the absence of 'cream-skimming' (i.e. covert selection) by schools – of which we have no evidence one way or the other. More crucially it depends on the existence of a school system that is not stratified along the lines of social class and although our data do not presently allow an authoritative statement on this issue, it is far from clear whether choice is a neutral mechanism.

FURTHER RESEARCH

A more rigorous examination of the dynamics of the quasi-market is needed to explore further the extent to which schools that have been less than successful in terms of recruitment, and have relatively weak GCSE pass rates, are in fact improving their examination results. Moreover a pertinent question is whether such schools are beginning to attract parental support. A feature of the education system reforms that has generated much concern relates to the promotion of 'league tables' of GCSE results as indicators of school performance. Although not conceding that this provides an unfair basis for comparing schools, the DfE do recognise that 'value-added' measures are preferable: '[They are] a better reflection of schools' achievements than raw performance tables since the effects of socio-economic factors will be largely cancelled out' (DfE 1995: 2). In the light of the hinted-at association between examination performance and pupil SES revealed by this study, the development of reliable 'value-added' measures of school performance would be more likely to lead to greater discrimination between 'good' and 'poor' quality schools. However the extent to which such information would influence parental decision-making remains to be seen.

In terms of methodology a widening of the definition of recruitment success to take into account sixth form intakes would be a useful adjunct. In addition to helping to distinguish the factors contributing to schools' recruitment success such a variable would no doubt go some way to help to explain the discrepancy between trends in this and financial success.

NOTES

1 As in practice the boundaries of neighbouring multi-school systems will tend to overlap, non-competitive schools will only realistically occur in single-school systems.
2 A ratio within this range (which allows for a small degree of error) indicates that the school is recruiting more-or-less at the level afforded by its local population.
3 Similar trends are found at the regional level and for schools categorised according to differences in financial success.

REFERENCES

Adler, M., Petch, A. and Tweedie, J. (1989) *Parental Choice and Educational Policy*, Edinburgh: Edinburgh University Press.

Ball, S. (1993) 'Education markets, choice and social class: the market as a class strategy in the UK and USA', *British Journal of Sociology of Education* 14(1): 3–20.

Department for Education (DfE)/Welsh Office (1992) *Choice and Diversity: A New Framework for Schools*, London: HMSO.

DfE (1995) 'Value added in education', Briefing Paper, London: Department for Education.

Glatter, R. and Woods, P.A. (1994) 'The impact of competition and choice on parents and schools', in W. Bartlett, C. Propper, D. Wilson and J. LeGrand (eds) *Quasi-Markets in the Welfare State*, Bristol: University of Bristol, SAUS Publications.

Le Grand, J. and Bartlett, W. (1993) *Quasi-Markets and Social Policy*, Basingstoke: Macmillan.

Levačić, R. (1994) 'Evaluating the performance of quasi-markets in education', in W. Bartlett, C. Propper, D. Wilson and J. LeGrand (eds) *Quasi-Markets in the Welfare State*, Bristol: University of Bristol, SAUS Publications.

Maclure, S. (1992) *Education Reformed* (3rd edn), London: Hodder and Stoughton.

OECD (1994) *School: A Matter of Choice*, Paris: Centre for Educational Research and Innovation (CERI), Organisation for Economic Co-operation and Development.

Woods, P., Glatter, R. and Bagley, C. (1994) 'Dynamics of competition: the effects of local competitive arenas on schools', paper presented at CEDAR International Conference 'Changing educational structures: policy and practice', University of Warwick.

10

THE EDUCATION MARKET, LABOUR RELATIONS IN SCHOOLS AND TEACHER UNIONISM IN THE UK[1]

Sharon Gewirtz

INTRODUCTION

This chapter discusses the impact of the marketisation of education on labour relations in UK schools. More specifically it is concerned with the effects of the market on the potential for organised teacher activity. I want to argue that, on the one hand, teacher unions have been emasculated by recent employment legislation and that the work of teacher unions has in many ways been made more difficult and complicated by the deregulation of schooling, competition between schools and the intensification of the labour process of teaching. On the other hand, I will suggest that the pressures on teachers – and students – generated by the market operating in conjunction with an increased workload accentuates the need for organised teacher responses. I begin with a brief description of the three-year investigation into the operation of market forces in education[2] from which the case study material used here is drawn. I then present a general discussion of the elements of the UK government's market policies which have an impact on labour relations in schools and union activity. I go on to consider the impact of marketisation on teacher unionism in one local authority, which, I argue, can be seen as a critical case.

Some preliminary words of caution are necessary. First, it is virtually impossible to separate out the impact of the market on teacher union activity from the effects of other contemporaneous policy developments. The market-creating policies of open enrolment, per capita funding, local management of schools (LMS), grant-maintained (GM) schools and school specialisation do not operate in isolation. They work in conjunction with the national curriculum and testing, regular inspections of schools by OFSTED (Office for Standards in Education) and with retrenchment in public expenditure to construct, as I shall demonstrate, an environment which is in many ways inimical to effective union activity. An appreciation of the historical context is also vital here. It is all too easy to slip into a kind of golden-ageism and to exaggerate the apparent disintegration of teacher unionism today by contrasting it with a romanticised past of untainted collegiality, when teachers are meant to have spoken with a united voice and acted together in unqualified solidarity. We need to remind ourselves that division is a persistent feature of teacher unionism (Coates 1972). The teacher action of the mid-1980s, for instance, exposed and fuelled enormous rifts and tensions within the teaching workforce. In addition, we shall see that whilst the market in many senses encourages the atomisation of the teaching force, it can also produce greater solidarity and the potential for stronger union allegiances.

THE MARKETS PROJECT

The data presented here is drawn from a study of the operation and effects of education markets in the secondary school sector. The settings and samples upon which the research was based were selected to provide a context in which choice and competition were likely to be significant factors in the local politics of education and a concern impinging upon schools and upon parents choosing a secondary school for their child. The research was conducted over a three-year period from 1991 to 1994. Data collection was focused on three competitive 'clusters' of schools in three geographically contiguous local education authorities (LEAs) in London: Northwark, Westway and Riverway. (All names used in the text are pseudonyms.) The project data base consists of interviews with 137 parents, interview, observational and documentary material from fifteen secondary schools, LEA documentation and interviews with LEA officials. I draw here on the schools part of the study. Our fifteen secondary schools, set in the three local competitive 'clusters', were selected on the basis of various criteria but particularly school type and market position. In each school we interviewed a cross-section of staff, 119 in all. The analysis of our qualitative data drew upon the techniques of coding and constant comparison developed by Strauss (1987). All of the school-based interviews have to some extent informed the analysis I present in this chapter. However, due to limitations of space I am unable to illustrate the arguments put forward here with as much of our data as I would like.

MARKET POLICIES AND LABOUR RELATIONS

There are four major planks of Government policy which have an impact on labour relations in schools: employment legislation; the deregulation of schooling via the LMS, GM and city technology college (CTC) initiatives and school specialisation policies; the fostering of competition between schools; and the intensification of the labour process of teaching caused by funding reductions, larger class sizes, the National Curriculum and assessment provisions of the 1988 Education Reform Act and the inspection of schools by OFSTED (Office for Standards in Education). To varying degrees, all of these developments may be seen to militate against organised teacher activity whilst at the same time enhancing the need for it. I consider each in turn.

Employment legislation

The Conservative Government's commitment to the application of market force principles in both the economic and social spheres was in the 1980s closely entwined with its employment policy. One of the ostensible reasons for the Government's attack on trade unionism was that organised worker activity was seen to stand in the way of the free operation of market forces – a view grounded in various neo-liberal theories and more specifically the work of Friedrich von Hayek. In education, trade unionism was presented as part of the wider problem of 'producer capture' where LEAs and schools were said to be serving their own interests rather than those of the users of schools, variously defined as children, parents and employers. Thus the employment legislation of the 1980s was a key component of the assault on producer capture in education. The 1980 Employment Act made secondary action and large-scale picketing illegal and balloting of members compulsory before strike action could be taken. The 1987 Teachers' Pay and Conditions Act, followed by a new Pay and Conditions Act in 1991, further emasculated the teacher unions by abolishing their legal right to negotiate on pay and conditions and by effectively removing the 'withdrawal of goodwill' as a strike weapon through the introduction of a legally binding contract of employment. One result of this legislation is that strike action on the issue of redundancies produced by LMS budgeting is now illegal beyond the affected schools. Thus, whilst successive National Union of Teachers (NUT) conferences have voted for strike action on this issue, the votes have been ignored by the executive on the grounds that illegal strike action would lead to the sequestration of union funds.

The deregulation of schooling

The impact on labour of the deregulation of schooling has been characterised by Seifert as follows:

[T]he high level of labour costs as a proportion of total costs means that, in the financially driven systems being adopted, a reduction of labour costs is essential. . . . [I]n order to achieve the promised higher quality and quantity of teaching within current and/or dwindling resources, there will have to be increases in labour productivity. This will be obtained through greater managerial controls over the labour process in schools and a more strategic approach to the utilisation of the labour force . . . Flexible staffing is . . . a major concern: more short-term contracts, more zero hour contracts (a system used with groups such as bank nurses), more planned use of supply staff and perhaps, more subcontracted labour. . . . Finally there is flexible pay. . . . There is your basic pay, but what proportion of total earnings comes from that? In the future less and less perhaps. Other elements of pay will include allowances, regional weightings, and merit payments/incentive allowances. Then there are the non-pay elements in the total reward package: subsidised health insurance, extra holidays, better pensions (private ones), and the range of satisfiers on offer.

(Seifert 1991a: 41–42)

Greater managerial control of the labour process was being exerted in a number of our case study schools through the techniques of target setting and performance monitoring (Gewirtz *et al*. 1995). And more 'flexible' approaches to staffing were also in evidence (see below) as in the study by Sinclair and colleagues (Sinclair *et al*. 1993). LEA school teachers continue to be paid according to a centrally determined pay structure. However, it is one which allows a fair (and increasing) amount of scope for employers' discretion. As is the case in some CTCs, GM schools are being encouraged to determine their own rates of pay and to agree individual contracts with individual teachers.

Whilst the deregulation of schooling intensifies the need for effective unionism, it also appears to make the work of unions more difficult. Under the LMS provisions, each school staff has its own employer – the governing body – which is responsible for appointments and dismissals. Whereas previously the local union association could negotiate with one employer – the LEA – on behalf of its members on local issues, the logic of the new system is for negotiation on issues affecting teachers to take place at individual school level. Deregulation thus complicates and increases the work of local union branches which have to develop relationships with many individual employers rather than just the one. In addition, the success of unions in defending the interests of their members is becoming increasingly dependent on the vigilance, expertise and skills of individual school representatives.

Competition between schools

Competition between schools can result in the deterioration and in some instances total breakdown of co-operative activities between staff based in different institutions, which in turn can have detrimental effects on students, as, for example, in cases where sixth form consortia have collapsed (Gewirtz et al. 1993b; Whitty et al. 1993: 146).[3] Where it is real and immediate, competition between schools can not only undermine collaborative professional activities; it also produces a potential point of conflict between teachers based in different institutions, because the job security of individual workers is dependent on the survival of the individual schools in which they are based. With formula funding, student numbers are converted directly into funding for schools which in turn translates into jobs for teachers and support staff. In many schools, workers in education are now being encouraged to see their jobs as dependent on the success of the schools in which they are working in relation to other local schools. This is part of the social psychology of self-interest upon which the success of market policies is seen by its proponents to depend. The competition between schools for students is also therefore a competition between the teachers in those schools for teachers' jobs. At first glance, this situation would not appear to be conducive to organised union activity across schools (although of course this is no different from the way things have traditionally been in the private sector).

Intensification of the labour process of teaching

A fourth factor which has a potential impact on the nature of organised teacher activity is the high levels of stress and low morale which teachers appear to be experiencing as a result of excessive workloads and a general climate in which teachers feel undervalued. The increase in teacher workloads is generated by the National Curriculum and associated assessment arrangements, preparation for OFSTED inspections, LMS, the need to market schools and larger class sizes. The contraction of LEA support services and of provision of in-service training exacerbates feelings of stress and low morale. Many of the teachers we interviewed felt ground down, demoralised, exhausted, apathetic, and a sense that any collective teacher action was futile. Competition itself can be stressful for teachers:

> the need to be more competitive, . . . that's detrimental, I think. . . . [Y]ou feel like you're always having to do better then the next school or every other school because you're competing and . . . I don't think . . . that's . . . very conducive . . . to the morale

and ethos . . . of the school because it means you're constantly worrying.

(NUT representative, Parkside School, Westway)

There is a sense of teachers being treated by management as commodities, of their being dehumanised (Ball 1994).

A number of the union representatives in our sample expressed resignation, and others anger, about the process of union residualisation which is seen to be taking place:

In the world of diminishing union power, this is all we can do, sort of knock the edges off things and save a job here and there, but you can't fundamentally alter the direction.

(NUT representative, Northwark Park School, Northwark)

[T]here's less of people joining together in union activities, there's poor attendance at union meetings, people don't see the union as having anything to do. They're more concerned just about individual issues like salaries and things as it affects them, but they're not very interested in getting involved. . . . I think people retain their union membership now for insurance purposes. If . . . you hit a child you've got some legal backing, or for advice of that sort, but not for anything very much . . . I feel quite angry that the union doesn't really address the issues that are important to people in the classroom. . . . They've been involved in logos and all sorts of issues which haven't really concerned people. I mean where people have wanted advice, it's always been difficult to find it on things like job descriptions, appraisal, all the issues where you're not sure what to do. I suppose it's being management led and unions haven't been very quick to respond to the issues that are being thrown at . . . you every day. You don't have time to go back and find out what the union's position is and what they'd actually do in the situation, so you deal with it yourself. Should I sign this document or should I sign this job description?

(Former NUT representative, Pankhurst School, Riverway)

The apathy that this teacher refers to was apparent in Fletcher School in Riverway where there was no official union representative because no one was prepared to take on the role. A growing lack of faith in the efficacy of unionism for purposes other than insurance is reflected at a national level in the redistribution of members from the TUC (Trades Union Congress)-affiliated NUT to the non-TUC Association of Teachers and Lecturers. The changing pattern of union membership raises questions about the amount of authority individual unions can mobilise at school level.

141

The stress, the low morale and the apathy arising from competition, deregulation and the intensification of teachers' work may well have a significant impact on the quality of education being experienced by students as well as on the physical well-being of teachers.[4] It would seem, therefore, that all of the arguments which have been traditionally advanced in favour of organised teacher union activity apply particularly strongly under the new conditions being generated within schools by the Government's market-creating strategies and associated policies. Is the potential for collective teacher action as bleak as the logic of the preceding discussion might suggest? There are two issues which need to be addressed here. First, what is the potential for union activity to occur, given the divisions that the market would appear to accentuate? Second, what is the potential for any action to be effective? In the remainder of this paper I deal exclusively with the first question which I explore by focusing on one LEA, Northwark.

UNIONISM IN NORTHWARK

Northwark LEA – where competition is fierce and deregulation particularly advanced – provides an interesting 'critical case' for the analysis of labour relations and unionism in schools in that it is at the 'leading edge' of market changes. If, in the longer run, the market takes hold elsewhere as it has in Northwark, then an understanding of the situation of unionism in Northwark today might provide some indication of the future of unionism at a local level more generally.

The intensity of competitive relations between schools in Northwark is fuelled by the existence of a significant number of surplus places, the constant threat of local authority budget cuts, the growth of the local GM sector,[5] and LEA-led school specialisation and selection. This situation has created a climate of fear about job losses in Northwark, particularly in under-subscribed schools. Whilst there had been no teacher redundancies during the period of our fieldwork, all of Northwark's cleaning and catering staff lost their jobs when these services were put out to compulsory competitive tendering in line with the authority's commitment to privatisation, deregulation and low local taxation. The new cleaners employed were paid at just over half the hourly rate of the previous workers and required to clean a larger area. Such changes have implications for standards of cleaning and catering in Northwark schools. The low quality of school meals was, for instance, a persistent topic of discussion at Northwark Park governors' meetings. But of particular relevance here is the contribution of the privatisation of support services in Northwark schools to the trepidation expressed by a number of

Northwark teachers in under-subscribed schools. These concerns were exacerbated when Northwark's announcement of a budget cut led to the handing out of redundancy notices at Milton School in 1992.

Northwark teachers are also feeling the impact of management 'flexible staffing' strategies. Specialisation policies being put into practice in Northwark are likely to exacerbate existing subject hierarchies and tensions between teachers of different subjects not only through differential pay but also as a result of differing levels of job security. As Ozga (1993) has pointed out: 'The emphasis on specialisation and diversity together allows considerable scope for diversity of treatment of the teaching workforce'. Whilst in particular subject areas, like maths and science, specialists are being sought out, in other 'low status' areas (like PE, sociology and special needs) specialisms are being 'diluted' and hence devalued:

> [T]here used to be slack in the timetable so you had free time, whereas now there's much less free time and people are split up between different things to fill up the gaps . . . so we've got people who usually teach art and come in here [the technology department] to do odd periods. . . . [T]hey've got no commitment to the department, so basically it drags the department down. I'm not saying that's their fault. I'm saying that if you do something, if you do it all the time, you're committed to it, you're interested in it and you get better results, the kids get better results. . . . The special needs bit also comes back to this using people and trying to fill the timetable so [the management will say] 'Ah Mr So-and-So teaches French, he's got three free periods, right we'll give him to special needs'. You know this sort of mentality is very prevalent and I think heads can't see a problem with it, they see it as good management, and I see it as short-sighted expedience, which can't be in the long term interests of either the school or the kids or the people who are doing it. . . . Special needs is particularly vulnerable to that sort of thing, I think, because [of the] 'Anyone-can-obviously-teach-special-needs . . .' syndrome.
>
> (NUT representative, Northwark Park School, Northwark)

The 'dilution' of subject specialisms is a difficult strategy to oppose because, although it is seen as detrimental to teachers' working conditions and to have negative educational consequences, it is viewed as an alternative to redundancies and therefore the lesser of two evils.

I now want to look at the effect of the developments described in the previous section on the role of the unions within individual schools and across schools in Northwark.

Unionism within schools

Deregulation means that the ability of unions to influence school decision making will now increasingly depend, at least to some extent, on
the management strategies of individual headteachers as well as the
market position of schools. School organisations are currently involved
in a process of transition as they adapt to the deregulation of labour relations. Within our sample some contrasts are already becoming apparent.
It is possible to divide schools into two 'rough and ready' categories –
those which wish to include unions in the decision-making processes of
the school and those which do not. As we shall see, unions are not
necessarily more powerful in schools which include them.

Inclusion of unions

The strategy of union inclusion corresponds to aspects of Seifert's
'liberal pluralist' model of 'human resource management': 'The corner-
stone of conflict avoidance here is the openness and formality of agreed
procedures on all aspects of managerial decision making, and the welcome participation in the process of the union representatives' (Seifert
1991b: 38).

In Milton, following a bitter conflict over the handing out of redundancy notices by the head, there is a move towards including the
unions in school decision-making processes. The labour crisis in the
school was ignited by the announcement by Northwark Council that
they would be cutting £7,000,000 from the education budget. The headteacher at Milton School immediately responded by issuing redundancy
notices to ten members of staff. The local NUT branch handed out
leaflets at the school gates informing parents of the redundancies. The
notices were withdrawn when the LEA reversed their decision to cut
the education budget. (The Conservative administration had apparently
become concerned about the possible negative consequences of the original decision to cut the budget on the local, and possibly national, Party's
success in the forthcoming General Election.) The dispute was a critical
event in Milton's recent labour relations history. It meant the head and
governors had to start to come to terms with their new role as employer,
however reluctantly:

> The head always gets angry when he's seen as the employer, he
> doesn't like that role at all. The governors . . . felt very difficult
> over all the budget stuff, because they felt they were doing the
> best job they could, and they couldn't understand why there was
> all this nasty stuff, people phoning them up and lots of pressure
> on them, because they thought they were doing the school a
> favour, so they didn't see themselves as a board of directors of a

company. They saw themselves as the friends of the school, trying to help the school and when they made the decision, which was a board of directors' decision, to cut a budget or to impose a budget cut based on the budget cut given by Northwark and then to name teachers, that changed their role and I don't think they were happy with that role.

(NUT representative, Milton School, Northwark)

The conflict produced new divisions in the school, in particular what the NUT representative called 'a massive breakdown in communication . . . between senior management and staff'. But new solidarities were also forged between the teaching staff and the office staff. Thus for example, during the redundancy crisis, unbeknown to the senior managers in the school, the office staff prioritised typing and photocopying work for the teaching staff over that for the senior management team (SMT). As a result of the conflict, new channels of communication between head and staff were developed which, according to the NUT representative, resulted in a new atmosphere of 'openness'. The SMT began to meet regularly with the union representatives (teaching and non-teaching) and staff were given access to the minutes of SMT meetings. In short, the SMT were making efforts not to be 'a closed board of directors'. As the NUT representative put it, 'they don't like that role and they don't want it'.

It is questionable how far such openness and communicativeness constitutes genuine participation or merely incorporation – what Hargreaves (1991) calls 'contrived collegiality' – and hence effectively emasculation. It is debatable first how open the 'openness' is – the union representatives at Milton are being given access to minutes of SMT meetings but such minutes rarely include everything discussed. Second, it is doubtful whether inclusivist strategies would enable the unions to prevent job losses in the future. All they would be likely to do would be to implicate the unions in any decisions regarding redundancies.

Exclusion of unions

This model conforms to aspects of Seifert's second management 'option' – 'new model unitarism':

The schools will develop corporate identities as teams of staff and the team spirit will be engendered through team building activities including outward bound courses for staff, and away days in brainstorming retreats. Shared objectives will be secured and teachers and other school staff will be rewarded and/or punished in line with these. . . .

The unions will be recognised for health and safety at work purposes, and for individual disciplinary matters. There will be no bargaining [in fact the 1991 Act precludes this anyway], no grievance/disputes machinery. Their role will be much reduced: full-time officials will be excluded from school grounds and school level representatives will have their facilities reduced. There will be no union meetings on school premises.

The thrust of policy is to emphasise the rewards available for 'loyal' and hard-working staff whose performance measures up to targets. Headteacher largesse will be at an all time high and this rediscovered power will be used to impose all school-determined conditions of service.

(Seifert 1991b: 37)

This model is most closely adhered to in the city technology college in Northwark. Although none of our other schools have so wholly embraced this option by the letter, the spirit is certainly apparent amongst particular heads, notably Mrs Carnegie, the 'Principal' at Martineau. The development of the school's corporate imagery, what the management textbooks call 'symbolic management', extends to a logo, a motto, a flower, a distinctive uniform and a school flag (Gewirtz *et al.* 1995). The head has not gone to the lengths of banning union officials or union meetings from school premises but she has gone some way to reducing the facilities of the union representatives by redefining a number of union issues as 'personnel' ones. The NUT representative is concerned about the 'down-playing' of the role of the unions in the school:

[M]y time for being a union rep has been decreased this year on the basis that we've now got a deputy head who is in charge of personnel and other things as well and therefore lots of these issues ought to go to him rather than to me, which I think, is a complete misunderstanding of what a union rep is and what a senior management in a school is, but that was the reason given to me.

(NUT representative, Martineau School, Northwark)

The unions would thus appear to be in a no-win situation. Either they are excluded from school decision making and so are unable to exert an influence, or they are included in the process, but risk being implicated in decisions which may adversely affect working conditions and job security.

The potential for teachers within individual schools to act collectively to defend jobs and improve conditions can also be affected by management strategies which are not directly related to the role of unions in schools. There are indications in some of our case study schools that

146

headteachers are operating, either consciously or unconsciously, policies of 'divide and rule'. Thus, in many schools, departments are being set against departments, creating a climate of competition between staff particularly at 'middle management' level. This partly operates through a competition over examination success, in which every department is encouraged to strive for the best results in and 'for' the school. But 'divide and rule' also operates through the creation of what can be seen as 'internal markets' within schools, that is bidding systems in which departments become 'cost centres' and heads of department have to compete for resources against other department heads. Thus teachers are being encouraged to see themselves, not as colleagues working in concert with each other, but as rivals whose interests are in conflict.

Unionism across schools

Because the majority of secondary schools in Northwark are no longer funded by the LEA, there are moves by NUT activists to establish a new federal structure of local union members in GM and LEA schools. Nigel Harris, the Milton representative, explains:

> From a union point of view across the borough there's a feeling we've got to try and keep the staff in the GM schools and the non-GM schools together. How do we do that, because obviously you're separated off as a GM school from a non-GM school? If there's a problem in one school we can't go on strike about it any more, so we've got to actually work somehow together on these things. There's beginnings, attempts, to set up a federation of the GM schools and the non-GM schools together. . . . I would quite like it if all the GM schools did the same negotiation because we're all starting from scratch, we haven't got the expertise in schools to do this, so where can we get the expertise from? Well the union can back up a group of schools together, provide the information for governors and for teachers to work together on it, that's the idea, so it's an attempt to stop the competition between the schools.
>
> (NUT representative, Milton School, Northwark)

The Northwark Teachers Association had belonged to the Inner London Teachers Association and is therefore part of a long tradition of active union membership which might be expected to provide a firm basis for resisting the atomisation of the teaching force which the market appears to encourage. However there is some doubt about how well the new federalism, which Nigel Harris refers to, will work in practice, given the competitive nature of the local school system and the tensions between teachers in different schools which that generates:

We're not in open competition with Hutton, it [has] very different pupils, from different places, so there's not that sense in which we're in competition, so we're willing to work with Hutton. We're a bit more in competition with Martineau, so how much can we work with Martineau, how much can people actually trust each other and share information?

(NUT representative, Milton School, Northwark)

As in the private sector, institutional survival is set over and against older cross-cutting interests and allegiances. However, it is important to distinguish between official union relationships, which Harris is involved in restructuring through attempts at federation, and the unofficial union activities of militant activists, for instance those involved in the Socialist Teachers Association. These latter activities may rest on stronger solidarities and may thus be more resilient to tensions created by the combined effects of open enrolment and per capita funding. Furthermore, despite the tensions within the Northwark teaching force alluded to by the representative at Milton, these did not prevent the Northwark Teachers Association organising against the threatened redundancies at Milton. However, had the budget cuts not been reinstated by the council, it is questionable how far Northwark teachers would have been prepared to go in opposing the redundancies, given the illegality of strike action.

CONCLUSIONS – IMPLICATIONS FOR FURTHER RESEARCH AND POLICY

The picture is therefore rather complicated. The market creates difficulties for unionism but also enhances the need for it. It accentuates tensions in the teaching workforce but also produces solidarities. However, teacher solidarity where it does exist is not enough to secure effective collective action, because of the constraints imposed by the employment legislation outlined at the beginning of this chapter. The impotence of the teacher unions was highlighted by the short-lived action over testing in 1993. The temporary victory of teachers in the boycott of the national tests[6] showed that up to a point collective teacher action could still occur and achieve things. Nick Cotton, NUT representative at Parkside School, Westway, commented:

We were all very much heartened . . . as union members . . . by the response to the boycott over the SATs [Standard Assessment Tasks] because that was positive, that demonstrated that we still had something in terms of power, that we could say, well this has gone far enough, because the overall feeling you get so often is that there's nothing you can do, this Government is going to steamroller through whatever they want and we just have to lie down and take it.

This was also the view taken by Hatcher and Troyna (1994) who argued that the boycott represented 'the most effective opposition so far to the government's ability to put its education policies into practice'. Such optimistic conclusions, however, turned out to have been somewhat premature. Although teachers' opposition to testing was essentially based on educational principle, the unions chose to take action on the grounds of workload (as to boycott on other grounds was deemed to have been illegal). The result of this is that following the Dearing Report (1994) (which recommended a slimming down of the curriculum and tests) the ostensible grounds for oppositional activity withered away and the tests, albeit simplified, went ahead in 1994, allowing the publication of league tables of test results, and the competition and resultant inequities which all of that implies (Gewirtz *et al.* 1995) to continue.

Hatcher and Troyna's analysis alerts us to the danger of premature evaluation of policy effects, and I would want to avoid falling into the same trap, as it is still early days. Our research indicates that school managers, teachers and unions are still in the process of grappling with their new roles in the changed policy context and it will be some time yet before we can make a definitive evaluation of the impact of the market on labour relations and union activity in schools. Meanwhile, there is certainly scope and a need for more in-depth research into how school managers, teachers and union activists are interpreting their roles in the market environment and into the impact those interpretations are having on employment relations.[7]

My reluctance to prematurely evaluate the impact of the market reforms on labour relations and union activity means that I am able to speak only cautiously of the policy implications of our research. However, one important conclusion that can be drawn is that policy makers need to rethink the relationship between teachers' interests and the interests of students. The assumption underpinning the market model of education provision which is now in place is that student interests are best served when teacher unions are weak and when teachers are acting as individuals in their own self-interest in competition with other self-interested teachers. This scenario of competitive individualism is seen by advocates of marketisation to be far superior to the corporate model of education provision which the reforms of the 1980s were designed to dismantle. Within the corporate model, according to its neo-liberal critics, teachers, through their unions, tended to act in their own collective interests and against the interests of students. My reading of our data leads me to conclude, however, that the current situation of competitive individualism in the context of reduced funding may well turn out to be detrimental to rather than facilitative of the well-being of students. The fear, anxiety, insecurity and loss of morale amongst many teachers which is being generated by the market model is, I contend, hardly likely to be conducive to a stable and productive learning environment for children. If I am right about this, then it follows that students' well-being at school is dependent, at least in part, on the collective security and well-being of teachers. That in turn, I would argue, depends, again at least in part, on the ability of teachers to act in an organised and collective fashion in order to pursue their collective interests. The simple, if tentative, policy lesson to be drawn here is that the market model, together with the associated residualisation of teacher unionism, is compatible neither with the well-being of teachers, nor by implication with the well-being of students.

NOTES

1 I am grateful to Stephen Ball, Alan Cribb, Meg Maguire, Carl Bagley and Philip A. Woods for their useful comments on an earlier draft of this chapter.
2 Directed by Stephen Ball and Richard Bowe and funded by the Economic and Social Research Council (reference number R000232858). This is one of a number of publications arising from the study. Others include Ball *et al.* (1994a; 1994b; 1995), Bowe *et al.* (1994; 1995), and Gewirtz *et al.* (1993a; 1993b; 1995).
3 Although, it is important to note, as two recent edited collections illustrate, that collaboration amongst schools is still possible in a market environment (Bridges and Husbands 1996; Macbeth *et al.* 1995).
4 It is interesting to note in relation to this issue of teachers' physical and emotional well-being, the increase of teachers leaving the profession before retirement age (DfE 1995).
5 By the end of our study Northwark had one CTC, four GM and only three LEA schools.
6 Otherwise known as SATs (Standard Attainment Tasks), these tests, to be taken by children at ages 7, 11 and 14 in the core National Curriculum subjects – English, maths and science – were introduced as part of the 1988 Education Reform Act.
7 Indeed, this is one focus of my current research with Stephen Ball ('Schools, cultures and values: the impact of the 1988 and 1993 Education Acts' – ESRC reference number R000235544).

REFERENCES

Ball, S.J. (1994) *Education Reform: A Critical and Post-Structural Approach*, Buckingham, Open University Press.
Ball, S.J., Bowe, R. and Gewirtz, S. (1994a) 'Competitive schooling: values, ethics and cultural engineering', *Journal of Curriculum and Supervision* 9(4): 350–367.

Ball, S.J., Bowe, R. and Gewirtz, S. (1994b) 'School choice, social class and distinction: the realisation of social advantage in education', ESRC Project Paper, Centre for Educational Studies, King's College London.

Ball, S.J., Bowe, R. and Gewirtz, S. (1995) 'Circuits of schooling: a sociological exploration of parental choice of school in social class contexts', *Sociological Review* 43(1): 52–78.

Bowe, R., Ball, S.J. and Gewirtz, S. (1994). 'Captured by the discourse? Issues and concerns in researching "parental choice"', *British Journal of Sociology of Education* 15(1): 63–78.

Bowe, R., Ball, S.J. and Gewirtz, S. (1995) 'Market forces, inequality and the city', in H. Jones and J. Lansley (eds) *Social Policy and the City*, Aldershot, Avebury House Press.

Bridges, D. and Husbands, C. (eds) (1996) *Consorting and Collaborating in the Education Market Place*, London, Falmer.

Coates, R. (1972) *Teacher Unions and Interest Group Politics*, Cambridge, Cambridge University Press.

Dearing R. (1994) *The National Curriculum and its Assessment: A New Framework for Schools*, London: School Curriculum and Assessment Authority.

Department for Education (DfE) (1995) Submission to School Teachers' Review Body.

Gewirtz, S., Ball, S. and Bowe, R. (1993a) 'Parents, privilege and the education market place', *Research Papers in Education* 9(1): 3–29.

Gewirtz, S., Ball, S.J. and Bowe, R. (1993b) 'Values and ethics in the marketplace: the case of Northwark Park', *International Journal of Sociology of Education* 3(2): 233–254.

Gewirtz, S., Ball, S.J. and Bowe, R. (1995) *Markets, Choice and Equity in Education*, Buckingham, Open University Press.

Hargreaves, A. (1991) 'Contrived collegiality: the micropolitics of teacher collaboration', in J. Blase (ed.) *The Politics of Life in Schools*, Newbury Park: Sage.

Hatcher, R. and Troyna, B. (1994) 'The "policy cycle": a ball by ball account', *Journal of Education Policy* 9(2): 155–170.

Macbeth, A., McCreath, D. and Aitchison, J. (eds) (1995) *Collaborate or Compete? Educational Partnerships in a Market Economy*, London: Falmer Press.

Ozga, J. (1993) 'Where are the teachers in the new framework for schools?', *Educational Review* 7(1): 44–45.

Seifert, R. (1991a) 'The conflict potential', *Managing Schools Today* 1 (1): 41–43.

Seifert, R. (1991b) 'Managing the conflict', *Managing Schools Today* 1(2): 36–38.

Sinclair, J., Ironside, M. and Seifert, R. (1993) 'Classroom struggle? Market oriented education reforms and their impact on teachers' professional autonomy, labour intensification and resistance', paper presented to the Eleventh Annual International Labour Process Conference, 1 April.

Strauss, A.L. (1987) *Qualitative Analysis for Social Scientists*, New York, Cambridge University Press.

Whitty, G., Edwards, T. and Gewirtz, S. (1993) *Specialisation and Choice in Urban Education: The City Technology College Experiment*, London: Routledge.

11

POLICIES FOR SCHOOL CHOICE
What can Britain learn from abroad?
Donald Hirsch

INTRODUCTION

Attempts to give parents and pupils a greater choice of school, and hence a larger influence on educational provision, have been widespread in OECD countries. The motives behind this general trend have not every-where been identical, and the policies that have resulted vary consider-ably according to the political climate and the institutional and cultural background. Nevertheless, the many features of approaches to school choice – both by supporters and critics – that are common to different countries make international comparisons worthwhile. In particular, the appearance of a number of comparable but relatively new policies across the developed world make it desirable for policy makers to ask 'How is this working elsewhere?' when considering options for the future.

In this spirit, the OECD's (Organisation for Economic Co-operation and Development's) Centre for Educational Research and Innovation recently undertook the first policy-oriented analysis of how school choice works in practice in a range of nations. The study took a snapshot of policy developments, research evidence and current debates in each of six countries as of mid-1993. These overviews covered Australia, England,[1] the Netherlands, New Zealand, Sweden and the United States. The study also looked more selectively at policies in Denmark and France. The resulting report (OECD 1994) analysed general trends, summarised developments in each country, and presented sixteen short case studies of different forms of choice in practice. (The present author, then an employee of the OECD, was responsible for the study.)

This chapter draws on the experiences described in the OECD report to explore the relevance of international developments for Britain. It starts by thematically reviewing the policies pursued in various countries. The second section comments briefly on observed market behaviour: on the one hand on the perception of choice by families as 'consumers' and on the other on the response to choice by schools as 'suppliers'. The third section discusses the issue of transferability: what relevance do the experiences of other countries have for British policy? The final section suggests some particular areas where foreign experiences offer apt lessons for Britain. Overall, the chapter argues that while the institutional and cultural differences between countries should not be ignored, an accelerated rate of institutional and societal change in Britain has made it more apt to draw lessons from foreign settings.

POLICIES FOR SCHOOL CHOICE IN OECD COUNTRIES

There are, very broadly, two main philosophical reasons for wanting to give citizens choice among schools in countries offering universal access to public education. The older reason, particularly strong in many continental European countries, is to preserve pluralism, and more particularly religious freedom, rather than impose a monolithic and secular framework for schooling on everybody. The second, much more recent reason is to replace a centrally planned, monopolistic local supply of schooling with greater competition among suppliers in order to make them more sensitive to the wishes of their 'consumers'. This second reason is strongest in English-speaking countries, especially those with neo-liberal governments, but exists in some form almost everywhere.

To these philosophical reasons must be added a third, more pragmatic one, which helps explain why the trend towards choice, although uneven, is all but universal. This third reason is that parents are becoming increasingly fussy about which school their children attend. Parents are more educated, schooling is seen as more crucial to life chances, than ever before. In some relatively homogeneous and stable cultures like Sweden's, the desire to choose actively is relatively muted, even now that free choice is available, partly because of the perception that school quality is extremely even. In France, a theoretically equal set of public institutions have come up against a highly competitive population who have never consented to regard every school as equal, and became adept at finding 'back-door' routes to choice until the government felt obliged to allow some choice officially into the public system. The Japanese government sticks more doggedly to an entirely equal set of schools for six to fifteen-year-olds, backed by rigid catchment areas and the rotation of teachers among schools. But intense competition to do well in the ninth-grade exams that give access to the best high schools finds a non-official outlet in *juku* – private crammer schools, whose growth is a constant concern for the Japanese Ministry of Education. In short, the official admission of choice can emanate not just from political principle but from pressures arising from the behaviour of parents – who to a growing extent regard themselves as consumers and their schools as 'service-providing organisations' rather than merely 'local institutions' (Ballion 1991: 18).

The new and old policies promoting school choice in various countries follow no neat pattern, but can be roughly classified as follows.

Public support for non-public schooling

Subsidies to 'private' schools (whose definition itself varies from one country to another) have long been used in certain countries as a mechanism for maintaining largely religious alternatives to the state system, at affordable prices to parents. Such subsidies are available to support mainly Catholic schools in France, Protestant, Catholic and secular schools in the Netherlands, and mainly non-religious schools (many with 'alternative' philosophies) in Denmark.

More recently, under the broad label of vouchers, there have been moves to support private schools more as a 'market' alternative, designed to subject public schools to educational competition rather than to underpin pluralism of belief. This idea has as a rule been more discussed than practised. Americans talk about it a lot but have experimented with it only in small-scale, isolated cases. A Swedish neo-liberal government (now out of power) introduced an adventurous voucher scheme without much discussion in the early 1990s. Private schools got 85 per cent of the local cost of a pupil in the public system (later reduced to 75 per cent by the Social Democrats), more or less unconditionally, for each student recruited. This quickly caused a doubling of private school enrolments – but to only just over 1 per cent of the school population. But the country with the highest enrolments in private schools receiving automatic cash transfers from government is Australia, where over a quarter of children attend such schools, which receive between a third and three-quarters of their income from the state and federal governments. Although the reason for introducing these subsidies in the 1970s was to rescue the failing Catholic school system, all recent growth has been in the independent (non-Catholic) sector, where enrolments are approaching 10 per cent of the total.

Liberalised enrolment rules in the public sector

The idea of allocating pupils to particular catchment areas remains strong in most OECD countries. Measures to allow enrolment regardless of residence have taken various forms. Like their British counterparts, parents in New Zealand, Sweden, the Netherlands and some parts of France (for secondary schools only) may apply for the school that they choose. But the choice is presented differently in New Zealand, where nobody is steered towards a particular school, than in France and Sweden, where choice only comes into play if a parent applies to over-ride the automatic assignment of a child to the local school. There is moreover a difference between the practice in Dutch state schools, which never turn students away, those in New Zealand, who must apply to central government to proclaim the risk of overcrowding before rejecting an application, and French ones, where choice is withdrawn not only if one's preferred school becomes too full, but also if one's nearest school becomes too empty.

Crucial to the operation of 'open' enrolment policies in practice is the means of selecting pupils for rolls that have had to 'close'. Britain is not alone in reverting primarily to the criterion that open enrolment is supposed to make irrelevant – residence – to select children for over-subscribed schools. New Zealand, however, gives greater freedom to such schools to define their own enrolment rules, and many use a wide range of criteria to give themselves effectively the power to admit more 'desirable' families (Bowden 1993; Gordon 1994a and 1994b). A number of American school districts, in contrast, operate allocation policies designed to avoid the concentration of more privileged children in high-status schools in wealthy areas – for example through differential admission rights by race, or through random allocation that removes the primacy of residence.

Policies encouraging schools to compete under liberal enrolment rules

Choice has in many countries been part of a wider process making schools into relatively autonomous institutions rather than mere units in centrally-administered provision. In New Zealand this has gone furthest – effectively giving all schools a similar status to Britain's grant-maintained schools. In continental European state school systems, devolution is more cautious, and limited in the medium term by the fact that in many countries schools do not traditionally have an independent consciousness, and the headteachers regard themselves as middle managers in a state bureaucracy. In the United States, even though schools often have a rather stronger self-identity than in Europe, school districts have a continuing tendency to run themselves as 'systems', and to restrict the scope for school-based initiative.

Crucial to the link between choice and autonomy is the relationship between enrolments and resources. The 'money follows pupils' principle is followed to varying degrees. In Sweden, for example (unlike in Britain), local authorities can decide how much money to put into capitation rather than spend on common services; one of the pioneers of pupil-based funding, Stockholm, only puts in around 50 per cent. France rejects the idea of money following pupils within the public sector: a school that attracts children from outside its catchment area simply has to cope with larger classes. But in those countries where some form of capitation does exist, three characteristics of the British system are commonly shared: each pupil carries the same weight (i.e. there are no major attempts to attach differential formula funding to pupils according to the presumed cost of educating them); payments cover recurrent rather than capital costs, limiting the incentives to recruit more pupils once physical capacity is reached; and payments relate normally to the average cost of educating a student rather than to marginal costs, arguably creating distorted rewards and penalties for fluctuation in student numbers.

Policies enabling schools to be different under liberal enrolment rules

Does choice have any meaning if all schools have similar objectives and characteristics? Arguably, even under a homogeneous system, schools might improve qualitatively if they are subjected to market discipline – i.e. competition will stimulate higher standards. Yet even if this were the case (and there is a singular lack of evidence internationally about whether it is or not), consumers who choose schools that are merely competing to do the same thing better than each other are certain to face widespread frustration. This is an important difference between school markets and markets for most goods and services. If supplier A is universally thought to make widgets better than supplier B, the latter quickly goes out of business and the former expands its supply. It is self-evident that schools do not work like that; so if school A is universally more popular than school B, and both are geographically accessible to the same families, many children will simply end up in their second choice of school. (The nature and consequences of imperfections in school 'markets' are explored further in Hirsch 1995b.)

One approach to this problem, giving resources to less popular schools to get better, may be desirable, but is unlikely fully to resolve the problem. Crudely speaking, league tables will never result in an across-the-league draw. Only if parents regard schools as qualitatively different rather than unequal might there be a relatively even distribution of preferences among those who do not automatically choose their closest school. It is this factor that makes the link between choice and diversity an important one.

How can policy makers encourage extra school diversity? In some European countries with tight national curricula and regulation, it is necessary in the first instance to *permit* diversity. In this sense we have recently got back from a five-year return trip to the continent: Sir Ron Dearing's loosening of the curriculum straitjacket (Dearing 1994) has helped reduce the contradiction of the 1988 Education Reform Act in attempting simultaneously to allow choice and increase uniformity.

In some countries education authorities have attempted to *decree* diversity – a rather risky project, practised for example by New South Wales in redesignating schools to specialise in languages, technology or teaching gifted children without always ensuring that they have acquired the competence or the ethos to do so. The ideal of *encouraging* diversity is the preferred model in Britain. As discussed further below, the question to be raised here is how genuinely schools are being encouraged to adopt different educational models, rather than merely competing for funds attached to labels such as 'technology college'.

Policies to make choosing schools more feasible

Any improvement in opportunities created by choice will be unevenly distributed if there is not a conscious effort to remove certain barriers to choosing schools. Information and travel possibilities in particular tend to be concentrated among the most privileged. So far the British Government has been more advanced than others in linking consumer information with choice (for example through the new style of OFSTED reports), but has done little to improve access to travel opportunities. The United States has a long-standing custom of funding school buses that lends itself well to choice; in the Netherlands, flat topography and good cycle lanes create a hard-to-replicate level of student mobility; New Zealand has departed from the common practice of skewing transport assistance to those attending their closest school, in a new system that approximates to portable school transport vouchers.

CONSUMER AND PRODUCER BEHAVIOURS

In observing these policies in action, it is worth reflecting on two issues of particular interest: how do families perceive their role as freely-choosing consumers, and how do schools respond to their new status as competing suppliers? There is no robust body of evidence on these matters at the international level, but some interesting indications arise from the fragments of evidence that exist.

In the case of families' response to choice, it is possible to risk six generalisations:

1 Attachment to local schools remains strong almost everywhere. Not only 'orderly' Swedes but also 'pushy' French people tend to treat the choice of school outside the home zone as the 'freedom of recourse': only 11 per cent exercised this freedom after it was first opened up to them in French *collèges* (middle schools) in the mid-1980s.
2 However, the degree of active choice may depend not just on local culture but also on the way that choice is administered. In Boston,

157

Massachusetts – where home zones have been abolished, allocation to over-subscribed schools is random, and parents must turn up at one of three parent information centres in the city to register their choices – a minority of families now opt for their local schools.

3 The criteria for making choices are highly diverse, and balanced between perceptions of educational quality, perceptions of ethos or atmosphere and situational factors such as location and the schools attended by siblings and friends. This picture, that emerges from surveys in various countries, makes it highly risky to take parental preference as a proxy for perceived academic quality.

4 Choice is not simply a matter for parents, but for intra-family discussion. Surveys indicate that children have a growing role in choice with increasing age – typically their preferences are at least an equal consideration at entrance to secondary education; in countries where choices are made at age 14 or above, their preferences become dominant.

5 Choices may be made by all social classes, but not always in the same way. Strong evidence from Australia and France supports the view that the professional classes are far more active as choosers than manual workers. But this evidence needs to be qualified by an interesting finding from France that the lower-middle classes are the most active choosers of all, because they are more likely than professionals to live in relatively poor neighbourhoods whose schools they wish to escape (Ballion 1991).

6 A significant influence in choosing a school is who else chooses it. The social factors influencing family choices were informally referred to by parents and teachers in every one of the six countries in the OECD study. The strongest formal evidence of this phenomenon has recently emerged from New Zealand (in research summarised in Gordon 1994a and 1994b), where socio-economic character is now probably the most important characteristic defining family preferences, other than proximity.

In the case of school responses to choice, it is far harder to pinpoint concrete evidence, since the availability of choice is only one of several influences governing any school's actions. There is plenty of informal evidence to indicate that competition does indeed affect schools' behaviour, superficially or otherwise; nobody living in Britain and observing the flood back to school uniforms and the explosion of glossy brochures should need academic proof of this fact. One of the biggest observed changes in countries like Sweden that are unused to the availability of choice is that parents say that schools listen to them more.

But perhaps the most significant observation about competing schools' behaviour is the limited extent to which they change their character in search of niche markets. Most diversity in state school systems, such as America's magnet school programmes, is led by the administrators of school systems rather than being a spontaneous market-based response by autonomous schools. This is perhaps not surprising, since most schools put a priority on retaining their sizeable semi-captive home markets – those living nearby – who might not happen to like particular changes in character or specialism chosen by a local school. Denmark's state-subsidised private sector is one of the best examples of schools independently adopting a variety of styles to cater for different tastes – but this sector provides only for the 10 per cent of the population who choose to opt for something other than the relatively uniform public *Folkeskole*.

ARE POLICY LESSONS TRANSFERABLE?

Any comparison of how, say, the Swedish and British governments devise policies for school choice needs to start with a raft of contextual qualifications. Sweden is a more harmonious society; the British are more obsessed with class; student performance is more evenly distributed among schools in Sweden than in Britain; Sweden has a more centralised tradition in terms of school administration; and so on. These caveats cause many to wonder whether international comparisons have any practical relevance to policy makers at all.

The problem with such arguments is that they look at the institutions, 'traditions' and perceptions of particular countries at a point in time and assume that they will never change. Yet when viewing societies and their educational practices over time, this is clearly not the case. Until the 1950s, Sweden had one of the most élitist education systems in the developed world: only about 10 per cent of children continued to upper secondary school; today over 90 per cent do so. Until the late 1980s, New Zealanders regarded their schools as of fairly even quality, and the scope for choice as limited; a neo-liberal government borrowing and exaggerating recent British policies has not merely caused much political rancour, but also helped change the way many New Zealanders view their schooling, opening up 'rich' seams of competitiveness and envy. In all countries, social relationships and attitudes to community and state institutions are being transformed by a host of changes: increased geographical mobility; growing average levels of education among the adult population; the reduced dominance of the nuclear family; and the cold winds of Thatcherism and its cousins blowing across state provision. In these circumstances, we may often learn more about our own future prospects and options by looking at how other countries are doing things today than by looking at how we did things yesterday.

Consider briefly how these arguments might apply to the relevance of the experience of school choice in countries that have, first of all, different cultural conditions, and secondly different institutional conditions from our own.

On the cultural side, it is evident that many of Britain's problems with the practice of school choice emanate from the readiness of its citizens to see schooling as a mechanism of sorting people by class, rather than offering potentially equal but possibly different kinds of education to everybody. The creation of a standardised national curriculum has therefore failed as yet to produce a presumption of equality, while narrowing the possibilities for diversity. Yet it is not entirely wishful thinking to propose that we should have a long-term objective to become more like Sweden in giving everybody an opportunity for positive and recognised achievement up to the age of 18 – in an era when all economic commentators agree that a precondition for prosperity is a more even spread of skills and learning through the working population. The introduction of GCSEs and GNVQs demonstrated that we at least wish to go in this direction. Nor is it Utopian to point to the toleration accorded to different pedagogical models in Denmark's 'free' schools (in contrast for example to recent government intolerance in Britain for adventurous styles of sex education, irrespective of local parents' views), at a time when growing heterogeneity in society militates against a single, state-given view of the world. In short, the cultural norms that determine our immediate responses today should not prevent policy makers and others from working towards long-term changes in attitudes that reflect changes in society.

On the institutional side, Britain's grammar school past may today cause any secondary school that attempts to take on a particular character or serve a particular clientele to be regarded with more suspicion of élitism than an American school that does the same. Yet the United States provides many examples of school systems that consciously attempt to combine fairness with diversity. (One of the best illustrations is Montclair, New Jersey, described in OECD 1994: 125–127; every school in the district has a special character, yet the allocation of places is carefully controlled to ensure equal chances.) It will be far more constructive for British liberals to accept enthusiastically differences among schools that add to educational richness, and to focus on redefining equity of access in this new climate, than to oppose outright any school that does not seem to be fully 'comprehensive'.

WHAT CAN BRITAIN LEARN?

In reviewing experiences of school choice in various countries in the context of British policy debates, this chapter has already hinted at possible

160

policy lessons. It is not intended here to give a detailed review of such lessons, but rather to present the case for looking in more depth at foreign developments when considering new directions for Britain. In this regard, it is worth dwelling more specifically on three areas where the comparative approach might be particularly instructive.

The search for diversity and pluralism

The second half of the title of John Patten's 1992 White Paper, *Choice and Diversity* (DfE 1992), was interpreted in large part as providing incentives for schools to adopt specialist characteristics, particularly in technology. This has led to a rather limited degree of diversity in practice, partly because special features are too easily used as an extra string to a school's bow of 'excellence'/popularity rather than creating genuine alternative approaches to teaching and learning. This has commonly been the case in city technology colleges (Whitty *et al.* 1993). Nor does the creation of an 'alternative' grant-maintained sector give any guarantee of diversity in terms of educational approaches, even though some grant-maintained schools may have clienteles and organisational styles that are different from what they might have been under local authority control.

Two aspects of foreign experience are particularly relevant for any attempts to combine choice with more genuine diversity. (The strong case for doing so was set out in the first section above.) First, some countries show more genuine toleration of difference than is often apparent in Britain. In Denmark, for example, 'free' schools are allowed to do more or less as they please with public money provided they are controlled by parents. In this setting, the Leeds case of tabloid censure of sex education leading to the banning of books would have been unthinkable. It is inappropriate to expect British governments to become as tolerant as Danish ones; rather, the Danish case brings into sharp focus the logic of following through the ideology of school choice by trusting local parents with more decisions about educational style. This question will arise repeatedly in the coming years with respect to religious education, the content of history teaching and other areas where cultural pluralism needs to be reconciled with a desire for national cohesiveness and hence homogeneity. If the stress is always put on the latter, choosers will end up with not much to choose between.

Secondly, foreign experience shows that mechanisms for achieving diversity need to balance some guidance from the centre with the encouragement of genuine local initiative. A variety of examples of system-wide diversity are bounded by two extremes. On the one hand, there is the New South Wales example referred to above, where the spirit of an alternative approach is often lacking from schools that have been merely designated to be different by the state government. At the other extreme is East Harlem, New York, where every school offers a special programme. Often misappropriated by free-market advocates as an example of how educational excellence can be created by freeing up demand through open enrolment, this is more than anything a textbook case of supply-side freedom: teachers with exciting ideas are given the scope to implement them. It would be hard to replicate the dynamism created in East Harlem: any bottom-up approach is by definition impossible to create from above. But the lesson here is that educational dynamism and diversity is more likely to be created by empowering teachers rather than over-defining their jobs. Such empowerment may nevertheless need to be combined with some degree of planning for diversity, given the disinclination in most cases for schools to seek 'niche' markets for competitive reasons alone.

The delineation between public and private education

Unlike in many other countries, most British debate about choice has focused on the creation of quasi-markets within 'public' institutions. But as illustrated by the desire of some private schools to 'opt in' to the state system and by the Labour Party's acceptance of the concept of several models of school governance, the division between public and private provision may start to become more blurred.

Other countries are more accustomed to the concept of systematic public funding for schools governed privately. The prime example is the Netherlands, where over two-thirds of children attend schools run by independent (mainly church-based) foundations but fully funded by the state. These schools are subjected to far more regulation than private schools in Britain, or indeed than state schools in New Zealand, which are fully controlled by parent-elected trusts. But an issue that has arisen in both the Dutch and New Zealand cases is how to combine such independence of control with coherent planning of provision. Holland's central and local governments are trying to create a more rational and efficient structure for planning all local provision, supervised by municipalities who would simultaneously step back from day-to-day running of their own schools. (This however is being resisted by the churches.) In New Zealand, fragmentation has had to be followed in many cases by 'Educational Development Initiatives' to co-ordinate provision in particular areas through a process of community consultation.

Criteria for allocating school places

However desirable a situation where all parents' and children's choices can be fulfilled, it has to be accepted that in the real world some schools will be more popular than others. So some method of selection to over-subscribed schools is necessary. In Britain, the dominant view of the education world is still that selection of pupils by ability or aptitude is an insidious route back to élitism through grammar schools, yet selection by residence is acceptable, even if it is leading towards the concentration of privilege among better-off families living close to more-desired schools. In thinking about choice and fair access to places, two contrasting scenarios in particular might be borne in mind.

The first scenario is that presented by New Zealand's state schools, every one now independently controlled by a parent-elected trust. Over-subscribed schools in New Zealand must publish 'enrolment schemes', defining admission criteria as they wish. This has increasingly led to the concentration of self-defining élites in the most desired schools, with the social composition of intake being a key criterion for choice. (Recent evidence of these trends is described in Gordon 1994a and 1994b.)

The second scenario is illustrated by several Massachusetts cities that have replaced access to schools by residence with a random draw to determine competing families' priorities. In one of these cities, Boston, there have been some interesting trends since the policy was introduced (Glenn et al. 1993; Willie and Alves 1993). Parents in Boston are required to go to one of the three district 'Parent Information Centres' to register their preferences on the basis of information given out about each school. Where not all preferences can be met, allocations are made on the basis of computer-generated random numbers assigned to each parent, determining their place in the queue. The scheme had to be modified somewhat after its start to ensure that those who only choose nearby schools are given some extra preference in getting places in them. But this kind of choice seems to have encouraged many parents to search further afield for the right school, without the problem of having a few popular schools desired by most parents. If anything, the hierarchy of preferences appears to have lessened, in that the majority of families are allocated their first choice of school, even though the majority do not choose their closest one. Another trend is that participation of white families in the public school system has actually increased. So it may be possible for some kinds of allocation policy to reduce the clustering of more-privileged groups around favoured schools, without necessarily causing a flight of the privileged to the private sector.

Again, these examples are not intended to illustrate models for import, but to point to important issues that need to be addressed in Britain. The New Zealand case shows the direction that Britain may be heading in if it ignores the issue of selection criteria. The Boston case, and many different measures taken locally in the United States, illustrate that a concern with equity in allocation can potentially be combined with a concern for choice. Indeed, many magnet school programmes attempt to achieve through voluntarism the more balanced and equitable distribution of opportunities that was unsuccessfully attempted by force through busing.

In this context, as I have argued in more detail elsewhere (Hirsch 1995a), it is possible to question the unthinking acceptance in Britain of the primacy of residence in allocating school places. Where there is competition for access to school places, must we accept a situation where residential élites form through the clustering of families around the best schools, reinforced by the common judgement by parents of schools with privileged intakes to be, prima facie, 'good'? The international experiences referred to above show both the danger of permitting such residential élites to form within public provision and the potential for using other criteria. Those who seek equality of opportunity in British education rightly argue that it is important for all schools to be made good. But we need to face the reality that when preferences are expressed they will never accord precisely to the distribution of places. Admissions policies that encourage a mixing of abilities, classes and races might ultimately help ensure that more preferences are met, by reducing the perceived differences among schools based on their intakes.

CONCLUSION

This chapter has started to illustrate some of the ways in which policies for school choice in different settings may have relevance for Britain. A notable feature of policies to create quasi-markets is the unpredictability of their results, depending as they do on decisions taken by a large number of producers and consumers. International comparisons at a time when many countries are attempting similar things might be seen as an imperfect but worthwhile method of market research.

This research shows that the tendency in Britain for choice to generate an increased awareness among parents of differences among schools, and hence a polarisation in their reputations that ultimately leads to frustration among those whose choices are not met, is repeated under similar conditions elsewhere. But it also shows that there are certain ways in which these conditions can be alleviated, notably by allowing genuine diversity and by designing admissions policies that reduce inequalities. These examples should influence our policy makers by encouraging them to explore measures that reduce the most harmful effects on school systems of increased parental choice.

NOTE

1 The OECD study chose to describe the case of England within the United Kingdom, in order to define precisely an example of UK choice policies in action. The present article, which focuses on the experience of countries outside the UK, uses 'Britain' and 'British' as a loose shorthand for prevailing UK attitudes and policies, and avoids reference to differences within the UK.

REFERENCES

Ballion, R. (1991) *La Bonne Ecole*, Paris: Hatier.

Bowden, R. (1993) *Trends and Effects of the Enrolment Legislation – A Comparative Study 1993*, Christchurch, New Zealand: Ministry of Education.

Dearing, R. (1994) *The National Curriculum and its Assessment: A New Framework for Schools*, London: School Curriculum and Assessment Authority.

Department for Education (DfE)/Welsh Office (1992) *Choice and Diversity: A New Framework for Schools*, London: HMSO.

Glenn, C.L., McLaughlin, K. and Salganik, L. (1993) *Parent Information for School Choice: The Case of Massachussetts*, Boston, MS: Centre on Families, Communities, Schools and Children's Learning, University of Boston.

Gordon, L. (1994a) 'Is school choice a sustainable policy for New Zealand? A review of recent research findings and a look to the future', paper, Christchurch, New Zealand: Education Policy Research Unit, University of Canterbury, New Zealand.

Gordon, L. (1994b) 'Rich and poor schools in Aotearoa, New Zealand', *New Zealand Journal of Educational Studies* 29(2).

Hirsch, D. (1995a) 'The other school choice – how should over-subscribed schools select their pupils?', open lecture, Institute of Education, London, May.

Hirsch, D. (1995b) 'School choice and the search for an educational market', *International Review of Education* 41(3–4): 239–257.

OECD (1994) *School, A Matter of Choice*, Paris: Centre for Educational Research and Innovation (CERI), Organisation for Economic Co-operation and Development.

Whitty, G., Edwards, T. and Gewirtz, S. (1993) *Specialisation and Choice in Urban Education*, London: Routledge.

Willie, C.V. and Alves, M.J. (1993) 'A report on the implementation of the revised Boston "controlled choice" plan', unpublished consultants' report, Boston, MS.

12

ADMISSIONS TO SCHOOLS
A study of local education authorities
Gulam-Husien Mayet

INTRODUCTION

The Government in its recent legislation, and particularly in the 1993 Education Act, made great play with the issue of choice and expressed the belief that greater diversity in the types of school available would enhance it: hence the developing policy of allowing schools to obtain grant-maintained (GM) status – outside the control of local education authorities (LEAs) – and gradually the granting of permission to those to introduce selection procedures in their admission policies.

The Society of Education Officers (SEO) had considerable doubts about whether the introduction of variety in this way would in fact improve the choice of school for most parents. They accordingly commissioned a survey by the author of this chapter who was at the time an Assistant Director of Education with the Birmingham Local Authority.[1]

The study sought to build on the work of Morris (1993) which found that open choice was becoming more limited. In some places successful first preferences had been at high, even very high, levels and scope for improvement had necessarily been limited. Some decline of numbers of successful first preferences had occurred, notably in urban areas. The number of appeals was increasing, but the proportion of successful appeals was declining – within a varied overall picture. The admission and appeals arrangements varied between and even within LEAs. It was clear that there were differences between urban and rural areas, and the definition of first preference clouded the statistical evidence. There was some indication that problems would increase in areas with GM schools, yet there was general optimism that co-ordinated admission arrangements could operate effectively. There was great diversity in the calculation of schools' capacities and there was evidence to show that it was difficult to find places for excluded pupils.

It was too early for any evidence of the fresh introduction of selection processes. There was evidence of great interest in these issues at the Association of Metropolitan Authorities (AMA) and the Association of

166

County Councils (ACC), which lent support to the project. Finally, the survey offered an excellent insight into the work of an LEA in relation to admissions and appeals. This showed and supported the view that the LEA has the crucial leading role in establishing co-ordinated local arrangements.

Since Morris's work there has been more time to see the effects of the Greenwich judgement, which removed the right of a local authority to use the authority's boundary as one of its criteria for admissions, allowing access to schools as if the boundary were not there. The Funding Agency for Schools (FAS) is also up and running. It has already taken over total responsibility for the planning of school places in those few LEAs where 75 per cent of pupils are in GM schools. In others, where more than 10 per cent of pupils are in GM schools, it shares responsibility with the LEA. This seemed to be a recipe for confusion, despite the efforts of officers in LEAs and the FAS to work together.

The SEO was keen to find evidence more substantial than the anecdotal, but it was unrealistic to attempt a major comprehensive exercise. Research was limited accordingly to evidence gained from local authorities about admissions to secondary schools only. The study was mainly based on eight LEAs, to which questionnaires were sent and in which relevant officers were interviewed in late 1994. Six of these were known to have a considerable proportion of GM schools and two other 'control' authorities were chosen which had none. Nine other authorities represented on the SEO Council also completed questionnaires, which offered useful additional information.

The research was conducted from October 1994 to February 1995.

ADMISSION SYSTEMS AND FIRST PREFERENCES

Two general points can be made:

1 There is huge diversity of admission arrangements ranging from fairly strict catchment areas to completely open systems, and even a lottery in one case. In some, applications are made direct to schools, in others religious preferences or selection clouds the issue, as indeed occasionally does geography. For these reasons even hard statistical evidence from particular LEAs is impossible to extrapolate into general patterns.
2 Where there were GM schools the gathering of meaningful statistics was not possible. Only in one or two authorities was formal co-ordination a reality and this was geared to avoiding duplication and securing places rather than gathering information.

For these reasons it is extremely difficult to offer satisfactory generalisations. Few LEAs had a run of figures over five years or so. However it did seem that where the LEA could not offer a comprehensive framework for organising admission arrangements because of the presence of GM schools, parents were confused and sometimes distressed by the process. There is also as expected a clear difference between the rural areas where one obvious school is available and acceptable to parents and inner city/town areas where the real competition exists.

What is obvious is that any planning of the provision of places or of admissions procedures becomes more difficult if schools are outside the LEA arrangements. At the same time there are greater problems for parents when there is no clear framework. The Secretary of State has refused at least in one case to impose co-ordination.

One authority allowed in its arrangements for both casual admissions and appeal successes and appeals were part of the allocation system. Leaving some places free for appeals and casual admissions may in the long term be challenged legally although it does enable certain parents to get access to the school of their choice. The position legally seems to be that if one informs parents in the admission arrangement of what the system of allocation is it is legal. In the light of this, many authorities would argue that either because of a moving population, or in one case because there was an RAF camp nearby, it is fair and reasonable to allow some places to be left vacant in the interests of the children who may, through no fault of their own, be moving into the area.

THE LOCAL AUTHORITIES

In *Gloucestershire*, the secondary school transfer procedure is extremely complex because parents are able to express preferences not only between LEA and GM schools, but also between selective and comprehensive schools. Of the forty-two secondary schools in Gloucestershire, twenty-nine are GM. There are also two voluntary aided (VA) schools.

In the more rural areas of the county, the secondary schools generally serve their own well identified priority admission areas. There are eighteen GM and four LEA schools. Four of the GM schools handle their own admission arrangements; two of these are grammar schools which also arrange their own assessment tests. In the Cheltenham area, there are five GM comprehensive schools, one GM grammar school and one LEA comprehensive school. The grammar school deals with all its own admission arrangements.

In the Gloucester City area, there are five GM schools and eight LEA schools. To emphasise the complexity, four of these are single-sex grammar schools, two LEA and two GM. One of the GM grammar schools and one of the GM comprehensive schools (which has recently become a technology college) handle their own admission arrangements.

It is not surprising in the light of this complexity that Gloucestershire is unable to keep complete details of the numbers of first preferences that are successful. Some schools are not included on the LEA preference forms. There is a general sharing of information with all GM schools, but not until after parents have been notified of places offered. While the situation is more predictable in the more rural areas, the difficulties experienced in Gloucester City and Cheltenham are similar to those which would occur in any urban area with a mixed economy of schools. The officers' general impression was that between 94 per cent and 96 per cent of parents were successful in obtaining their first preference overall, although in the Gloucester City area the figure would generally be lower.

In a *London borough*,[2] the authority manages the secondary admissions process only in relation to producing information in a booklet for the whole of the borough – and without using its logo! The total number of schools in the borough is fifteen, of which twelve are GM. The FAS is now responsible for providing sufficient school places as more than 75 per cent of secondary pupils are in the GM sector. The position is even more complicated as there are concerns about whether there are sufficient places in the borough and the FAS is consulting with the community regarding extension of places in the secondary phase. It is interesting to note that they seem not to be obliged to use the basic needs formula (which is a complex and very tight calculation of the capacities of schools) imposed on authorities by the Department for Education and Employment (DfEE), but can make a much more generous assessment of the need for extra places.

The parents in the secondary phase apply directly to the schools. Open evenings are held in September/October, with the closing date for applications in early November and offers are made in December. After Christmas, a meeting is held between all the schools and the LEA, to share information and to identify duplicate applications. There are about 2,500 Year 6 pupils.

In December there are usually about 450 pupils without any offers; this would reduce to 200 by January, and by July it would be about eighty. The LEA does not have figures for first preferences, as these are impossible to ascertain. They are only aware that there are anything up to eighty pupils who could be without a school at the beginning of September although, by the time the term starts, they are confident that this would be less than ten. Clearly, accurate research in these circumstances is not possible.

In *another London borough*, the authority produces a booklet for all parents, but they ask parents to apply direct to a particular school or schools that they wish their child to attend. According to some, this is a power market because it enables parents to apply to any school that they wish their child to attend.

There is a range of admissions policies. For example, some schools have a selective system, whilst some GM schools select 10 per cent of pupils with some special talent such as music. Some schools will admit pupils with music, dance, movement or academic abilities, while others have a straight selective system. Some schools have within their admission arrangements compassion as a criterion, but this seems similar to the medical and social reasons which most other authorities have. There is in addition, a voluntary aided Catholic school with complex admission arrangements and, finally, the LEA all-ability schools.

As parents apply direct to the schools they wish their child to attend, places offered account for 99 per cent of the transfer cohort. However, only the parents actually know whether the school they have accepted is their first preference. The increasing number of GM schools has had an impact on LEA appeals because in 1989 there were 202 appeals, but this had fallen to seventy-one in 1994. The numbers have reduced essentially because this London borough has reached Stage 3 in terms of secondary education and therefore has over 75 per cent of its pupils in the GM sector and there are likely to be many appeals within that sector. It is not possible to say how many there are or what the success rate is.

The LEA designed a self-completion questionnaire which was sent to 23 per cent of parents of children attending primary schools within the LEA and who eventually accepted places for September 1993 in any of the fifteen all-ability schools. Of the parents who replied 82 per cent stated that they had achieved the school of their first preference and 13 per cent indicated that they had accepted the school of their second preference.

In *Lancashire*, places are allocated at secondary schools upon an open preference system. Parents are encouraged to express three preferences and priority is given in all cases to first preferences. In some cases school catchment areas are described so that preferences from within these areas have priority over other preferences of equal status. Otherwise, after allowing for brothers and sisters and any special medical or social cases, priority is given either to those who live nearest to their preferred school or to those who live furthest from the nearest alternative school. At two out of 100 secondary schools in the authority random selection is used instead of a geographical factor, reflecting decisions made at the time of comprehensive reorganisation.

The proportion of parents who obtain their first preference school continues to exceed 90 per cent. A general impression is that this number may be falling slightly since the late 1980s. Certainly, the number of appeals for both September and mid-year admissions is increasing. The

popularity of individual schools, as expressed by the ratio of first preferences to places available, varies from year to year. Whilst demographic
factors clearly play a part other issues such as recent school building
improvements, successful OFSTED reports, changes of senior staff and
improved marketing all appear to have an effect. Lancashire also has a
significant number of aided Roman Catholic and Church of England
schools and most of these continue to be over-subscribed and indeed
many are gaining in popularity.

Kingston has a mixed economy of selective and non-selective schools.
Most children are assumed to want to participate in the selection procedure but parents can 'opt out' their children from the procedure. The
tests are administered during the school day within primary schools and
specially designated centres. Until recently the primary schools marked
the papers but this is now organised centrally.

The authority has problems in satisfying the demand for single-sex
girls' school places. Overall flexibility amounts to only twenty to thirty
places.

The authority has four GM schools and six LEA schools and has established a common closing date for applications, offer date and an informal
'clearing house' arrangement. All schools are involved in this and parents
are given fourteen days in which to make decisions on 'double' offers.

The LEA officers interviewed indicated that first preferences have
increased both for the selective schools and the single-sex girls' schools.
In 1988 the authority was able to meet 98 per cent of first preferences
but currently this is only 80 per cent. Officers believe that this is due to
a combination of a natural increase in numbers, the effects of the Greenwich judgement and the popularity of Kingston schools.

In *Birmingham* parents can choose any school. They have a choice
between LEA and GM schools (both selective and non-selective in each
case), a city technology college in Solihull, and other schools there and
in other neighbouring LEAs. They decide whether to take selection
tests. Within the authority's arrangements they can choose up to three
comprehensive schools in priority order and this selection is not affected
by any of the other choices, as parents are not required to tell the LEA
about these.

Clearly there are duplicated offers arising from this process and it is
difficult, therefore, to interpret the figures which Birmingham has of
successful first preferences. The figures of 93 per cent (1989), 88 per
cent (1990), 88 per cent (1991), 86 per cent (1992), 86 per cent (1993)
and 80 per cent (1994) show a very clear declining success rate. In 1994,
however, the figures were adjusted to 86 per cent, once parents had
refused duplicate offers. The authority has to take a calculated guess on
how many places to allocate at some schools, to allow for successful

application elsewhere. There is clear evidence that less favoured schools have to retrawl the authority's lists to fill up their places.

East Sussex, one of the control authorities, has nearly 8,000 pupils who transfer to secondary schools each year and thirty-five secondary schools. It is building more schools to take account of a rising population. It has no GM schools. East Sussex operates two different admission systems, one for rural schools and another for those in urban areas (where parents have easy access to a number of schools).

For schools in rural situations, the system operated is based on traditional areas. Most parents seem to understand what this traditional area means. Details of the traditional area are published in the admissions booklet and priority is given to children living in those areas.

In the urban situation there are no pre-determined areas. Having taken account of siblings and 'special' reasons, admission arrangements are made by geographical restriction based on the spread of applications and the drawing of an area to satisfy as many parents as possible. The area drawn will vary from year to year and will also take account of the availability of spare places at under-subscribed schools. This approach to admissions was challenged in the High Court but the challenge failed and the DfEE, although unhappy with the system, is unable to change it either.

East Sussex is also unusual in that a review stage is operated whereby parents can meet with officers to discuss their case in greater detail and officers then make a decision as to whether the case falls within strong medical or other special reasons. Places are held back specifically for this purpose. This system also reduces the number of formal appeals.

Acceptance rates of first preferences have remained constant over recent years at over 95 per cent. Although East Sussex has no GM schools there are some in border authorities and where these exist there is an impact on admission arrangements.

Doncaster, the other control area, has a catchment area system with the option of choosing out of an area. Like East Sussex, it is able to satisfy over 95 per cent of the first preferences. Out of the very small number of parents who express a preference outside their catchment area, the success rate (in 1989) was 88 per cent, (1990) 92 per cent, (1991) 85 per cent, (1992) 83 per cent, (1993) 85 per cent and (1994) 76 per cent.

The two control authorities without GM schools are the most successful in terms of achieving first preferences for parents.

APPEALS

There is clear evidence of a rising number of appeals in most of the authorities. There are problems with this evidence as many authorities did not have information or are not clear if the information is accurate since it does not include GM schools. In Birmingham, like other urban authorities, there has been a substantial increase. The number of secondary appeals in 1988 was 234 whereas in 1993 it was 935 and, although every year substantial numbers withdraw when accepting a duplicated offer, the trend is very clear. Many county authorities with catchment areas do not have the same level of increase as in urban authorities although in Gloucestershire, in urban areas like Gloucester and Cheltenham, appeals have increased. There is a significant number of authorities which had very few appeals. Wolverhampton had very few appeals and in addition nearly 90 per cent of the appeals were successful. The general impression is that against the background of rising appeals, the proportion of those which are successful is falling, particularly in urban areas. It seems reasonable to claim that meeting first preferences in urban settings led to less successful appeals because the schools were already full to their standard numbers.

The appeals information that LEAs now have is generally incomplete as it does not include figures for GM schools. It is clear that no one is aware of how effective or fair the appeals systems in GM schools are.

GRANT-MAINTAINED SCHOOLS

Out of the seventeen authorities which completed questionnaires, there were six which had no GM schools in their areas. The position in these areas was not very different from 1988 with the exception of those parents who did not like their local catchment area. Most of these authorities were able to satisfy up to 97 per cent of their parents, although one could argue that if you are allocated a catchment area school you are not necessarily exercising choice or preference. The counter argument is that choice was exercised by allowing parents to opt out from their catchment areas. In some authorities, this led to the guarantee of a place in the catchment area being withdrawn, while in other authorities this did not happen.

The major impact of GM schools is that many authorities, for example Gloucestershire and the two London boroughs, do not have figures any more for the successes at first preferences or at appeals. Schools have their own admission arrangements and on the whole the authorities are only picking up appeals or unsuccessful parents and assisting them in finding places for their children. On the whole, the relationship with the GM sector is good although there are quite a few areas where difficulties remain. In some areas there is full co-operation, while in others there may be just one or two GM schools which do not want to co-operate. There are also authorities where there is no co-operation at all; for example, there is no common timetable in relation to admission closing dates or allocation dates or even common information. The general impression must be that slowly co-operation is improving although many GM schools, like VA schools, are not willing to be part of a co-ordinated admissions arrangement because they feel their independence may be sacrificed. There is a clear impression of covert selection by some schools, although there is very little evidence except when parents complain to the LEA. Some LEA officers were clear that there was some element of selection in GM schools although others did not think that this was happening in their areas.

The role of interviews before a decision on placement was made was seen as the process by which covert selection took place. This was increasingly the position in VA schools as well.

SCHOOL CAPACITY AND SURPLUS PLACES

Most LEAs were not happy with the DfEE calculation for establishing standard numbers under the open enrolment legislation. They felt that this was not a reasonable measure whereas the physical capacity of the school was a better yardstick. Many have been pressing directly and through their associations for a better definitive measure.

Clearly LEAs did not feel able to answer the question on desirable capacity for enhancing choice. Most of the LEAs who responded gave rounded figures, 5 per cent over physical capacity being the favourite figure to enable more preference to take place.

CASUAL ADMISSIONS

The majority of authorities, particularly in the county areas, did not have problems finding places for children who moved into their areas. In fact, as mentioned above, some authorities actually allowed vacant places to be held on the basis of some estimate of the number of casual admissions that they were likely to have in the area.

The issue that most of the authorities had difficulty with was in finding places for children who had been excluded from a local school. A very strong concern was expressed by most of the authorities that it was getting harder to find schools to accept pupils or that the schools that had to accept these children were the under-subscribed schools. This was both unfair to those schools and also laid the basis of what seems clearly to be happening in certain urban areas, namely the development of a 'sink' reputation for the school. This led to many of the local schools in inner city areas being regarded unfavourably by their local residents and the impact of this was that they were vulnerable to closure as their numbers were falling quite dramatically. This led to one or two schools being closed.

One London borough has particular problems in this area, because the FAS now has control over the number of places available.

EXTRA-DISTRICT OR OUT OF COUNTY PLACES

Most of the respondents expected the parents to apply directly to the LEA in which their child wished to attend. There appears to be no significant difference among LEAs in how they deal with extra-district or out of county preferences. The London boroughs and some of the urban boroughs still felt that the Greenwich decision was a major cause of concern, as it sometimes led to a local authority being unable to provide school places for all its own residents. One London borough particularly suffers: in 1992, 300 places were offered to extra-district children, leaving 55 children from the borough without places. As with casual admissions they are powerless to provide places, since the FAS has taken over planning powers. Kingston has similar problems.

The difficulty is aggravated in these authorities by the fact that some schools are selective.

OTHER RELEVANT ISSUES

Although admission policies themselves were the prime focus of this study, it is obvious that other factors influence the ability of parents to choose a school.

Transport policy

If there was a school deemed suitable within three miles of the pupil's home, it was extremely unlikely that any LEA would give support with transport costs. If a school outside the local catchment area or in another authority was chosen, no help was given. Choice and preference was, therefore, limited by finance and only those parents who could afford transport costs had an effective preference. The only exception was usually for Catholic parents.

Funding Agency for Schools (FAS)

The FAS is not meant to deal with admissions, only the planning of provision. In two London boroughs it has total control of this, which leaves the authority quite unable to guarantee any parent anything.

Special educational needs (SEN) pupils

No authority expressed particular concern on this issue, in that they were able to secure places for children with statements. Many LEAs however, were experiencing increasing problems in placing children who were excluded, especially those who had emotional and behavioural problems, but no statements.

CONCLUSION

It is not easy to produce accurate factual information, but some indications shone through the investigation:

1 Choice does not seem to be increasing. In rural areas the issue has always been academic: only in urban areas is it realistic for parents to declare a preference. In those areas without GM schools the situation has changed little over the past five years and LEAs are quite successful at meeting 95 per cent or more of first preferences. Where there is a range of different types of school the successful choice of some parents is balanced by the increasingly unsuccessful choice of others. At the extreme one parent might have five successful choices and another none.

2 The number of appeals has increased in most LEAs, as parents have become more inclined to assert their rights. More appeals have generally meant proportionately less success for parents.

3 The lack of freely available information from GM schools obfuscates the picture for parents. The need to duplicate applications further confuses the situation. Where further options of voluntary aided schools and single-sex schools are added there is even more difficulty. Varying forms of selection (without clear methodology) compound incomprehension and distress amongst parents.

4 The lack of accountability of GM schools is already impeding parents in exercising their preferences and in gaining fair access to appeal hearings.

5 The lack of synchronisation and transparency in admissions processes in GM areas is a major problem for parents and local authorities which are left picking up the pieces and not always able to do so adequately.

6 In GM areas there is no longer any accurate picture of how successful parents are in obtaining their first preferences. It is imperative that research is done in this area and the DfE should undertake a survey to see what the impact of recent legislative changes has been in the area of parental choice. The study by Jowett (1995) for the National Foundation for Educational Research (NFER) might help to provide a better picture of what is happening. The study focused on the

outcomes of first preferences and the way that parents make choices. It looked to see if parents are satisfied with the allocation and appeal systems, how LEAs have organised the information which they must provide to parents and also the usefulness of school prospectuses and performance tables. The study examined the degree to which the LEA-controlled and GM secondary schools involved in the allocation of places operate co-ordinated admission arrangements. Although it, too, found difficulty in producing very hard evidence, it seemed to do little to support government claims about increasing choice.

7 In summary, it is obviously extremely difficult for anyone to know exactly what is happening on the ground. It behoves the DfEE to set up arrangements whereby full and accurate information is forthcoming for all the parties involved in the process of admitting pupils to schools, particularly secondary schools. In the absence of such evidence claims by government that parental choice has increased lack any credibility. The SEO looks forward to the time when an honest appraisal of the results of legislation affecting parental choice of schools can be made.

NOTES

1 The Society is grateful to Tim Brighouse, Chief Education Officer of Birmingham, and the Authority for releasing time for this project, Bob Morris, the staff of LEAs and the Education Management Information Exchange (EMIE), and Sylvena Nelson (Birmingham) and Jane Haythorne (SEO) for their advice and administrative support.
2 The two London boroughs in the survey wished not to be named.

REFERENCES

Jowett, S. (1995) *Allocating Secondary School Places: A Study of Policy and Practice*, Slough: National Foundation for Education Research.

Morris, R. (1993) *Choice of School: A survey 1992–3*, London: Association of Metropolitan Authorities.

13

CHANGING ADMISSIONS POLICIES AND PRACTICES IN INNER LONDON
Implications for policy and future research[1]
Anne West and Hazel Pennell

INTRODUCTION

In addition to introducing a series of far-reaching reforms into the education system of England and Wales, the 1988 Education Reform Act provided the legislation for the abolition of the Inner London Education
Authority (ILEA) and the transfer of the education service to the twelve
inner London boroughs and the Corporation of London. This chapter
focuses on the admissions policies to secondary schools in the area
formerly covered by the ILEA and how these have changed since the
ILEA was abolished in 1990. In the first section, the research methodology that was adopted is outlined. This is followed by a description of
the system of 'banding' that was used in the ILEA to try and ensure
that secondary schools received a balanced (i.e. comprehensive) intake.
The next section focuses on how the new inner London local education
authorities (LEAs) have changed their admissions policies and the
reasons for these changes – for example, political, administrative, or to
increase parental choice. Issues related to individual school admissions
policies and practices are then explored with the aim of trying to ascertain to what extent these can be attributed to such factors as parental
choice, LEA policies, and broader issues related to the 1988 Education
Reform Act (e.g. the introduction of grant-maintained schools and city
technology colleges). Key findings from the research are then presented
and the implications for policy and for future research studies are highlighted in the final part of the chapter.

METHODOLOGY

The research reported in this chapter is based on an analysis of a range
of policy and other documents and not on a conventional piece of
empirical work. Documentation produced by the former ILEA was
examined and analysed as were Education Development Plans produced by the newly created inner London LEAs that replaced the ILEA.

Information relating to the admissions criteria for secondary schools in the inner London area (for entry in September 1995) was obtained from LEAs and in the case of grant-maintained schools and city technology colleges, from the schools themselves. Additional detailed information was obtained directly from LEA officers and from the Department for Education and Employment (DfEE).

BANDING IN THE ILEA

Background

The ILEA was unique in that it used a system of banding to try and ensure that its secondary schools had an intake that was balanced in terms of ability. The 'banding' system took priority over all other criteria (notably siblings, distance, medical/social need). No other LEAs, other than a number of successor authorities to the ILEA, have been identified that use a banding procedure or any other assessment procedure designed to provide comprehensive schools with a balanced intake. In fact, when the 1975 Education Bill was before Parliament, the ILEA expressed its concern at the Government's declared intention to end banding on which its comprehensive policy hinged. At first the Secretary of State resisted pressure for an amendment which would allow banding to continue, but this was eventually conceded. The amended wording of the 1976 Education Act was carried over to section 6(3)(c) of the 1980 Act which in effect relieves the LEA of its duty to comply with parental preference if to do so would be incompatible with its arrangements for achieving a balance of intake based on ability.

The banding system and comprehensive schools

The first purpose-built comprehensive school in the ILEA opened in 1954. By 1961, there were fifty-nine comprehensive schools in inner London. However, it was not until 1977 that all secondary schools received a comprehensive intake. Prior to this, in 1972, the ILEA decided that in order to provide each secondary school with a reasonable balance of ability, all pupils transferring from primary to secondary school should be assessed by the primary headteacher as Band One (above average), Band Two (average) or Band Three (below average). For inner London as a whole, 50 per cent of the *total* number of children transferring were assessed as Band Two, 25 per cent as Band One and 25 per cent as Band Three.

Each secondary school was given a quota of places for each band and recruited pupils only up to that limit. The quotas were not exactly in the proportions 25:50:25 as they were adjusted to reflect the number of pupils in each band of ability leaving local primary schools. In order that assessments would have comparability within all the ILEA's schools, a verbal reasoning test was carried out with the aim of validating the head-teacher's own judgement of each individual pupil's level of ability (in terms of the bands described above). This test was taken by all classes in which there were pupils due for transfer to secondary school; it was taken anonymously by every child in the class, marked by the school staff and a record of all results forwarded to the ILEA centrally. From the results of this test, schools were informed of the number of pupils who might be expected to fall within each band. No child's performance in the test directly affected the band to which the headteacher of the primary school allocated him or her; the verbal reasoning test was taken as a group test, not as a test for assessing individual children. It was for the headteacher, as far as she or he thought necessary, to adjust pro-visional bandings in the light of information from the test about the dis-tribution of numbers in each band. Although headteachers had discretion to allocate more or fewer children to a particular band, there was generally a fairly close correlation between the intended ratio and the ratio actually achieved. In this respect, it was considered to have served its purpose.

There were a number of problems with the use of the verbal reasoning test that have been discussed elsewhere (Pennell and West 1995) and, in autumn 1987, it was agreed by the ILEA that the verbal reasoning test should be replaced from autumn 1988 by a reading test – the London Reading Test – as a means of determining a balanced intake to secondary schools. On the basis of the test results cut-off points on the raw score scale for allocating pupils to three reading performance groups were computed. The highest attaining 25 per cent of readers were allocated to the first reading performance group, the middle 50 per cent to the second group and the lowest 25 per cent to the third group.[2]

CHANGES SINCE THE ABOLITION OF THE ILEA

Since the twelve inner London boroughs[3] took over the education service in April 1990 a number of changes to secondary schools' admissions policies have taken place. The most significant of these has been that the system of banding used by the ILEA has been discontinued by the majority of LEAs.

Banding by LEAs

An early decision to end banding was made by the Conservative-controlled LEAs (Kensington and Chelsea, Wandsworth and West-minster). Wandsworth signalled its intention to end banding in its

Education Development Plan, in which it was noted 'Because of an over-provision of secondary school places in [Wandsworth], banding is no longer an effective means of ensuring a spread of ability in secondary schools. It is, moreover, a denial of parental choice which the Council cannot support' (Wandsworth Borough Council 1989: 59).

The Education Development Plan for the City of Westminster simply stated that the Council intended to discontinue banding whilst that for the Royal Borough of Kensington and Chelsea noted that a banding scheme was not considered to be appropriate or necessary for its only county school. However, one Labour-controlled LEA, even at this stage, also expressed concern about the banding system, on a number of grounds including the fact that 'it rests on the same principle as the 11+ exam, namely that ability is a fixed and measurable quality' (London Borough of Camden 1989: para. 148).

The first Labour-controlled LEAs to end banding were Hammersmith and Fulham and Islington with Camden following in 1992. There has, to some extent, been a 'knock on' effect as regards the discontinuation of banding, largely because of a substantial transfer of pupils across borough boundaries at the secondary school stage. In practice, it is not feasible to band pupils from schools in LEAs not using such a procedure themselves and the decision to end banding in the three Labour-controlled LEAs to the west and north of London appears to have been influenced to some extent by the ending of banding in neighbouring boroughs. It is also interesting to note that among the first LEAs to cease banding in inner London were those which had a high propor-tion of voluntary aided schools with their own admissions criteria – for example, Westminster, Hammersmith and Fulham and Camden (Pennell and West 1995).

Since 1992, two more Labour LEAs (Southwark and Lambeth) have ceased to band pupils. In Southwark the main reason given for doing so was the difficulty of obtaining a balanced intake using the banding procedure as there was an overall surplus of Band One places and insufficient Band Two and Band Three places compared with the expressed preferences of parents. Another problem was the imbalance between county and voluntary aided schools with the latter achieving on average 14 per cent more Band One pupils and 14 per cent fewer Band Three pupils than schools in the county sector (London Borough of Southwark 1992).

Lambeth discontinued banding most recently (in 1994). The decision by the neighbouring borough of Southwark to stop using banding was one factor, whilst another was the growing number of grant-maintained schools in the borough (responsible for their own admissions). The remaining number of schools was too small to make the system feasible, particularly as the neighbouring boroughs to the east (Southwark) and the west (Wandsworth) had stopped using banding. Another factor was that none of the remaining LEA schools was over-subscribed so that any parent applying to one of these schools would eventually succeed in obtaining a place for their child notwithstanding the existence of the banding system in the authority.

The four boroughs that have retained banding (Greenwich, Hackney, Lewisham and Tower Hamlets) appear to be committed to using it at least in the short term. Significantly, for each of these four boroughs, the neighbouring borough, with which it has most cross-borough movement, continues to band, although not necessarily on precisely the same basis (Pennell and West 1995).

ISSUES RELATED TO INDIVIDUAL SCHOOL ADMISSIONS POLICIES AND PRACTICES

Grant-maintained schools and changes to admissions policies

In September 1995, there were twenty-one grant-maintained secondary schools in the inner London boroughs; these were concentrated in a small number of boroughs. While five boroughs had no grant-maintained secondary schools, three had one, one had two, one had four and two (Wandsworth and Lambeth) had six each.

Over half of the twenty-one grant-maintained secondary schools (twelve) in inner London are former voluntary aided Roman Catholic schools, whilst just over a quarter (six) are former county schools (the remainder were other types of voluntary schools). This pattern is consistent across inner London with the exception of Wandsworth, where four of the six grant-maintained secondary schools are former county schools. Wandsworth Borough Council was at the forefront of the Government's education policy changes to increase parental choice of school and in particular to increase the types of schools from which parents could choose.

A number of grant-maintained schools have sought to change their admissions policies so that they have a guaranteed intake of able children. Some have become bilateral schools, selecting part of their intake by means of tests administered by the school, and two have reintroduced a form of banding.

Bilateral schools

Three grant-maintained secondary schools (two in Wandsworth and one in Lambeth) have sought to change their admissions policies in order to become more academically selective. These are former county schools. Only two of these applications were agreed by the then Department for

Education (DfE) and as a result these schools are now bilateral – that is, they select a proportion of their intakes on the basis of ability tests; in the case of one of the schools, half the pupils are now selected on the basis of their ability, whilst in the other about one-third are selected in this way. The question arises as to why these schools felt that there was a need to change their admissions policies. Since the abolition of the ILEA, these two schools had been selecting pupils using criteria that were almost identical to those in operation in the LEA area in which they are located – siblings, special medical/social need and proximity. One of these schools[4] reported in a consultative document on its admissions policy that it was 'impossible to guarantee a balanced intake, i.e. an intake with a fair proportion of able pupils'.[5] The headteacher of the other school noted that the application for a partially selective intake was necessary to 'achieve a balance of pupils necessary to retain its comprehensive ethos in the Wandsworth context' (*Education Guardian*, 24 January 1995). It can thus be inferred that the admissions criteria in operation were unable to guarantee an academically balanced intake in the way that the banding system had.

Re-introduction of banding

Two grant-maintained schools in Lambeth were given approval by the former DfE to re-introduce a form of banding. One has been quoted as justifying its application on the grounds that 'since the abolition of the ILEA the ability banding system ensuring their intake was balanced has broken down'[6] and this had led to 'a high proportion of new pupils requiring remedial education' (*Education*, 21 October 1994). The aim of the application from this school was to use tests to reintroduce a form of banding skewed towards pupils of higher ability rather than the full ability range.[7]

Both in the case of the schools that have sought to become bilateral and in the case of the schools that have reintroduced a form of banding, it is likely that the cause of an unbalanced intake was the widening of parental choice without an effective system of banding. The schools involved were demonstrably concerned about the reduction or possible reduction in the proportion of able pupils being admitted. One reason for this is undoubtedly the publication by the DfE of annual performance tables of public examination results. It is nevertheless important to bear in mind that, as yet, relatively few grant-maintained schools have gone down the road of selectivity. As one former voluntary school, for example, states: 'Whilst striving to maintain a comprehensive intake, priority will be given to children from practising [Roman Catholic] families.'

County schools and changes to admissions policies

Whilst most interest in becoming a bilateral school has come from the grant-maintained sector, one county school (in Wandsworth) has also sought to select half of its pupils by reference to their ability. Whilst the application for a change of character was not successful, the reasons for seeking this change were similar to those given by the grant-maintained schools. A new consultative document has been produced by the LEA on its plans for the school to become bilateral and this is explicit in stating that under the present arrangements the school is receiving fewer more able pupils and a greater proportion of less able pupils than might be expected. Under the former banding procedure this was not the case.[8]

As well as new types of schools, the Government has encouraged existing schools to specialise in particular curriculum areas (DfE 1992) such as music, art, drama and sport. A model of this development is a special music course which was established many years ago (before the abolition of the ILEA) which 'exists to provide an intensive musical education for students who want music to be a specially important part of their lives' (City of Westminster 1994: 10). The setting aside of a small number of places (no more than 10 per cent) for pupils who have an aptitude in music has recently been taken up or is proposed to be introduced by a small number of voluntary aided or grant-maintained schools in inner London.

However, the policy of specialisation within schools has been more generally developed by Wandsworth Borough Council (1992), where one county school now specialises in art and design and modern European languages, and another in technology. In contrast to the situation with grant-maintained schools, neither of the specialist county schools proposed to become specialist themselves. Rather, it was the LEA that promoted this concept. It was concerned to provide diversity and choice in the secondary schools within the LEA as part of its belief in the role of market forces in improving the quality of education. In its view an ability to choose 'contribute[s] to higher standards in pupils' behaviour, motivation, attendance, examination results and employment prospects. But there can be real choice only if parents are able to choose between genuinely distinctive schools' (Wandsworth Borough Council 1992: 3). The desire to increase parental choice was thus one of the key factors for the LEA in promoting specialist schools.

City technology colleges

There are three city technology colleges in inner London all of which opened in 1991 and all of which are located in south London (in

Lewisham, Southwark and Wandsworth). City technology colleges are required to admit pupils 'spanning the full range of ability' (Whitty *et al.* 1993: 66) and within their catchment areas to admit pupils representative of the ethnic and social composition of the area. However, city technology colleges are also expected to serve a substantial catchment area and to recruit pupils who are 'demonstrably willing and able to benefit from the special character of the education' they offer (Whitty *et al.* 1993: 66).

The admissions policies of city technology colleges are perhaps one of the most interesting aspects of recent government policy as they are the only form of schools that are required to have an academically-balanced intake. However, as in the case of most voluntary aided schools, interviews are held prior to the allocation of places.

Voluntary aided schools and 'banding'

In several LEAs where banding has ceased, voluntary aided schools make it explicit in their admissions criteria that they seek to obtain a comprehensive intake (in those LEAs that still retain banding, the majority of voluntary schools are part of this system).

The voluntary schools that fall into this category tend to be located in those LEAs that were amongst the first to cease banding – Westminster (three schools), Kensington and Chelsea (two), Hammersmith and Fulham (three) and Islington (one). Whilst religious criteria are present in many cases, there can be little doubt that some voluntary schools are either committed to retaining a comprehensive intake or are attempting to maintain such an intake as the following examples taken from individual school brochures, show:

All students applying for [School X] are placed in an ability band following a verbal reasoning assessment to ensure a balanced, mixed ability intake. The school accepts 25 per cent Band One, 50 per cent Band Two and 25 per cent Band Three. Having placed all the students in Bands, [School X uses] the same criteria as the maintained schools in [the LEA].

Within this over-riding priority [religious], the governors seek an intake that is truly comprehensive in terms of academic ability. To achieve this purpose they will place applicants in one of three ability bands following tests administered at the school.

The school will admit [N] pupils in Year 7 and in so doing will endeavour to preserve its comprehensive character by establishing a balanced intake across the ability range including those with special educational needs in the ratio of 25:50:25. The means taken

185

to achieve this will include information gained from a non-verbal reasoning test.

It is apparent that these schools are actively seeking to maintain an intake of much the same type as banding achieved prior to the abolition of the ILEA, although they differ in terms of whether they test prospective pupils themselves or use other (unspecified) means to assess ability.

Covert selection

Whilst the issue of selection on the basis of academic ability has been addressed previously, there is another issue that warrants discussion, namely that of 'covert' selection. Any *school* that operates its own admissions policy is in a position to use some form of covert selection to try and ensure that its intake is as favourable as possible. In practice, LEA schools that administer their own admissions arrangements are accountable to the LEA. The situation in relation to grant-maintained schools, voluntary aided schools and city technology colleges is somewhat more complex, and procedures that may be considered to be forms of covert selection exist.

One of the most widespread of these is the practice of interviewing pupils or parents prior to allocating a pupil a place. This is common particularly in voluntary aided schools, where schools wish to establish whether religious criteria are met. Another concern is the application form for the school. In some cases the nature of the application form is such that certain parents may not be able to complete the form (for example, those with English as a second language). Forms as long as four pages exist, with parents being asked to provide a range of information, that does not have any bearing on or any relationship to the published admissions criteria (e.g. parental occupation, musical achievements, hobbies and interests). Once schools have such information, it is not unreasonable to suppose that they will use it in the event of the school being over-subscribed and in the knowledge that there is no system in operation that requires schools to be held accountable for the decisions that they have made. Indeed, it is likely to be the case that such forms were introduced so as to increase the ability of schools to choose the children that they feel are most desirable.

KEY FINDINGS

It can be seen from the above discussion that the system of banding that operated in the ILEA until its abolition, was used to try and ensure that there was a comprehensive intake to secondary schools in the authority. It is perhaps not surprising that the Conservative-controlled LEAs –

Wandsworth, Westminster, and Kensington and Chelsea – should have been amongst the first to abandon the system, either on political grounds or on the grounds that it was incompatible with 'parental choice'. For various other reasons, a number of Labour-controlled LEAs have also abandoned the policy, but this has largely been on administrative rather than ideological grounds.

In the circumstances of the new 'market' in education and the absence of banding across inner London, there have been radical moves to change the admissions policies at a small number of schools. These steps have taken place in that part of inner London where the market is most developed, namely in Lambeth and Wandsworth. It appears that the lack of banding may well have affected the intake to certain schools and a few schools are beginning to take action to obtain a more academically able intake by introducing selection.

Nevertheless, in other parts of London, there have not been any radical changes in relation to banding and in a number of voluntary aided schools, published admissions criteria make specific reference to the desire to achieve a balanced intake. In these cases, the indications are that, on ideological grounds, comprehensive intakes are still sought.

IMPLICATIONS FOR POLICY

Overall, the admissions procedures in inner London have become fragmented over time, with the various inner London LEAs, voluntary aided and county schools, grant-maintained schools and city technology colleges having their own policies and practices. These changes mean that the process of secondary transfer has become more complex. A number of policy implications arise from this research:

- Whilst LEAs are required to produce information about individual schools that they maintain (i.e. county and voluntary schools) they are not obliged to provide information about grant-maintained schools or city technology colleges. Although within inner London, a few LEAs do make this information available in brochures, the majority do not. Given the importance of information for informed parental choice and for equity, it would seem appropriate for details of *all* state-maintained secondary schools and their admissions criteria to be made available for *all* parents. In densely populated city/urban areas information about all schools in the city/area should be available, as there is considerable movement of pupils across local authority boundaries.
- It is important that only schools that are clearly designated as 'selective' act in a selective manner. Policies and practices should be transparent to aid equity.

- In the ILEA, parents completed just one form to express their preference for a secondary school for their child; now parents may have to complete multiple application forms. Some of these forms could be used to enable the covert selection of pupils. To discourage covert selection, application forms should not ask for details of pupils' achievements (e.g. in music) or their hobbies, which are likely to be advantageous to certain groups of parents and pupils but not to others. To facilitate the whole process, it is worth considering a more streamlined admissions system requiring just one application form (naming the preferred schools) to be completed, and with a 'clearing system' being established (much as happens with higher education applications). This would avoid the need for multiple applications which can be inequitable particularly for those who have English as a second language or low levels of functional literacy.

- Prior to 1990, parents across the whole of inner London used to have interviews with the primary school headteacher who explained the process of secondary transfer to them. The practice of interviews with the headteacher of the child's primary school is no longer an inner London-wide phenomenon. This is at a time when the whole secondary transfer process is much more complex with parents often making multiple choices and not necessarily having an adequate appreciation of schools' admissions criteria (see West *et al.* 1995; David *et al.* 1994). Parents need to be able to obtain advice about appropriate schools – in terms of the schools' admissions criteria and parents' preferences for different types of schools – to which they could apply and an advisory service needs to be offered; this service could be provided by headteachers, but could also be offered by the LEA or an independent agency.

- To assist parents with the process of choosing a school, information about the Year 7 intake for the previous year should be provided in brochures. This information should comprise the number of siblings accepted, the distance over which pupils were accepted, the number of children accepted because of medical/special needs and so on. Details about whether and to what degree a school is over-subscribed should also be given.

- To address equity issues, information on the social class and ethnic background of all applicants should be collected (as currently happens with higher education applications); this could be used as part of an overall monitoring process and to relate the social class and ethnic background of applicants to those offered places. Alternatively (or additionally), information on National Curriculum assessment results could be collected on all applicants, for the same purpose. Such information could discourage covert selection especially if accompanied by appropriate audits of schools' admissions practices as they relate to stated policies.

IMPLICATIONS FOR FUTURE RESEARCH

- One area that needs to be examined is whether the ability intake to secondary schools is changing. It is important to know whether some schools are becoming more academically selective, either on the basis of overt or covert criteria, or as a result of parental choice and if so whether this is confined to certain types of schools or is a process affecting all schools. Information relating to national assessment results or other tests carried out across an LEA area could be used to measure changes over time.
- If schools are changing their policies in order to become more selective, it is important to know whether this is the result of the school selecting pupils or parents selecting the school.
- It is not clear precisely how the admissions process is carried out by voluntary aided and grant-maintained schools that have responsibility for their own admissions and how these practices vary between schools (but see Whitty *et al.* 1993 for a thorough review of city technology colleges' admissions procedures). There is also concern about the accountability of admissions procedures that are administered by such schools where practices are not open to outside scrutiny.
- Whilst the number of appeals has increased markedly in recent years, there is little data available about how the system operates, who is appealing and why, and whether they are successful.

NOTES

1 We would like to thank John Wilkes for his help with the preparation of this paper and Ann Edge for helpful comments. Thanks are also due to the Department for Education and Employment, the inner London local education authorities and individual schools for providing information.
2 The banding system was not, in practice, as effective as it might have been in delivering a balanced intake (see Pennell and West 1995 for further details).
3 The Corporation of London has no secondary schools.
4 In 1988, this school received 29 per cent Band One pupils (ILEA 1989).
5 Sources are not cited where to do so would identify individual schools.
6 This can be contrasted with the LEA's view that one of the reasons that a decision was made to end banding was the unwillingness of grant-maintained schools in the borough to continue banding (London Borough of Lambeth 1993).
7 The aim was to obtain an intake on a ratio of 40 per cent above average ability, 40 per cent average ability and 20 per cent below average ability.
8 In 1988, the school received 23 per cent Band One pupils (ILEA 1989). In 1993, 11 per cent of its pupils were classified by the LEA (Wandsworth Borough

Council 1994) as being in reading performance group A (representing the highest 20 per cent of the scores). In 1996 the DfEE agreed to this school's application for a change of character.

REFERENCES

City of Westminster (1994) *Your Choice for Secondary Education September 1995*, London: City of Westminster.

David, M., West, A. and Ribbens, J. (1994) *Mother's Intuition? Choosing Secondary Schools*, London: Falmer Press.

Department for Education (DfE)/Welsh Office (1992) *Choice and Diversity: A New Framework for Schools*, London: HMSO.

ILEA (1989) *Transfer from Primary to Secondary School 1988, ILEA Schools Sub-Committee S8218*, London: Inner London Education Authority.

London Borough of Camden (1989) *Education Development Plan*, London: London Borough of Camden.

London Borough of Lambeth (1993) *Secondary School Admissions Policy. Report to Education Committee 20.7.93*, London: Lambeth Education Department.

London Borough of Southwark (1992) *Secondary Admissions Policy. Report to Schools Sub-Committee 5.5.92*, London: Southwark Education Department.

Pennell, H. and West, A. (1995) *Changing schools at 11: Secondary Schools Admissions Policies in Inner London in 1995*, Clare Market Papers Number 9, London: Centre for Educational Research, London School of Economics and Political Science.

Wandsworth Borough Council (1989) *Education Development Plan*, London: Wandsworth Borough Council.

Wandsworth Borough Council (1992) *Diversity and Choice. A Consultative Document*, London: Wandsworth Borough Council.

Wandsworth Borough Council (1994) *Secondary Intake Analysis for Wandsworth Schools September 1993 REU 43/94*, London: Wandsworth Education Department.

West, A., David, M., Hailes, J. and Ribbens, J. (1995) 'The process of choosing secondary schools', *Educational Management and Administration*, 23: 28–38.

Whitty, G., Edwards, T. and Gewirtz, S. (1993) *Specialisation and Choice in Urban Education: The City Technology College Experiment*, London: Routledge.

REVIEW AND IMPLICATIONS

Ron Glatter, Philip A. Woods and Carl Bagley

INTRODUCTION

The purposes of the invitation seminar (see Chapter 1) on which this book is based were:

- to review research findings
- to identify their implications for policy
- to draw up an agenda for future research.

This final chapter will draw together some of the main themes and issues emerging from the previous chapters and from the discussions during the seminar, looking in turn at the three purposes identified above. It will conclude by drawing attention to the importance of dialogue between the research and policy communities.

REVIEWING THE RESEARCH

General observations

A particular feature of much of the research reported in this volume is its focus on the *interaction* between parents and schools over the question of choice of school. Previous research had concentrated on the qualities of schools which parents said were important to them in influencing their choice (Johnson 1990; Glatter *et al.* 1993). The competitive 'market' introduced by the Education Reform Act 1988 posited a dynamic and responsive interplay between 'consumers' and 'producers', and its evaluation required a much more sophisticated and multi-faceted set of research strategies.

This raises many problems of scope and methodology. The area is a highly contentious one. Values on many of the issues within it are strongly held. Researchers have to determine how far their own values are to influence the conduct and interpretation of their study, and how explicit they will be about this dimension. One of the authors repre-sented here commented that the findings of their study contradicted their own ideological position on the relevant topics – a rare and striking observation.

A particular problem concerns the identification of causation. Schools in England and Wales have been subject to a range of radical policy initiatives in recent years. Some of the most significant of these, notably the National Curriculum and its associated assessment requirements and the major restructuring of the school inspection system, have argu-ably little to do with parental choice and are not consumer-driven. In such a complex situation it is difficult to separate out the effects of one strand of policy from those of others.

Many of the policies will take some time to show their consequences. Methods need to be employed that are capable of evaluating change which is dynamic, both in terms of time and in relation to the interaction of different policies at school level. Here larger, longitudinal studies are likely to have an advantage, as will those which have employed a mix of qualitative and quantitative methods.

Overall, qualitative approaches predominate in this collection. This is perhaps understandable and justifiable in view of the subtlety of the factors that are being investigated and the need for methods which pro-vide insight into the complex multi-faceted and multi-layered process of parental choice and organisational change. However, it was noted that it is important to use research methods which reveal what parents and school staff actually did, and not simply to rely on statements of their views and preferences. The study by Hardman and Levačić, Chapter 9, employed sophisticated quantitative techniques and there was a feeling at the seminar that such approaches had been under-exploited so far and that they had considerable potential, particularly in terms of relating the competitive market to educational outcomes.

With regard to scope, much of the work reported here as elsewhere focuses on entry to secondary school. In this it reflects the overwhelming emphasis in the educational and political debate. There has been very little research on choice at entry to pre-school or to the primary phase (Hughes et al. 1994, is a rare exception on the latter), nor at the crucial sixteen-plus 'bridge'. Moreover, the question of choice of programmes or pathways within phases of schooling is almost completely overlooked, although Goldring (Chapter 7) implicitly asks whether choice ends when the school is chosen by examining the level of parental involve-ment in specialist or magnet schools compared with others.

There is also little on choice in relation to the private sector of school-ing, yet some of the policy initiatives of recent years could be seen as attempts to offer alternatives to private education within the state sector, and a revival of grammar schools has been advocated as a means of attracting middle-class parents back to the state system (Hutton 1995). However, the essay by Edwards and Whitty (Chapter 3) helpfully analyses movements in the two sectors in relation to each other.

Three themes appeared particularly prominent in the work reported here: responsiveness, diversity and traditionalism. Although they are discussed under separate headings below, in practice there is significant overlap between them.

Responsiveness

A central debate initiated by the present studies concerns whether schools are becoming more responsive under the pressures generated by competition, as predicted by advocates of market approaches. A firm position is taken by Levin and Riffel (Chapter 4). Drawing on a wealth of literature in the field of organisational analysis as well as their own empirical work carried out in Canada, they argue powerfully that schools and their staff are poorly equipped by history and organisation to respond to changes in their environment, that they will seek to minimise the impact of such changes on their practice and that consequently schools' responses to a competitive environment will be limited and short-term in nature, rather than the far more radical effects predicted by advocates of competition. At the end of the chapter, they make a series of predictions about the reaction of schools to a market-like environment, many of which have been borne out by research and experience. A related argument, that schools exist in an environment dominated by factors such as university entrance requirements and government curricular regulations, giving them the impression that, far from being autonomous, they are in fact caught in nets, seems very relevant to the context of England and Wales.

However, it was argued at the seminar that such an analysis, based as it is on experience in the relatively non-competitive context of Canadian education, under-estimates the ambition of the market advocates to confront and demolish the very conservatism and professional and organisational constraints which Levin and Riffel identify. Evidence suggests that the wide-ranging responsiveness to consumers which was sought has not been achieved. Hughes (Chapter 6), for example, argues on the basis of findings reported in his chapter, that teachers' sense of professionalism and their perceptions of the role of parents are a barrier to responsiveness. It would be wrong to assume that schools and their staff have not been affected by competition. For example, Gewirtz (Chapter 10) concludes that it has generated a more inward-looking approach among teachers based upon a 'social psychology of self-interest'. Other studies reported here indicate that it may have reinforced rather than challenged professional conservatism and insularity. We shall return to this latter issue when we discuss traditionalism below.

It is evident too that academic aspects of schooling are not the only factors influencing parents' choice of school. There is clear evidence that parents attach considerable importance to the impact of the school's social environment and organisation on their child's happiness and sense of security (Glatter *et al.* Chapter 2). Thus, if the schools are to be responsive to a market-like environment, there is more to be concerned with than performance in examinations and other academic assessments.

Market responsiveness is only one aspect of schools' responsiveness to a changing world, and discussion at the seminar increasingly interpreted the term in a wider sense. Could schools be helped to assess and respond to the impact of the massive social, economic and technological changes which are occurring in their environment? How could they be encouraged to take a longer-term, more strategic approach? It appeared that at least one aspect of the marketisers' proclaimed agenda – to bring schools to a more outward-looking stance – seemed a valid and extremely important one, but it was not clear whether the competitive market provided a solution or compounded the problem.

The impact of incentive systems, most notably funding formulae, on responsiveness, needs to be understood more clearly. On the one hand it might seem that they have powerful and subtle effects on institutional behaviour, and that, for example, changing the character of the local management of schools (LMS) formula so that it gave more weight to social need factors and less to pupil numbers could significantly change the 'market' without eliminating competition. On the other hand, discussion of the paper by Hardman and Levačić (Chapter 9) in particular suggested that school budgets are less sensitive to short-term changes than might be supposed, in that schools could in the short term only try to influence the pupil numbers in their intake years (generally Year 7 for secondary schools and Year 12 where they have a sixth form). It might therefore be a weaker instrument than was often assumed.

Diversity

There were indications in a number of the chapters (for example Halpin *et al.* Chapter 5, and Glatter *et al.*, Chapter 2) that so far the competitive system had promoted uniformity rather than diversity, and that it had become almost unacceptable, or at least hazardous, to be different except in relation to government initiatives such as the Specialist Schools Programme (DfE 1994).

However, it became clear that diversity is an ambiguous term, and is often used in a rhetorical manner. It can imply different things to different people: what looks like diversity to one observer may appear to another to be patchiness. More important, it is multi-dimensional, as the typology in Table 2.1 in Chapter 2 indicates, and this prompts the question: assuming that diversity is bound to be limited in practice by financial and other considerations, what *kinds* of diversity do we want to promote? It is not established that most parents want a diverse system, as distinct from a high quality one, and it is certainly not clear that parents generally want a secondary system containing a substantial proportion of 'specialist schools', each emphasising a particular area of the curriculum.

Hirsch (Chapter 11) argues on the basis of US experience that diversity can best be created by empowering teachers, putting the emphasis on a bottom-up approach, albeit within a broad framework of planning for diversity because the evidence indicates that schools will not seek to be different purely for competitive reasons. In this view, supply-side freedom is more likely to generate educational dynamism than parental choice.

The relationship between diversity and equity is a crucial one. The question raised by Hirsch's chapter and others is whether schools can reflect genuine educational differences on an equal basis for all, so that the idea of diversity does not simply act as a cover to create a 'new improved sorting machine' (Moore and Davenport 1990) for the active choosers. This requires types of schooling that are different but 'equal' in the life chances they are perceived to confer, otherwise a distorted form of choice arises, in which preferences are significantly shaped by non-educational considerations.

Traditionalism

A number of the chapters address the impact of the competitive system on the content of school education, notably those by Edwards and Whitty (Chapter 3), Glatter *et al.* (Chapter 2), Halpin *et al.* (Chapter 5), Hirsch (Chapter 11), and Levin and Riffel (Chapter 4). This is a particularly topical issue because of the current political debate about the relative significance of structure and content in securing educational improvement. For example, a Labour Party policy document asserts: 'We have had a concentration on structures, when we need to concentrate on getting the content right' (Labour Party 1995: 34). It may, however, be difficult to sustain such a distinction in practice. If, as is argued in some of these chapters, structures and content turn out to be related to one another then the attempt to treat them separately becomes questionable.

Generally it is being suggested that the structural reforms in England and Wales since the late 1980s have led to a renewed emphasis on traditional approaches within school education. Interpretations of this development vary. It can be seen, following Halpin *et al.* (Chapter 5), as a form of escape from conditions of radical social upheaval (and an attempt to rediscover a lost national role?). Edwards and Whitty (Chapter 3) stress the entrenched prestige of the traditional academic forms of schooling and the better prospects they are perceived to offer. Levin and Riffel (Chapter 4) comment more generally that public images of what schools should be are usually influential in a conservative direction.

If this general analysis is correct, then it may not only be the reforms normally associated with the competitive market (LMS, more open enrolment, grant-maintained schools and the publication of performance tables) which are responsible, but also regulatory innovations such as the introduction of the National Curriculum and assessment arrangements and the restructuring of the inspection system. These latter, regulatory mechanisms are often seen as distinct from, and even to an extent in conflict with, the instruments designed to promote competition. However, one of their goals is to secure a degree of standardisation, and if the competitive system is also achieving this, instead of the pluralism with which competition is often associated, then the two groups of mechanisms could be reinforcing each other rather than opposing each other in creative tension.

The outcome could be an unimaginative orthodoxy, with risk-taking discouraged and alternative visions of state schooling unable to gain a foothold. Perhaps more importantly, if the dominant model is, as Halpin *et al.* (Chapter 5) contend, taking the form of a retreat into the past, then it is questionable whether many of the products of such a system will be employable in the international economy of the twenty-first century.

Before coming to such a cataclysmic conclusion, however, we need to be clearer than is possible on the basis of the present studies about what is meant by 'traditionalism'. We need to understand in much more detail how the curriculum actually experienced by pupils in England and Wales, or in other systems which emphasise choice and competition, is balanced between 'traditional' and 'modern' elements (in Edwards and Whitty's terms, see Chapter 3). The curriculum 'labels' can often mask what is being offered and give a false impression of reality, as respondents to our PASCI study (see Chapter 2) have suggested to us.

The relationship of competitive systems (and school structures more generally) with pupil learning and school performance is clearly an area of major importance. We shall return to it in later sections.

POLICY IMPLICATIONS

Towards the end of the seminar, each participant was asked to identify, in no more than ten words, one policy priority that stood out for them on the basis of the research that had been reported. The following examples give an indication of the range of topics covered:

- a fair admission policy for all schools;
- achieving school improvement following the failure of 'the market' to deliver;
- extension of home-to-school transport provision to any chosen school;
- developing different and exciting new curricula to choose from;
- change incentives for school recruitment and practice by formula alterations.

Although the range was wide, there was a very noteworthy clustering around one topic area. Almost half the priorities chosen (fifteen out of thirty-two) concerned policy on school admissions in relation to equity. Most of this section will focus on these two overlapping issues.

It seems unlikely that the political significance of parental choice will be substantially reduced in the foreseeable future. Although in Britain particularly there has been a distinctive ideological component to the debate, it is clear that wider social and economic factors are generating a demand for greater choice in many countries (OECD 1994). Levin and Riffel refer to some of these at the end of Chapter 4. Dennison's assessment of the political realities seems accurate:

> Governments of all persuasions having been seen to sponsor consumerism become committed to its furtherance. Rights and choices, once conferred, are difficult to deny in a democracy. More significantly, the transfer of some consumer power in itself increases demands for further transfers.
>
> (Dennison 1993: 220)

If choice and competition are here to stay, it is important to develop systems and frameworks which operate fairly in the interests of all. We will comment first on the general question of equity and then on its particular manifestation in the case of admissions to schools.

Equity

The issues here are clearly complex (Simkins 1995). The close linkage of schools with their immediate localities may promote inequity. In Chapter 11, Hirsch castigates the dominant educational view in Britain that selection by ability or aptitude is wrong but that selection by residence is acceptable, arguing that this allows residential elites to form around favoured schools. He also claims that in Britain much less has been done than elsewhere to improve pupils' access to transport to more distant schools, although policies on consumer information are more extensive than in other countries.

The findings from Goldring's study (Chapter 7) are of particular interest in this connection. She finds clear evidence of a 'creaming effect' by social class in specialist and 'magnet' schools in two very different contexts – Cincinnati and Israel. Such an outcome should perhaps give us pause before contemplating further extensions of the 'specialist school' concept if we are concerned with issues of equity and access. She concludes that the study indicates the complexity of combining choice with class diversity. Access to transport and information, and fair admission processes, are all important for addressing equity: her research suggests that they are necessary but not sufficient criteria. In addition to these policies operated by central and local authorities, she argues that schools themselves should interact with all parents in ways that would ensure a broad social class distribution within their pupil profile. But this might require a redesign of incentive systems to encourage all schools to value such a broad representation.

The significance of incentive systems for equity is highlighted by Evans and Vincent in their chapter on parental choice and special education (Chapter 8), in which they conclude that over-subscribed schools are 'pricing' children. Marginalised and disempowered groups of consumers, such as those whose children have special needs, may be perceived within a competitive environment as 'difficult' to provide for and expensive in terms of time and resources, and less attractive than more 'valuable' consumers. The operation of such informal or covert 'pricing' mechanisms would need to be addressed in any policy which sought to reconcile choice with equity.

Admissions to schools

Although a number of chapters touch on this topic, two focus on it directly. The survey of a group of local education authorities (LEAs) reported by Mayet (Chapter 12) indicates the difficulties and confusion that can arise in areas where there is no single admissions authority, and in particular where there is a significant number of grant-maintained (GM) schools. Both this study and that of admissions procedures in inner London by West and Pennell (Chapter 13) highlight the issue of accountability in relation to schools such as GM and voluntary aided schools which are responsible for their own admissions, whose practices may not be as open to public scrutiny as those of LEA schools where the responsibility lies with the authority. It was suggested at the seminar that in some areas of England there are almost as many admissions systems as schools.

Two of the criteria for an acceptable admissions system are simply stated and might command widespread assent. First, that it should be easily understood by all parents, including those with limited 'cultural resources' (Gewirtz *et al.* 1995), and all should be able to participate in it without undue difficulty. The adjectives 'clear' and 'transparent' are often used as shorthand for this requirement. Second, it should be fair and equitable, in the sense that no pupil or parent, and no group of pupils and parents, should be unjustifiably advantaged in the attempt to secure a place at a school. Thus, adherence to the relevant faith is accepted as a justifiable advantage in seeking admission to a religiously-based voluntary (state) school, and the demonstration of appropriate academic attainments is regarded in the same way in relation to a selective school (DfE 1993). Even though the principle of selective or state religious schools may be disputed, so long as such schools exist, arrangements of this kind do not breach the second criterion concerning fairness. Many would regard any form of social selection, as might be achieved through a process of interviewing pupils or parents before admission, or requiring complex and demanding application forms to be completed (see Chapter 13), as conferring unjustified advantage.

A third criterion that might be advanced, that admissions systems should be structured so as to secure a broad balance of ability in schools' intakes, would be more contentious. This is the principle which underlay the banding system operated by the Inner London Education Authority (ILEA) prior to its abolition in 1990 and which a number of its successor authorities have maintained. The connection between admission criteria and the academic balance of schools' intakes has become a particularly significant issue since the national publication of annual performance tables of examination results. It is interesting that some GM schools in West and Pennell's study (Chapter 13) introduced forms of selection avowedly as a defensive measure, to ensure that they received a fair proportion of able children and hence a reasonably balanced intake. The research evidence has long indicated a connection between balanced intakes and school effectiveness (Mortimore 1995), and the renewed interest in school improvement and effectiveness might lead to this issue being given closer attention in debates about admission policies.

It is easier to propose criteria for admissions systems than to suggest viable schemes to meet them, both because of logistical complexities and the high political and media sensitivity surrounding the issue. West and Pennell (Chapter 13) make a range of proposals, emphasising the need for full information to be made available to parents, for advisory services to be established and for streamlining application processes, perhaps by the use of a clearing system as exemplified in the higher education applications system. Much stronger national specification of criteria would be welcomed by some (Forrest 1995) while others would be wary of the further centralisation implied by such an approach and place emphasis instead on local co-ordination. A major question is whether any school should have almost total responsibility for its own criteria and procedures, subject only to legal constraints, broad national advice and a degree of central approval.

Specific suggestions made at the seminar ranged from complete randomisation of admissions to a 'choice guidance' approach using a careers guidance model involving partnership between teachers, parents and, where appropriate, pupils (Adler 1993).

Quality

A commitment to improve all schools, and particularly to raise the performance of the weaker ones, through a partnership between the schools, local authorities and central government, was proposed as a positive approach to enhancing parental satisfaction and would perhaps lead to fewer 'negative' choices. This raises again the issue of the link between structural arrangements and educational quality. Clearly, successful school improvement is dependent on action taken by those within the school with the support of appropriate external stakeholders and agencies. But equally clearly, the structural framework can promote or inhibit that process. Its importance should be recognised. The challenge to policy makers is to devise and test structures which can reinforce improvement in all schools.

FUTURE RESEARCH

The most prominent themes to emerge as important areas of future research activity in relation to choice and competition, deriving largely from the previous discussion, were the process of family choice, intake patterns, school performance and equity.

Family choice as a process

Parents are a highly diverse group, and choice is often a complex and ambiguous process for families. We need to understand much more about its dynamics and micropolitics, taking into account the characteristics of particular families, their resources and the fact that the task is not simply to choose a school but to consider the child in relation to available schools.

The relative contributions of mothers and fathers is one aspect of this (David *et al.* 1994) as well as how the choice of single-sex as against co-educational provision for daughters and sons is made, where such a choice exists. The choice process might be conceptualised as involving a series of trade-offs, for example between concerns for the child's 'happiness' and well-being as against the perceived significance of examination results or test scores, or between closeness to a school and other features. It would be well worthwhile looking at such trade-offs and seeing how they are resolved within different families.

It is important to understand not just why parents choose certain schools but also why they reject others, given that choice is thought often to be a vote against one or more schools rather than (or as well as) a vote for the chosen one. A related consideration, highly relevant to the 'market' idea, is how many of the factors involved in rejection are within the school's control (for example its geographical and socio-economic location). How does this 'key-factor-controllability' vary between 'winning' and 'losing' schools?

We need to know more about how perceptions of different schools are influenced or mediated and by whom. For example, what is the role of the grapevine, and of officially produced information? How does the influence of these and other external sources vary amongst different families? Which of the many types of information now available about schools are genuinely informative to parents and help them in their choices? In the conclusion to Chapter 7, Goldring raises a number of important queries about the possible effects of informal counselling processes and social networks on parents' perceptions of which schools are 'appropriate' or worth considering for their children.

School intake patterns

Close and regular monitoring is needed to provide up-to-date information on key indicators such as the proportion of parents obtaining their first preference school and the volume of, and success rate in, appeals. These data should be collected and published by the Department for Education and Employment (DfEE), and should be classified by LEA area and cover all publicly-funded schools. They should be published within a short and defined period, say three months, of the end of the annual transfer process to which they refer, much as the school performance tables appear within a few months of the public examinations whose results they report.

There is also a need to monitor closely and regularly the pattern of ability intakes to secondary schools, to see whether the picture is changing under the influence, for example, of choice and competition and greater selectivity, overt or covert. It is important to know whether there is increased or reduced polarisation among our schools in terms of their ability profiles. This follows a proposal by West and Pennell (Chapter 13). The introduction of testing at Key Stage 2 might provide a basis for this monitoring. Again these data should be collected by the DfEE and published soon after the completion of the relevant transfer process.

More generally, the impact of greater selectivity both on the selective schools themselves and on the non-selective schools in the locality should be assessed. Overall, we need to examine whether competition is increasing or decreasing the differences between schools in terms of their pupils' educational and family characteristics. This should include research into whether increased ethnic segregation is resulting from parental choice (Bagley 1995).

School performance

Future research should look at education outcomes, and attempt to measure the impact of parental choice and related policy initiatives on standards and on inequalities. For this, we need to use indicators of success that are more sophisticated than raw examination results in order to help us to understand the connection (if any) between schools' success or failure in the market and the quality of education they provide. By what criteria this 'quality' should be assessed is itself a matter of debate and requires careful examination (including fundamental questions such as *who* ought to determine what constitutes 'good quality'). As we have already noted, parents' criteria for assessing schools are wider than academic performance alone.

Ultimately the two key hypotheses in this area could be stated as: 'The competitive system rewards educational quality and improves performance' and 'It reinforces socio-economic differences'. (In thinking about the relationship between the 'market' and performance, it might be salutary to bear in mind the remark of the business entrepreneur who said: 'We would not enter a market in which we did not have an unfair advantage'.) Can a more market-like school system benefit the broad swathe of children, or are there inevitable tendencies for the benefits, where they do exist, to favour the children of already advantaged families?

Further issues

As implied earlier, future research could usefully focus on choice and decision points at stages other than secondary transfer. The connection between choice and subsequent parental involvement and influence would be a worthwhile subject for investigation. In relation to responsiveness, the relative effects of 'market' and other variables on school change would be a fruitful topic. A study could helpfully examine the costs and benefits of vigorous school marketing activity, and whether such activity correlates with high or improving performance.

TOWARDS AN AGENDA FOR DIALOGUE BETWEEN THE RESEARCH AND POLICY COMMUNITIES

The seminar concluded with some general reflections on the relationship between research and policy in areas such as the present subject. There could be said to be something of a culture gap between researchers and policy influencers. Perhaps this has always been so, because of the two groups' different goals, frames of reference and ways of working. However, in recent years the notion of 'trialling' new education initiatives before full implementation has become much less common ('every school a pilot school'), immediacy has tended to rule and the contribution of reliable research findings or evaluation studies to policy has often seemed minimal.

The different time-scales of research and policy development is a well-recognised factor: research requires substantial lead times to have an impact on policy. Differing research aims are also relevant, between those who wish to influence the development of policy and practice in the short term and those with a longer-term agenda, say of contributing to knowledge development or the confirmation of pre-determined social and political stances. This is a tension neatly caricatured in Ian McEwan's novel *The Child in Time* in this description of the expert members of a committee set up to give policy advice: 'The committee divided between the theorists, who had done all their thinking long ago, or had had it done for them, and the pragmatists, who hoped to discover what it was they thought in the process of saying it' (McEwan 1988: 10).

The relationship between analysis and action is elusive and ambiguous. Policies are stimulated by a variety of contextual factors, and this process too needs to be researched. It seems vital however that policies such as those examined in this volume are subjected to rigorous analysis and scrutiny, so that lessons can be learnt from experience and knowledgeable policy development set in train. Even when politicians are so certain of their ground that they forecast outcomes with complete confidence, researchers have a duty to say, 'It's more difficult than that.' This may seem less than helpful, but it is a crucial function of the research community. The dialogue between researchers and policy influencers on which this chapter has been based represents one attempt to seek a mutual understanding.

By way of conclusion, it is appropriate to reaffirm that the pre-eminent concerns of the research and policy communities – despite their differences – are shared and to underline this by summarising some of the key points under three broad headings.

First, there is the *process* of choice. This includes the process of selecting or attempting to select a school, the administrative procedures laid down for this, the information and guidance made available to families, and the outcome in terms of the size and nature of school intakes. Improved admissions procedures are needed. It is equally clear, however, that what is also needed is (a) regular and reliable data on the parental success rate in obtaining their preferred place and on the composition, year by year, of individual school intakes, and (b) in-depth studies of the process of choice as experienced by families.

Second, there is *provision* – that is, the range of educational opportunities and the learning that these facilitate – which must be the central concern of all. Accumulating evidence suggests that a more competitive system does not of itself increase diversity or produce schooling which is more responsive to parents and children. If we wish to move in this direction more decisively, specific policies are required to encourage this. Accordingly, there are important policy choices to be made about the *extent and nature* of diversity and responsiveness – and innovation – which is desirable. Research into the variety of views on this and on the practical effects of different policies is needed. This must include studies into defining and evaluating the quality of education, encompassing not only academic indicators of high quality.

Third, there is the issue of *inequality*, which is concerned with the extent to which choice and competition may exacerbate social divisions and whether their benefits (where apparent) may be unequally distributed in favour of the already advantaged. Research evidence to date gives no reassurance that this is not happening: indeed, some evidence suggests, as we have seen, that an emphasis on parental choice can foster socially unbalanced school populations. Practical policies to counter such trends, and a willingness to develop and try out new approaches, are required. They need to be informed by research that examines inequalities in both *process* and *provision*.

Continuing research and innovative thinking on all of these matters is essential. The more dialogue there is between the research and policy communities, the more likely it is that a proper and beneficial balance between the individual right to choose and the public need to plan will be achieved.

REFERENCES

Adler, M. (1993) 'An alternative approach to parental choice', NCE Briefing 13, London: Paul Hamlyn Foundation/National Commission on Education.

Bagley, C. (1995) 'Black and white united or flight? The racial dimension of schooling and parental choice', paper presented at the symposium 'Home and school: an equal partnership', at the European Conference on Educational Research, University of Bath, 14–17 September 1995.

David, M., West, A. and Ribbens, J. (1994) *Mother's Intuition? Choosing Secondary Schools*, London: Falmer Press.

Dennison, B. (1993) 'Performance indicators and consumer choice', in M. Preedy (ed.) *Managing the Effective School*, London: Paul Chapman.

Department for Education (DfE) (1993) *Admissions to Maintained Schools*, Circular 6/93, London: Department for Education.

DfE (1994) 'Specialist schools programme extended – Shephard', *Department for Education News* 296/94, London: Department for Education.

Forrest, K. (1995) 'A way forward', *Education*, 6 October.

Gewirtz, S., Ball, S.J. and Bowe, R. (1995) *Markets, Choice and Equity in Education*, Buckingham, Open University Press.

Glatter, R., Johnson, D. and Woods, P.A. (1993) 'Marketing, choice and responses in education', in M. Smith (ed.) *Managing Schools in an Uncertain Environment: Resources, Marketing and Power*, Sheffield: Sheffield Hallam University for the British Educational Management and Administration Society (BEMAS).

Hughes, M., Wikeley, F. and Nash, T. (1994) *Parents and their Children's Schools*, Oxford: Blackwell.

Hutton, W. (1995) *The State We're In*, London: Jonathan Cape.

Johnson, D. (1990) *Parental Choice in Education*, London: Unwin Hyman.

Labour Party (1995) *Excellence for Everyone*, London: Labour Party.

McEwan, I. (1988) *A Child in Time*, London: Pan Books.

Moore, D.R. and Davenport, S. (1990) *Choice: The New Improved Sorting Machine*, in W.L. Boyd and H.J. Halberg (eds), *Choice in Education: Potential and Problems*, Berkeley, CA: McCutchan.

Mortimore, P. (1995) 'The balancing act', the *Guardian*, 28 February.

OECD (1994) *School: A Matter of Choice*, Paris: Centre for Educational Research and Innovation (CERI), Organisation for Economic Co-operation and Development.

Simkins, T. (1995) 'The equity consequences of educational reform', *Educational Management and Administration*, 23: 221–232.

INDEX